DATE			
10/94			

Shadows Dancing

Shadows Dancing

Japanese Espionage
Against the West
1939–1945

TONY MATTHEWS

St. Martin's Press
New York

"A Thomas Dunne Book"

ISBN 0-312-10544-4

First published in Great Britain by Robert Hale Limited.

First U.S. Edition: April 1994
10 9 8 7 6 5 4 3 2 1

Contents

Illustrations

PICTURE CREDITS

US National Archives: 1,2. Oficina de Informačion
Diplomatica, Madrid: 3, 4.

This book is dedicated to my brother, Tom Matthews

Preface

This work deals primarily with the espionage activities of various Japanese diplomats and secret agents operating – principally in Europe – during the Second World War.

I have attempted to detail, as far as possible, all the known events which led up to the formation and the operations of the various spy nets, and to offer an insight into the lives of many of those people who were heavily involved in the events.

To describe persons such as Morito Morishima or Yakichiro Suma, two of Japan's leading diplomats and spy-masters, as evil incarnates or in any other derogatory fashion, would be to veer unnecessarily from the truth. It is true that these men were dedicated to their cause, perhaps fanatically so. It is also true that – according to my research – some of the Japanese agents and spy-masters would not stop, even at the possibility of murder, in order to achieve their aims. This is clearly demonstrated in the case of Japanese defector Sakimura (see page 160, 161).

Both Suma and Morishima were certainly deeply involved in espionage activities, as were dozens of other leading Japanese diplomats accredited to many embassies, consulates and legations during the war. As such they succeeded in infiltrating agents into Allied and neutral countries, and inflicting irreparable harm on the Allied prosecution of the war, supplying an enormous mass of vital information to Tokyo on a wide diversity of subjects, including troops and convoy movements, Allied arms and equipment manufacture, and even the state of Allied morale.

It is, however, important to acknowledge that these men were working diligently and earnestly, under the direct orders of their superiors at the Japanese Foreign Office in Tokyo. Despite often incredible difficulties, especially towards the end of the war, these diplomats and spies carried on with their dangerous missions until ordered by the Japanese Foreign Office to cease subversive operations in 1945.

The research to uncover these events and the details of the lives of these people, has been diversified. The primary sourcing, as detailed in the text, comes from thousands of previously secret reports now held at the National Archives in Washington DC. Other information has come from Australian, British and Malaysian archives, and from a wide variety of sources in the Philippines. When I arrived in Manila in December 1989 to conduct some of the research for this book, I was almost immediately embroiled in the sixth coup attempt against the presidency of Mrs Corazon Aquino. The city was in turmoil as the bloodiest fighting since the Second World War took place. As a result, archives, libraries and many public institutions of learning and research were closed, thus making the research project a considerable difficulty. However, despite these problems, the research was able to proceed with the aid of the following persons and organizations, to whom I would like to offer my sincere thanks: Staff of the Filipiniana Capital Division, National Historical Institute of the Philippines; Florrie S. Carino and Alexander F. Favila, of the Serials Division, National Library of the Philippines; Filipe Romanillos and Pio A. Penaflor, Research Division of the National Historical Institute of the Philippines; Alicia M. Sison, Chief of the Research and Publications Division, National Historical Institute of the Philippines and Teresita R. Ignacio, Chief, Archives Division, Philippines National Archives.

My research in Great Britain was aided by: The librarians and staff of the Bristol and Swansea Public Libraries, and the Imperial War Museum.

In Australia I would like to thank: K. Browne, Assistant Curator, Information Services, Australian War Memorial; The librarians and staff of the Warwick and Maryborough Public Libraries; Staff of the Microform Division of the State Library of Queensland, and my wife Lensie for her untiring efforts in assisting in microform research and checking the various drafts.

Appreciation to the US National Archives for their willing help and advice. Finally, special thanks to my literary agent, Tina Betts, of Andrew Mann Ltd, London, who made it all possible.

Tony Matthews
1993

Introduction

Had it not been for a group of highly intelligent and dedicated American crypt-analysts, working under difficult conditions and under very high pressures of work during the Second World War, this book could not have been written. *Shadows Dancing* is derived from the many thousands of top-secret intelligence reports sent between the Japanese Foreign Office and the various Japanese diplomatic embassies, consulates and legations – principally in neutral or Axis countries – during the war. It details how the United States military was aware, often before many Axis departments – of enemy moves, positions and future intentions. These signals, intercepted and decrypted by the US counter-intelligence authorities, became known as the *Magic* Summaries.

But what exactly did *Magic* do? In effect the messages were largely responsible for Allied superiority on every military front during the war. They provided the Allies with information on Japanese, German and Italian espionage activities around the world. The Allies were aware of almost every move made by German ships running the Allied blockade as they attempted to get vital supplies to and from the Far East.

Magic supplied vital intelligence on top-secret technical information, the design of German, Japanese and Italian aircraft, the power of their engines and the composition of metals from which they were made. It gave the Allies intimate knowledge of Axis subversive and propaganda campaigns, the movements of troops and ships, the total contents of stores, the reserves of oils, coals and metals. It supplied the complete economic structure of Axis nations and how those nations were coping with difficult economies ravaged by war. *Magic* gave details of resistance movements in occupied countries, what damage they were doing to Axis powers and how those powers were dealing with such activities. It supplied fascinating insights of key personalities, and – almost at the end of the war – it even provided President Harry S. Truman with sufficient vital information about the Japanese psyche and their determination to continue the fighting at whatever the cost to enable him to decide that the only alternative to landing Allied troops on the Japanese mainland was to use the atom bomb.

This book, however, chiefly concerns itself with the details of Japanese espionage activities against the Western nations and their allies which were revealed as a result of *Magic*. Had it not been for *Magic*, little of these details would have been available today, for, as the war came to its predictable close in 1945, the Japanese Foreign Minister in Tokyo, through whose office most of the Japanese intelligence reports had been channelled during the war, sent a series of top-secret messages to all of his remaining embassies and consulates ordering that their diplomatic files, their archives of coded messages and their financial records were to be destroyed. This order was, of course, immediately carried out by the diplomats accredited to these posts. In these files had been details of all espionage activities organized through each diplomatic post during the war. Particulars included the names of spies, their controllers (usually Japanese diplomats or nationals of neutral countries), how the various spy networks had been organized, how much the spies had been paid and where the funds for payment had come from. With the destruction of these files, there was little record, apart from the *Magic* messages, of what the Japanese intelligence nets had achieved or had attempted to achieve during the war.

The following pages endeavour to set out, primarily in chronological order, the set-up of each of the Japanese espionage nets and, where possible, the personnel involved. Details of the *Magic* Summaries were kept secret for more than thirty years after the end of the war, and even today numerous elements are still highly classified and have not been released by US authorities, including the names of many of the spies who operated principally from the embassies in Portugal, Sweden, Switzerland, Turkey, Russia, Germany, Argentina, Chile and Spain.

1   The Axis Spy Network

A Spanish link with Axis espionage was revealed in a US report on fifth-column activities which detailed widespread spying operations in June 1942. The Spanish were quick to refute the allegations stating that the report had been fabricated.[1] In Buenos Aires, the Spanish Embassy issued a statement with the express authority of Madrid, making the charge that American governments, including those of the United States, Argentina and Chile, were using 'falsehood and forgery' to bolster up allegations that Spain was cooperating with the Axis in espionage, by making Spanish diplomatic pouches available for the transmission of documents.

Further details of Spain's involvement in the establishment of Axis espionage nets were released by US Under Secretary of State Sumner Welles during a highly controversial speech given at Boston in October 1942. Sumner Welles charged that, according to secret documents in his possession, Axis agents in Chile and Argentina were forwarding spy reports through agents in Cuba and Barcelona. The existence of this espionage system was only one of many pieces of information which showed a connection between Axis activities in Chile and Argentina with the sinking of numerous Allied vessels.

The contents of Welles' speech had already been sent in a memorandum to the Chilean and Argentine authorities, causing a political furore.

The memorandum stated that there were at least thirty Axis agents operating in four groups and reporting to Axis diplomatic missions. Each of the four groups had its own illegal radio transmitter and, as a direct result of their activities, ships, merchandise, petroleum, munitions and foodstuffs worth millions of dollars had been sunk, and the lives of hundreds of men, women and children had been lost. Shortly after the speech given by Welles, arrests were quickly made of secret agents in Santiago and Havana, and confessions were 'extracted'. One of the agents arrested in Santiago was named Carlos Robinson. He had obtained information regarding ship movements and passed it on through unnamed channels until it finally reached an Axis agent named Luning in Havana. Luning was also arrested and subsequently confessed to Cuban authorities that he had operated a radio station through which he had passed on information regarding Allied ship movements. He also acknowledged that because of his information, many of these ships had been sunk.

Among those arrested in Santiago was Alfred Kleiber, the director of the Banco Germanico of Chile, who also confessed to sending messages on ship movements to an Axis agent in Barcelona. There was also evidence which showed that many seemingly innocent commercial messages sent from Argentina and Chile were in fact coded messages to Axis agents. Other agents arrested were Dr Hans Borchers, the former Consul General in New York, an influential banker named Kreiber who reported shipping movements directly to Axis agents in Barcelona, and two other agents. A Santiago news dispatch stated that the spies had been arrested when counter-intelligence operatives caught them sending information to the spy net in Cuba

Insinuations that Spanish diplomats particularly were closely involved in espionage activities began to appear in the Western press as early as 1942, as the following *Times* article demonstrates:

Madrid, November 4.
The Spanish Foreign Office which had already issued various refutations of charges that Spanish ships help Axis submarines and that Spanish diplomatic and consular representatives abroad work for the Axis, has now published another official explanation of the humanitarian work being done by Spain on behalf of the subjects of belligerent countries and a restriction of 'twisted interpretations' of this country's attitude.

Since the entry of Japan into the war, when Spain assumed the protection of the interests of Germany, Italy and Japan in America, there have been insinuations in the press of certain American countries that Spanish diplomatic missions in that continent were working in the service of those powers ... The [Spanish] Foreign Ministry emphatically declares that these charges are false.

The actions of Spain, it says, are fully in accordance with international law, and based upon the humanitarian and gentlemanly principles which should rule among all civilized nations. She is ready to assume with equal zeal and in the same humanitarian spirit the protection of the interests of either side.[2]

Within weeks, Argentine authorities announced that an official investigation into the espionage activities of Axis nations was under way. They stated that the initial stages of the investigation included raids on Axis centres and the closure of at least one secret radio station.

The following month, after an interrogation of six of thirty-eight agents arrested during the anti-espionage sweep, the Argentine Public Prosecutor, Senor Belisario Gache Piran, admitted that Axis diplomats in Buenos Aires were widely involved in espionage activities directed against Argentina itself, and also against the United States. He stated that because Axis diplomats were involved, the cases would have to be referred to the Argentine Supreme Court. Argentine Judge Miguel Jantus ordered preventive imprisonment for the captured spies, and all the remaining Axis agents were detained at police headquarters for interrogation.

The next day the Argentine government issued a decree bringing into effect State control of telegraphic, telephonic and wireless communications to prevent Axis diplomats and agents from communicating in codes with their respective foreign offices. After the decree was issued, private radio became the only method then available to the Axis embassies because of the cut in telegraphic, telephonic and postal communications. The Argentine Cabinet decreed that from that time on, the State would have full control of all telegraphic telephonic and wireless communication entering or leaving Argentina. The preamble to the decree stated that the national territory 'must not be used to injure the military interests of American countries.' A few days later the Argentine Department of Posts and Telegraphs announced new regulations complementing the decree. However the restrictions of Axis messages was in fact rather less drastic than had been anticipated. Diplomatic messages in secret code by radio were not to exceed 100 words daily, or 700 words per week, and any of the quota of words unused in one week could not be carried over to the following week. The number of words in plain language messages remained unlimited.

It may be worth noting the volatile state of Argentine politics at this time when various Argentine governments fell because of professed pro-American policies and, even as late as 1944, Argentine officials were still prevaricating in reports detailing the activities of Japanese espionage agents operating within the country. A typical example is that of the fall of General Pedro Pablo Ramirez (who himself had taken office following a coup), who surrendered his presidential power to his Vice-President, General Edelmiro J. Farrell, in February 1944. Despite his own affiliations with fascist groups, Ramirez had been the driving force behind the unpopular decision to sever diplomatic relations with Germany and Japan on 26 January that year, and was himself forced from office by a swiftly executed military coup. The action was allegedly taken because of rumours that Ramirez was about to declare war on the Axis powers. Paradoxically, Farrell himself finally relented to US pressure, and on 27 March 1945 he announced that Argentina was officially at war with the Axis.

Also, at this time, the US authorities released a document which detailed the activities of an Axis spy ring operating through diplomatic posts in Chile. The document was published by the Inter-American Committee for the Political Defence of the Continent, a body representing all South American republics. The publication was preceded by a five-hour debate during which the Chilean delegate strove to prevent the information reaching the public. The document was based largely upon messages intercepted by the US Federal Communications Commission. These messages included the arrivals and departures of ships, details of military aid given by the United States to various Latin-American countries, names of Axis agents working through diplomatic posts, commercial businesses, news agencies and shipping companies, etc. The release of the report resulted in the widespread expulsion of Axis agents from Chile. Commenting on these expulsions, US Secretary of State Cordell Hull remarked:

> ... All true friends of Chile must have read with great satisfaction of the vigorous steps taken by the Chilean government in the last few days to smash the operating centres in Chile of Axis espionage, sabotage and subversive activities, which were being carried on in Chile, as elsewhere in this hemisphere.

Hull added that he had always been confident that President Rios [of Chile], when fully aware of the danger and scope of these activities, would act decisively and forcefully to bring them to an end.[3]

Spy nets were also working, to a limited degree, from the Cuban capital Havana, although shortly after the release of the Chilean report, General Manuel Benetiz of the Cuban Army – who was visiting the United States at the time – praised the work of the FBI in fighting Axis espionage and stated that Cuba would do everything in its power to stamp out Axis nets in his country.

Despite diplomatic and political moves to have these spy nets removed, Axis agents were to continue their work in South American countries, and especially in Argentina and Chile, throughout the entire war. In February 1944, General Wolf, the Military and Air Attaché to the German Embassy, and Rear Admiral Yokishita, the Japanese Naval Attaché in Argentina, were both arrested in their homes. An Argentine announcement stated that investigations by the police had shown that the two men were the heads of all Axis espionage operations in Argentina, and that conclusive proof of their guilt had been carefully gathered. Axis agents who had been expelled from other South American countries usually found their way into either Argentina or Chile. Large amounts of money were transferred from Axis nations to some of the major newspaper corporations and news agencies in those countries for the purpose of paying correspondents acting as agents, and also as payment for propaganda articles deriding the Allies and Allied war efforts and reaffirming the inevitability of an Axis victory.

In October 1941, as war with Japan loomed closer, nine wooden cases containing radio transmitter parts were loaded aboard the Japanese ship *Tao Maru* and shipped to the Naval Attaché in Argentina. The goods were later forwarded to Rio de Janeiro for intelligence work.

In 1942 the Mexican Department of the Interior assigned 400 carefully chosen counter-intelligence agents to travel through the country seeking out Axis agents and to suppress Axis propaganda, particularly among industrial workers.

In Brazil the problem chiefly concerned the Japanese, and the government enlisted the cooperation of the press in withholding news of a large round-up of Japanese aliens. Publicity given to an earlier round-up had resulted in several key agents being allowed to escape into Argentina. Brazilian officials stated that they had the German and Italian espionage nets well under control, but that they were still far from satisfied with the situation caused by the large Japanese colonies in the country, many of which harboured spy nets.

The earlier round-up which took place in March 1942, captured 300 Axis agents, among them a German Army colonel and a Japanese admiral who had been disguised as a farmer. The spy rings had been operating primarily in the states of Sao Paulo and Santa Catharina. Also seized during the raids were six clandestine radio stations, of which one – operating close to the Cattete Palace, the executive office of the President of Brazil in the heart of Rio de Janeiro – had a transmitting range of around 12,400 miles. Police had kept this radio station under surveillance for quite some considerable time before pouncing, waiting for many of its operators to make themselves known so that they could be captured in the swoop. Those arrested included a Swede who was reputed to have been the chief Axis radio expert in Latin America, and a Hungarian operator attached to the Hungarian Legation.

Payment for many of these operatives was made through the German Transatlantic Bank. Money for the purchase of the radio equipment – which had been bought in the United States – also came through the same bank. All those arrested were imprisoned on Flores Island, the notorious gaol in Rio de Janeiro Bay.

Most of the people taken into custody were Japanese, Germans or Italians. According to Brazilian officials, the Japanese: 'who disguised themselves as waiters, house-boys, laundry men, pedlars, canvassers and farmers were the most dangerous of the lot.'[4] According to Brazilian police, the disguised Japanese admiral had commanded a large fleet of fishing boats operating in Santos and along the coast of Sao Paulo, and it was said there was a plan to fit these boats with torpedoes and to send them out to sea to attack unarmed Allied merchant shipping.

Documents seized during the raid showed that Axis groups operating in Brazil were organizing their espionage nets like a well oiled and disciplined military machine. The police stated that the network was extremely extensive and well organized, and that there was a regular flow of intelligence information being transmitted to various Axis espionage headquarters in Europe, including 'digested and re-transmitted British and American news'.

There were about 250,000 Japanese nationals living in Brazil at this time, and the difficulties in keeping control over them – short of placing them into internment camps – were enormous. In August 1942, after German submarines had sunk nineteen Brazilian ships, Brazil declared war on Germany and Italy, but no declaration of war with Japan was made because of the difficulties involved over the large Japanese population living in the country. Many arrests were made however, and those interned were sent to the immigration detention centre on the Ilha das Flores in Rio de Janeiro Bay. Some of those arrested included General Yusci Tonogawa who had been disguised as a farm labourer, and a captain in the Japanese Army who had cleverly disguised himself as a woman to gain work as a cook in the household of a wealthy Brazilian businessman. Incredibly, his ruse worked for five years before he was discovered by the Brazilian police.

Japanese plans to establish espionage nets in South America were long term and of vast proportions. The establishment of such nets began some twenty years or so before the Second World War. The years between the two World Wars were important to Japan in establishing such nets – especially so in North and South America where, at this time, American counter-intelligence authorities – especially those of the Navy and Army – were understaffed, and evaluation of available intelligence was being made by men who, on the whole, were untrained in intelligence and counter-intelligence techniques. For example, in the mid 1930s the US Office of Naval Intelligence was staffed by only eighteen men. Two of these, aided by one clerk, were responsible for the entire Latin American region. With Japanese espionage teams virtually flooding into these countries at this time, such staffing levels were clearly extremely inadequate.

Large Japanese fishing fleets were gradually built up along the Mexican and Californian coastlines. These fleets were partially comprised of former British Coastguard vessels. The vessels were crewed by Japanese nationals or American nationals of Japanese descent. They were equipped with radios and ship-to-shore communication systems, and were under instructions from Japanese Naval Intelligence to report on US ship movements. They also made reports on soundings along the coastline and made recommendations regarding possible landing sites for a proposed Japanese invasion of California.

In Tijuana, not far from the Mexican–US border, the Japanese operated a well known brothel named the Molino Rojo, the 'Red Mill'. This establishment was used as a meeting place for Japanese agents where intelligence conferences often took place.

One of the leading Japanese agents operating in this region at the time was Toshio Miyazaki, a lieutenant-commander in the Japanese Navy who had studied as an exchange student at Stanford University. Miyazaki was responsible for recruiting as a spy a former US Navy yeoman named Harry Thomas Thompson. Thompson was a disgruntled unemployed farmhand when he met Miyazaki in San Pedro. Miyazaki gave Thompson US$500 with monthly payments of US$200 for his espionage services. Thompson used a yeoman's uniform to get aboard US Navy warships where he would pump the crews for information. He was later tracked down and arrested by the Office of Navy Intelligence after a friend of Thompson's had given information to the O.N.I. about Thompson's spying activities. Thompson was convicted of selling secrets to a foreign power and sentenced to fifteen years imprisonment.

Children were probably Japan's most effective means of propaganda in South America during the first thirty years of the century. A few years prior to the Second World War an Argentine Naval training ship called at several Japanese ports during the course of a world cruise. The ship was met by hundreds of Japanese children, dressed in white, who marched down the quay to hand flowers to the Argentine officers and crew. When Japanese immigrants arrived in Brazil, as the ships approached the quay, the Japanese children often sang, firstly the Brazilian National Anthem, and then the Japanese Anthem. Japanese settlements in Brazil were frequently visited by Japanese 'officials', representing their government. According to *The Times* correspondent in Buenos Aires in January 1942, the Japanese colonies in Latin America were definitely planned with a view to strategic importance. Investigations in Brazil had shown that of the 250,000 Japanese colonists, most went to the state of Sao Paulo and settled along the railway lines and roads leading to Sao Paulo City. Similarly, the Panama Canal was the centre of attraction for many Japanese settlers. Several years prior to the war, Japanese settlers requested permission of the Colombian government to found agricultural colonies along the valley of the River Cauca, not far from the frontier with Panama. The Colombians refused permission but allowed the Japanese to fish along the Colombian coasts. Later there was reason to believe that the Japanese were not so much interested in fishing as in photographing and sketching the coasts, allegedly to lay the groundwork for the future laying and sweeping of mines. Authority was also requested of the Costa Rican government to establish Japanese settlements along the Panamanian frontier. A frontier dispute between Costa Rica and Panama seemed to favour the plans, but to the Japanese the attraction of the locality was enhanced by the proximity of two ideal naval bases in the Pacific Ocean, the Gulf of Nicoya, and Coco Island, both belonging to Costa Rica. Like Columbia, Costa Rica refused the Japanese requests for settlement, but gave fishing privileges.

By November 1941, the Japanese Minister to Panama, Masatoshi Akiyama, was reporting that canal officials were investigating all known nationals of Axis nations, these included 2000 Germans, 700 Italians and 400 Japanese. Fearing a Japanese attack on the canal region, Panamanian authorities had stepped-up patrols, boosted fortifications, and had increased the garrisons in such areas as locks, spillways, and especially the spillway control tower on Lake Gatun, its electricity plant and the huge Gatun locks. Very precise details of these events – and most shipping movements – were being transmitted back to Japan by Akiyama.[5]

Prior to the outbreak of hostilities, Panama revised its laws concerning immigration and took a firm stand against Japanese nationals. The Japanese took their grievances to the Panamanian President, pro-fascist Arnulfo Arias, who, under strengthening Japanese diplomatic pressure, finally stated that Japanese interests would be taken care of and that Japanese nationals within Panama would be treated as any other foreign nationals. For a while Japanese espionage continued unhindered, but on October 8, 1941, Arias was deposed by *coup d'état* and replaced by the pro-American leader Ricardo Adolfo de la Guardia. This unexpected change of government signalled a rapid transformation to Panamanian/Japanese attitudes, and relations between the two countries quickly turned bitter.[6] At the time the Japanese Embassy in Rio de Janiero (then also representing Panamanian interests) stated: 'Thus we were not allowed any time to dispose of the stock of Japanese goods which we had ordered, and as a result 300 Japanese are out in the cold. If they cannot go elsewhere in South America or return to Japan, they will lapse into the condition of beggars or vagabonds.'[7]

JAPANESE NETWORKS IN THE UNITED STATES

Japanese spy nets were, of course, operating in the United States from before the beginning of the war. As early as December 1940, the Japanese were seeking the cooperation of a number of organizations in efforts to gather intelligence in the United States. On 10 December that year, shortly after the appointment of Kichisaburo Nomura as Japanese Ambassador to America, Yosuke Matsuoka, the Japanese Foreign Minister sent a secret cable to the Japanese Embassy in Washington:

> With the appointment of Ambassador Nomura we wish to formulate a definite plan for your propaganda and information gathering work by seeking cooperation of Japanese bank and business officials in the US.[8]

This message was relayed to all other Japanese consulates within the United States, and the following day Sadao Iguchi, a counsellor based in New York replied:

> ... The set up of the Press Attaché should be concentrated on the task of assembling information and of widening the intelligence net and its personnel. Special effort should be made to establish

personal contacts with members of the press and persons influential in American politics and business. The intelligence net should be so organised so as to be able to function even if there should be a severance of diplomatic and commercial relations between Japan and the US.[9]

Six days later Iguchi also stated:

As propaganda and enlightenment organs here we have the Japan Institute, the Tourist Bureau, and the Silk Office of the Ministry of Commerce and Communication. Other groups whose importance we cannot ignore for collecting information are the financial adviser, the Army and Navy Inspection Offices, representatives of Domei, Asashi, Nitiniti and Yomiuri [newspapers and agencies], the Bank of Japan, the Specie Bank, Mitsui, Mitsubishi...In order to obtain the fullest cooperation from the above it is well to establish an information committee centring around the press attaché.[10]

By the end of January 1941, as Japanese-American relations steadily worsened, the Japanese Foreign Office had decided to 'de-emphasize' all propaganda work then being carried out by their agents in the United States, and to concentrate instead on intelligence gathering. In consultation with the Japanese Intelligence Bureau, they had mapped out a comprehensive outline of objectives and had sent this outline to their embassy in Washington. The objectives included the establishment of an intelligence organ which was to function primarily from the Washington Embassy. This intelligence organ was to be directed towards determining the total strength of the United States – divided into three general classifications, political, economic, and military. They also planned to make a survey of all US persons or organizations of importance who openly or secretly opposed participation in the European war, and to make investigations of all anti-Semitic movements, Communists, movements of Negroes and labour organizations. The other major aspect of their plan was the recruitment of US citizens of foreign extraction (other than Japanese), Communists, Negroes, labour union members and anti-Semites for intelligence-gathering purposes, especially people who had access to governmental establishments, laboratories, factories and transportation facilities.

Also planned was the recruitment as espionage agents of 'second generation' Japanese persons then living in the United States. After war was declared, it was expected that many espionage nets would be moved to Mexico, making that country the nerve centre for all Japanese espionage activities directed against the United States. Therefore it was planned to set up facilities for a US-Mexico international intelligence route. This net was to cover Brazil, Argentina, Chile and Peru. Negotiations had already taken place with the German and Italian authorities to provide for close cooperation between the three countries in their intelligence gathering endeavours.

By early February 1941, Japanese Foreign Minister Matsuoka had instructed his embassy in Mexico City to begin upgrading its espionage activities. The embassy staff had been ordered to appoint several persons to direct espionage investigations and to set up the necessary information-gathering machinery ready for the time when the United States would be drawn into the war. Mexican consular staff advised Tokyo that additional 'advisers' should immediately be sent to Mexico City, particularly personnel with air and technical backgrounds.

On 8 February, the New York Japanese Consulate advised Tokyo that because of worsening American-Japanese relations, it seemed likely that a financial freezing order would soon be made on Japanese funds (much of which were used to finance espionage operations), and that in the light of this possibility several of the leading Japanese banks had already begun reducing their staff.

A few weeks later, by mid-February, Tokyo had advised its embassy in Washington of its information requirements. Some of these requirements included the amount of strengthening of military preparations on the Pacific Coast and in the Hawaii area, ship and aircraft movements, especially large bombers and sea planes, whether or not merchant vessels were being requisitioned by the US government, and the calling up of army or navy personnel and their training. At this time too, Tokyo appointed Colonel Hideo Iwakuro to the Japanese Embassy in Washington, ostensibly as 'Aide to the Military Attaché', but actually to assist with espionage activities which were being directed through the embassy. Shortly afterwards, Tokyo announced the appointment of Secretary Taro Terasaki as the Chief of Intelligence and Propaganda in the United States. Terasaki, whose brother was the Director of the American Bureau at the Japanese Foreign Office in Tokyo, was given wide powers in order to perform his duties effectively. In a message to the Washington Embassy in mid-March, Foreign Minister Matsuoka had stated:

> Please put secretary Terasaki in full charge of directing information and propaganda in the United States. Please have him maintain close contact with all our offices for the purpose of co-ordinating information-gathering through these channels, also

please have him convene or visit officials concerned whenever he deems it necessary. Please allow him to travel to South and Central America whenever he feels it necessary to contact our information officials in these countries. Bearing in mind that sufficient funds have been provided to give him a reasonable amount of freedom of action in pursuing his work, please offer him every assistance at your disposal.[11]

By the following month, Terasaki, having gained a significant insight into American foreign policy, warned Tokyo that, in his opinion, the United States was preparing for war. He asked the Japanese Foreign Office to prepare for this contingency by securing sufficient espionage funds and the rapid employment of more spies.

At this time too, Tokyo advised its consulates and embassies of the need to dispose of sensitive documents in the event of the United States entering into a war with Japan, and on 11 March the Minister in Santiago advised Tokyo that local Japanese merchants had withdrawn the greater part of their funds from America.

By now, the Japanese themselves were becoming increasingly aware of the need to protect themselves against Allied espionage, and in a message to his embassy in Rome, Foreign Minister Matsuoka informed the Japanese Ambassador there that, under the current world conditions, Japan was redoubling its counter-espionage activities. Matsuoka ordered the Rome Ambassador to make a thorough investigation of all applicants for Japanese visas, and that all news correspondents, magazine writers, military officials and any other person of doubtful political leanings were not to be issued with visas unless their objectives had been painstakingly checked and verified.

Plans to have the US espionage nets more strongly formulated proceeded with speed and efficiency. Various clandestine recruitment operations were undertaken, couriers were employed.

In May 1941 the Japanese Consul in Los Angeles, Kenji Nakauchi, advised Tokyo that they were doing everything within their power to establish outside contacts and to recruit possible espionage agents. Nakauchi was in the process of establishing close relations with various organizations in the aircraft manufacturing industry and military establishments. He had engaged reliable Japanese second-generation citizens in the San Pedro and San Diego areas to keep a close watch on shipping and aircraft movements, and other agents had been employed to watch the US-Mexico border. He had also succeeded in employing the services as agents of several US servicemen of Japanese descent then in the US Army, and had spies working in several aircraft manufacturing factories. Nakauchi's staff were working with anti-Jewish movements and were trying to establish contacts with persons within the movie industry who had openly professed strong anti-war feelings. Contact had also been established with influential Negroes who had promised to keep the Japanese informed about the operations of Negro organizations.

The leading Japanese agent responsible for building ties with such Negro movements was Deniti Hikida, a recognized authority on the Negro problem within the United States and a highly experienced agitator. By June 1941 however, his primary role of recruiting Negroes for intelligence and propaganda work had largely been negated because of intensive surveillance by US counter-intelligence staff. Early that month the Washington Embassy sent the following message to the Japanese Foreign Office:

> Deniti Hikida – an authority on the Negro problem in the United States we have been utilizing for propaganda work among the Negroes, gathering general intelligence, investigations, and in various other capacities – expresses his desire to return (to Japan) on the *Tatsuta Maru*.
>
> Recently he is being subjected to strict surveillance by the authorities of this country, and for this reason we feel that it is in our interest to have him return home. In view of his excellent record of cooperation with this office in the past, will you please give consideration to our advancing him his passage for his return voyage. (We are paying him his discharge allowance from our secret intelligence fund.) Because the time of departure is fast approaching, please advise us immediately.
>
> Will you give consideration to employing this man upon his return home to our offices there. We feel his specialized knowledge will be of value to us.[12]

Japanese plans to carry out sabotage in the United States involved Negro movements and – originally at least – an ultra-nationalist right-wing subversive movement known as the Silver Shirts. This organization, rabidly anti-Jewish and anti-Communist, had been disbanded in 1940 after six years of disturbing existence. Its members went underground however, and continued to print various publications which were widely distributed throughout the country from the organization's base in Indianapolis. According to these publications, members of the society believed that the Roosevelt administration was riddled with international Judaism and Communism and was under the influence of British royalty. The publications claimed that America should be defended from such destructive forces and that US foreign policy should be formulated in such a way to save the human race from the, 'enslaving grasp of the international Jews.' However, even the Japanese baulked at the unfavourable reports they obtained about the activities of the Silver Shirts, and they turned instead to the American Negroes, a massive force of largely disgruntled citizens, many of whom had a racial axe to grind against white Americans. The Japanese allegedly worked in cooperation with several powerful Negro groups to establish espionage and sabotage operations, including the Negro Congress, the Negro Alliance and the National Association for the Advancement of Colored People.

Mexico

By early June 1941 the plans to establish a formidable espionage net operating from Mexico were moving rapidly ahead. On 2 June, Foreign Minister Matsuoka informed Yoshiaki Miura, his Ambassador in Mexico City, that 100,000 yen had been appropriated for the exclusive use of espionage against the United States, with Mexico as its base. Matsuoka stated that Miura was to work in close contact with agents in Los Angeles, Houston, New Orleans and New York. Miura's subordinate – himself an expert espionage agent – was Jisaburo Sato, the Naval Attaché then based in Mexico. Sato was working towards training locals in espionage, and was preparing to send to Tokyo several men, including José Llergo, 'an outstanding Mexican news reporter', whom Sato believed would be capable of greatly influencing the Mexican press. The formation of a regular intelligence route was investigated. This route was to run through Laredo, El Paso, Nogales and Mexicali to Mexico City. However, it was later decided to abandon plans to use Mexicali as one of the bases, as the border town was a sensitive point and Japanese nationals living there were under close surveillance by US and Mexican counter-intelligence operatives. It was also planned that after war had been declared, and if Mexico then officially became an ally of the United States, a scheme would be devised to establish a secret radio transmitter in Mexico City. If the transmitter were discovered, the operatives would be instructed to plead the rather unlikely protection of diplomatic immunity.

On 17 June, arrangements were made by the Japanese to secure copies of charts and maps detailing the locations of military installations and equipment in Panama. A Japanese espionage agent had successfully managed to get Italian officials to provide him with copies of the charts. However, as Japanese codes were suspect, he was concerned that if he should send details over the air, the US authorities would know that the charts had been obtained, and therefore make arrangements to alter the siting of military hardware and personnel. The only way to have the documents arrive securely in Tokyo was by courier. The plan was subsequently dropped because at least some Japanese diplomats were being searched by airline officials. Some months later, however, the plan to forward details was revised. The maps were then forwarded to Japan via a circuitous and secret route. They were carried to Chile by Japanese Minister Yamagata. From there they were carried by Assistant Attaché Usui to the Italian Ambassador in Buenos Aires. A Japanese courier named Tatuma then took them with him when he boarded the steamer *Buenos Aires Maru*, bound for Japan.[13]

Details of exactly how the South American Japanese spy nets were being formulated were revealed to US authorities in August 1941 when Taro Terasaki, the head of Japanese intelligence activities in the United States, who was co-ordinating all Japanese espionage in the Americas, ordered all Japanese offices to give immediate attention to the recruitment of qualified espionage agents. Terasaki stated that each Japanese spy office was to be equipped with a radio which would be capable of receiving US domestic broadcasts, and that a central listening post would be established in Brazil where persons proficient in English shorthand would be on duty around the clock. Subscriptions to many important US newspapers and magazines, particularly military, science and engineering magazines, were to be taken out in South American names and sent for analysis to experts in Brazil, Argentina, Chile and Columbia. Terasaki advised his agents that telegraphic sections of diplomatic posts were to be enlarged and the intelligence sources within the Domei news agency, and Spanish and Portuguese correspondents, were to be utilized to their full capacity. He stated that Japanese merchants were to be used to report on US economic conditions, and that if German and Italian diplomatic staffs were ordered out of the country, then their informants were to be hired as spies by the Japanese.[14]

The Philippines
In the Philippines, Japanese Consul Katsumi Nihro was carrying out a highly successful espionage operation, informing Tokyo of the movements of US ships and troops. His staff, also trained

agents, were keeping members of the American military under surveillance, and at the same time keeping a close watch on several persons who had entered the country as temporary tourists. They were aware that they themselves were under surveillance by Allied agents working through the British Embassy. The Japanese were also interested in the large increase of Chinese immigrants to the Philippines during June 1941. In fact 1,013 Chinese immigrants had entered the country, as compared with a monthly average of just 250. The Japanese believed that these men were to be used as Allied fifth-columnists in the event of a Japanese invasion of the archipelago.

Japanese intelligence reports were primarily concerned with the archipelago's fortifications, especially on Luzon, the construction of airports, and the movements of warships. On 20 August, Foreign Minister Toyoda instructed his intelligence agents in Manila to make weekly reports. Two months later Toyoda instructed his agents to make a special report on all the new defence works which were being built by the Americans along the east, west and south coasts of Luzon

In July 1941, Mr Negishi (first name unknown), a Japanese secret agent, was appointed to engage in intelligence gathering in the Philippines. After this there was a detailed flow of information streaming from Manila to the Japanese Foreign Office. The Japanese were aware of the size of the Philippines armed forces, its reserves, the number of American troops stationed on the islands, the number of aircraft and ships and many other top-secret details.

Financing for these espionage activities, especially after a monetary freezing order following the Japanese invasion of Indo-China, was made from a secret fund controlled by Consul Nihro. Such secret funds, always controlled by diplomats and used specifically for espionage subversion and propaganda, were commonplace in Japanese diplomatic posts. On 11 August 1941, the Japanese Ambassador in Washington sent a detailed message to his superiors in Tokyo which listed all of the secret funds then held in the United States. These included two accounts of $17,425 and $20,556 held in Washington, and three accounts in San Francisco totalling $106,606.[15]

The following day Tokyo announced that several 'assistant military attachés' had been appointed to the Legation in Washington, these included Colonel Kenkichi Shinjo, Major Kita Yoshioka and Hinkai Ko. The term, 'assistant military attachés' was generally accepted as being a euphemism for espionage agents.[16]

During the whole of 1940 and 1941, Japanese diplomatic missions in the United States, Great Britain, South America, the Philippines and the Hawaiian Islands continued to forward vast amounts of intelligence to Tokyo. For example, on 16 August, 1941, Consul Kenji Nakauchi in Hollywood reported that a ship named the *St Claire* had loaded 95,000 barrels of aviation gasolene and had sailed from Los Angeles for Vladivostok, and was scheduled to rendezvous with several other American vessels in the Pacific, all of which were carrying fuel or military supplies. At the same time a Japanese spy named Jisaburo Sato (formerly based in Mexico and now based in Seattle), reported that the British warship *Warspite* had entered the port of Bremerton.[17]

Sato's reports were invariably accurate, and he sent many such valuable intelligence items to his superiors in Tokyo.

On 16 October 1941, the Japanese Foreign Minister, Teijiro Toyoda instructed Sato to begin making reports every 10 days, and specifically ordered that all movements of American flagships-of-fleet or scouting forces were to be reported immediately.[18]

At this time too, US authorities were stepping up their counter-intelligence activities against the Japanese. In August 1941, several members of the FBI and the US Treasury Department raided offices of the Yokohama Specie Bank, and the Sumitomo, Mitsui and Mitsubishi branch offices in Los Angeles. They made detailed inspections of all files and even checked letters and documents of private individuals. Employees of the Yokohama Specie Bank were forbidden to enter their offices during the inspection, to prevent them from burning incriminating documents.[19] Japanese diplomats in all US cities were kept under close surveillance and had their travel rights severely restricted. In California, US immigration officials arrested approximately 100 Japanese nationals who had been caught in possession of false passports, most of these were quickly deported.[20]

By September 1941 Morito Morishima, the Consul-General in New York who closely assisted Taro Terasaki – the Head of Japanese intelligence in the US (Morishima later led the espionage net operating out of Lisbon), had advised the Japanese Foreign Office that because of the US freezing of assets and the subsequent lack of funds, he had decided to dismiss all minor agents, those who were not supplying him with valuable information, and to transfer all of the valuable agents from the legation to the Japanese Cultural Institute (a front for subversion and Japanese propaganda). Morishima stated that these people would be diverted from the task of disseminating propaganda to the exclusive employment of gathering intelligence and other espionage activities, such as the recruiting of spies. Morishima also advised that the Japanese propaganda publications *Living Age*, *Foreign Observer*, *Far Eastern Trade*, and the *Culture of Wheels Library* would cease publication. Also scrapped because of the lack of funds was the distribution of propaganda films through the YMCA offices and other agencies. Morishima stated that while these reductions would mean that many Japanese nationals would be out of work, he intended keeping several such employees on the pay-roll, although at greatly reduced wages.[21]

In Panama, the Japanese Minister, Masatoshi Akiyama, was responsible for all intelligence reports. His Ministry was strategically positioned to report on all shipping movements through the Panama Canal, reports which were quite invaluable to the Japanese military. In September 1941, Akiyama forwarded to Tokyo an estimate of the money he would require for his espionage activities during the forthcoming year. These expenses included bonuses for spies assigned to watching the canal and payments to be made to newspaper correspondents and other espionage recruits. Akiyama's total estimate per month amounted to $730.00.[22]

In San Francisco, the Japanese intelligence agent was named Yoshio Muto. He too was a valuable source of information, primarily concerning the shipping movements in San Francisco harbour, dates of arrivals and departures, and especially details of cargoes and the movements of troopships.

As early as 1942, just months after the Pearl Harbor attack, agents of the FBI, acting on 'very definite suspicions of espionage,' among enemy aliens in California, made a series of raids in February that year, one of which was at Vallejo, suspiciously close to the US Navy's base at Mare Island, and arrested nine Japanese, one of them a woman. They seized several cameras and radio sets, some weapons and a quantity of naval signal flags, maps and flares. During a raid a few days previously, they had arrested fifteen Japanese spies and seized a small arsenal of firearms and a cache of dynamite which the Japanese claimed they used for land clearing. Several other Japanese aliens were also arrested, all of whom were in the possession of illegal firearms, maps and short-wave radios.

Also at this time FBI agents raided Terminal Island in the centre of Los Angeles Harbour where up to 2000 Japanese aliens were living in a slum of old huts. 383 men were arrested and interrogated.

On 19 February 1942, President Franklin Roosevelt signed Executive Order 9066 which allowed the US Army to intern any alien believed to be a potential threat to the nation's security. What followed later became a tragic scandal in United States history, as thousands of people of Japanese descent were rounded up and herded into temporary camps at show-grounds or race-tracks while more permanent accommodation at concentration camps was being constructed. There were ten camps spread through the United States, in California, Arizona, Utah, Idaho, Wyoming, Colorado and Arkansas. All of these camps came under the control of the Civilian War Relocation Authority. Most of the camps were surrounded by barbed wire, and guards manned the watch-towers armed with automatic weapons. Conditions were not harsh, some of the cooks, for example, were well known chefs in their own right. The internees complained primarily of boredom, and most stated that being in the camps was simply their part in the American war effort. In November 1942, Colonel Karl Robin Bendetsen was awarded the Distinguished Service Medal for moving more than 110,000 Japanese from a 150 miles West Coast strip to 16 temporary assembly centres in Washington, Oregon, California and Arizona. In 1942 the largest camp was at Manzanar in the Owens River Valley where, at that time, around ten thousand Japanese and Japanese/Americans were incarcerated. It was not until 1980 that the Commission on Wartime Relocation and Internment of Civilians found that the incarceration of these people had been a grave injustice. Eight years later, in 1988, President Reagan signed a bill which made allowances for $20,000 to be paid to each of the 60,000 surviving internees.

THE JAPANESE SPIES

However, during those early years of the war there was little doubt that espionage activities were steadily increasing. But how were these widely diversified spy nets formed, who were the men responsible for their creation? As we shall see, the Axis powers worked closely together on many occasions in setting up their spy nets, this is particularly true of Germany and Japan, although there is little doubt that in Europe and the Americas at least, Germany certainly led the field and was far more successful in its spying endeavours than Japan could ever hope to be. Japanese spy masters, however, were diligent and determined, despite the many difficulties they faced in setting up their nets. The men responsible for these nets included a rich pastiche of principal personalities.

Yakichiro Suma

Firstly, there was Yakichiro Suma, the ambitious and dedicated minister who headed the Japanese Legation in Madrid. Yakichiro Suma's diplomatic career was a long and honourable one. Prior to the war he served four years as Japanese Consul-General in war-torn Nanking, and was transferred to Washington in October 1937 as a counsellor, where he was second in rank to Ambassador Saito. That year Suma made numerous statements claiming that the Japanese war in China would be contained in China and that the war was being fought to protect Japanese interests from misgovernment by Communist elements. Suma was one of the primary movers in instigating Japanese espionage activities against the Allied powers during the Second World War. A career diplomat, highly intelligent, perceptive and a fanatical believer in the power and right of dominance of the Japanese people and the establishment of a Greater East Asia Co-Prosperity Sphere, he became the driving force behind what was to become the most successful of the many Japanese espionage posts in Europe. There is no doubt that he worked diligently and earnestly to place agents in various parts of America, both north and south, and to glean intelligence from a wide variety of sources. As the war drew to a close in 1945, he became even more motivated, fighting diligently to maintain his intelligence net, often under difficult and dangerous circumstances. However, under mounting diplomatic and political pressure he, like many of his colleagues in the Japanese Diplomatic Corps, was forced to abandon his post and his espionage net as the tide of war swung irretrievably in the Allies' favour.

Morito Morishima

The second most important man in charge of Japanese intelligence-gathering from Europe was almost certainly Morito Morishima, formerly the Consul-General in New York who, prior to the outbreak of hostilities, had assisted Taro Terasaki, the head of Japanese espionage in the United States. Morishima was transferred after Pearl Harbor to become Minister of the Japanese Legation in Lisbon. While in New York, Morishima had been an integral part of setting up the Japanese intelligence organization in that country, working with a variety of highly experienced Japanese espionage agents. Like Suma, Morishima was a dedicated career diplomat with more than twenty years of service behind him. Both he and Suma realized early in the conflict that Lisbon and Spain, being neutral countries, strategically placed on the Iberian Peninsula, would become virtual hotbeds of intelligence-gathering for both Axis and Allied powers.

The key to the Mediterranean was Gibraltar, and whoever controlled the Mediterranean also controlled the Indian Ocean, so Gibraltar became of vital importance. It was protected by the Iberian Peninsula and the Allies worked long and diligently to maintain the status quo and to keep both Portugal and Spain neutral. Had either of them swung into the Axis camp, Hitler could have walked through and captured Gibraltar, virtually cutting off the Allies from the Mediterranean.

In addition to these dangers, control of the Iberian Peninsula was vital to the security of the Azores. If the Azores had fallen into German hands, Great Britain would have been cut off from the eastern South Atlantic. The vital shipping route to North Africa – where the campaigns against Rommel were being carried out – would have been closed.

Fortunately, both countries maintained their neutrality – albeit somewhat reluctantly at times, Spain, having received substantial military aid from both Germany and Italy during the bloody Spanish Civil War, quite obviously favoured the Axis – at least until the tide of war began to turn in 1943/44. Thus these two countries were swamped with espionage agents, both Allied and Axis, as political and diplomatic manoeuvres were made to swing the balance in favour of each party. Morishima – emulating Suma in Madrid – quickly established a comprehensive spy net which operated directly from his legation in Lisbon. Much of his information was code named *Fuji* intelligence, some of it was excellent material and of real value to the Japanese, but much of it was only poor quality, often inaccurate or misleading. Yet on several occasions the various Japanese Foreign Ministers in Tokyo warmly congratulated Morishima on the value of the information he forwarded in code to Tokyo. Later, however, the security of Morishima's legation was to come under critical examination by the Japanese.

Hiroshi Oshima
Hiroshi Oshima was the Japanese Ambassador to Berlin during the war, serving firstly as a military attaché and later being promoted to Ambassador. As such it was his arduous responsibility to maintain relations with Hitler's government, and

to relay all of the mountain of messages and correspondences which passed back and forth between the two powers during that time. Oshima was a close friend of General Tojo (later executed by the Allies for war crimes). Oshima, Tojo and General Tomoyuki Yamashita, the so called Tiger of Malaya, were all classmates during their training at the Staff College in Tokyo, graduating in 1916. (Yamashita too was executed for war crimes in the Philippines at the end of the war.) During the First World War these three men formed a close bond and were part of the Young Officers' clique, the members of which generally believed that Japan should profit from the war by making military advances into China. All three men were early advocates of a strong militant German/Japanese alliance. During the early 1940s Oshima was an intense protagonist in favour of Japan's entry into the war on Germany's side. He was also a close friend of Admiral Canaris – the highly respected head of the Abwehr, the German military intelligence arm. (Canaris was later executed by Nazis for his involvement in the 20 July 1944 plot to assassinate Hitler.) As the head of an embassy, Oshima outranked both Suma in Madrid and Morishima in Lisbon, and quite naturally much of the intelligence gathered by the two spy-masters was forwarded to Oshima in Berlin. This information was often then shared with the various German intelligence and counter-intelligence services who would reciprocate by sharing (at least some of) their own intelligence with the Japanese. But Oshima was not merely a conduit through which the information passed, he too was very closely involved in establishing an espionage net which operated from the Japanese Embassy in Berlin. This net was not nearly as successful as the two in Spain and Portugal, for it was far from the centres of Allied information, yet it did achieve some significant successes.

At a session of the international military tribunal for the Far East, held in Tokyo in 1946, the prosecution introduced an important secret document, drawn up by the German Reichsführer Heinrich Himmler, which had been discovered by American investigators in 1945. The document, dated 31 January, 1939, stated that Oshima had confidentially informed Himmler that he had succeeded in sending ten Russians armed with bombs across the Caucasian frontier in an attempt to assassinate Stalin. The document also disclosed that Oshima had been undertaking – in collaboration with German subversive agencies – the long-range task of 'the disintegration of Russia from the Caucasus and Ukraine'. The prosecution introduced a report of an interrogation of Oshima in which he admitted that he had been deeply involved in the organization of espionage against Russia in Poland and elsewhere. Oshima stated that fear of Russia was uppermost in the minds of Japanese military leaders, to the extent that they wanted any mutual aid pact to be directed primarily against that country. He admitted, however, that when he became Ambassador to Germany in October 1938, he and his co-defendant at the military tribunal, Toshio Shiatori, the former Ambassador to Italy, in an agreement with the German government, and in violation of the desires of their own government, worked for a pact aimed against the rest of the world.

If Suma and Morishima were the acknowledged spy-masters in Europe, then Oshima was the driving force. It was Oshima who, shortly after the attack on Pearl Harbor, called together all of the leading Japanese diplomats in Europe for a special intelligence meeting in Berlin. At that meeting these diplomats studied espionage strategies and objectives which were to carry them through until the end of the war.

Ramon Suner

Ramon Suner was the Spanish Foreign Minister based in Madrid. The brother-in-law of General Franco, he was a shrewd and clever diplomat. Suner fully endorsed the establishment of a Japanese espionage network on Spanish soil and did everything in his power to assist Suma in his intelligence-gathering activities.

Suner had begun his career as a lawyer, graduating from the University of Madrid. He became the vice-president of *CEDA*, (the Spanish Confederation of the Autonomous Right), and later embraced the Falange Party doctrines.[23] During the Spanish Civil War he was captured by the Republicans in Madrid and held in the notorious *Model* prison where he witnessed a mass execution of prisoners of war. He escaped from the prison hospital and fled to Nationalist territory in February 1937.

Described by the US Under Secretary of State, Cordell Hull, as '... flamboyant'[24] both Suner and General Franco firmly believed in the inevitability of an Axis victory and that such a victory was in the best interests of Spain. Of course, German espionage agents were also pouring into Spain – especially during the first months of the war – and Suner served the intelligence-gathering interests of both Axis countries equally, indeed he himself was often a superb source of secret material and willingly disclosed to Suma (and presumably to German agents) details of highly confidential and sensitive communications which constantly flowed through his ministry. It was Suner who introduced one particular spy to Suma, a Spanish national, and an acknowledged expert on espionage activities, which allowed Suma to establish his highly successful *TO* spy net in the United States.

Count Gomez Jordana

Count Gomez Jordana, a monarchist, was Suner's successor after Suner had fallen into disgrace following a violent argument with General Franco. Far more cunning and wily, Jordana from the very beginning of his term in office, informed the Japanese that while he was, of course, aware of the espionage activities being carried on right under his nose, he had decided to do nothing about them. He stipulated that, ostensibly at least, he wanted no part in the activities. Yet throughout his term he was to aid Japanese intelligence-gathering in Spain.

PROBLEMS FACING ESPIONAGE AGENTS

It may also be worth noting here the dangers and difficulties facing espionage agents during the Second World War. Perhaps more than any other war, spies were very active during the 1939-45 years – the reasons for this were varied. The more countries to become involved in the conflict naturally meant that more intelligence and counter-intelligence services were also involved. The war covered vast territories on many fronts, and of particular importance was the very speedy technical advances being made in weaponry, aircraft, radar, anti-submarine devices, and rocketry. A typical example, of course, was the development of the atom bomb. The agents sent into enemy territory to sniff out these technological advances were, on the whole, brave men, no matter what their nationality, for, if caught, they faced almost certain death.

Britain, for example, was ruthless in its treatment of captured spies and dozens went to the gallows, including the Japanese spy of Dutch descent, Charles Albert Van den Kieboorn. Den Kieboorn is a classical example of how ill prepared the Axis spies were for the task they had set out to achieve. He was landed with two German spies, Karl Meier and Rudolph Waldberg at Romney Marsh, on England's south-east coast on the night of 2 September, 1940. The men separated, as they believed it may have seemed suspicious for them to be seen walking together. That morning Meier knocked on the door of a public house and asked for a bottle of cider. His training in Germany had not provided him with the knowledge that British public houses did not open until at least 10.30 a.m. The landlord, suspecting Meier had recently landed, called the police. Meier was arrested and thoroughly interrogated. Twenty-four hours later Waldberg was found and arrested – principally through information supplied by Meier. The Japanese spy Van den Kieboorn was remarkably unsuccessful in his spying endeavours. Shortly after landing he carelessly walked into a patrol of a company of the Somerset Light Infantry. Because of his distinctly Asiatic features he was questioned by the platoon leader, and, as he could not supply plausible answers, he was arrested. Waldberg and Meier were found guilty of espionage and hanged on 10 December. Van den Kieboorn went to the gallows a week later. One agent landed by submarine on the east coast of England, stole a bicycle and rode away on the wrong side of the road. He was almost immediately arrested and later hanged.

Axis Agents in Britain

Agents were introduced into Britain in various ways, firstly through the accepted routes of Portugal, Ireland and Spain, and later through other neutral countries not quite so pro-Axis, such as Sweden and Switzerland. One of the favourite methods of getting agents from Spain to Britain was aboard the regular boats bringing cargoes of oranges.[25] Suspected agents were interrogated at the Royal Victoria Patriotic School in Wandsworth, which had been set up as a special investigation centre for the flood of European refugees fleeing from Nazi control. The centre was extremely successful. Few spies, if any, managed to evade the lengthy and exhaustive procedures which would eventually place them on the road to the gallows.

At the outbreak of war there were several Axis spy nets in Britain, two German nets, and the burgeoning Japanese net operating from the Japanese Embassy in London. The most efficient of these three were the ones belonging to the Germans. The first of these consisted of German au-pair girls – and there were several thousand of them – whose principal task it was to report on everyday life and on the households (often of important people) in which they were employed. The second net consisted of around thirty-five or forty experienced and hardened German spies. At the outbreak of hostilities most of these people were known to British counter-intelligence and they were quickly rounded up. The Japanese believed (primarily because they had been told so by the Germans), that the Germans had an efficient spy net operating in England. In fact the only spies the Germans had in England were those who had been caught by the British and turned into double agents – these agents were used to feed the Germans with false information for many years.

The Japanese spy net in London was never very efficient. Even before the outbreak of hostilities the British were suspicious of the Japanese. Those few who remained in the country were rarely in positions of trust and so their opportunities for intelligence-gathering were limited. Thus they were often constrained to rely upon the services of German agents. In 1941, before the attack on Pearl Harbor and when the Japanese Embassy in London was still operating, the Japanese were regularly paying the Germans for intelligence or making financial drops on behalf of the Germans, who, of course, did not have any diplomatic posts in England at this time. Such a financial 'drop' was to be made at 16.00 hours one evening at the terminus of the Number 11 bus route at Victoria Station. The German spy was a double agent named Wulf Schmidt whose code-name was Tate. Tate had been parachuted into Britain in 1940 and quickly captured by British counter-intelligence. He had been 'turned' and for the remainder of the war he supplied the Germans with false information while still drawing a substantial amount of German pay. Tate had been instructed by the Abwehr[26] to meet a Japanese agent for a payment consisting of £200. The Japanese was to carry a copy of *The Times*, in which the money was to be concealed. In his other hand he was to carry a book. Tate was to wear a red tie and also to carry a newspaper and book. After the fifth stop, both men were instructed to leave the bus and then to continue their journey on the next bus which came along. On the bus, after an agreed exchange of code-words, the money would be paid. Unfortunately, the Abwehr was unaware that the bus from Victoria Station no longer ran and the meeting was postponed. Supposedly desperate for money, Tate signalled the Abwehr to arrange another meeting, this time suggesting the Number 16 bus. That meeting finally took place several days later – observed and photographed by the Special Branch of Scotland Yard. The Japanese agent was tailed back to his embassy and recognized as Assistant Naval Attaché Lieutenant Commander Mitinory Yosii.

The Germans, on the other hand, while having an excellent counter-intelligence system, were never as successful in catching Allied agents. The reasons for this were simple. Allied agents in France had the advantage of having the Resistance movement to work with. Those who were sent to Germany were well prepared and trained, and carried forged papers of such perfection that only one or two were actually caught because of them. Most captured Allied agents were, not unexpectedly, quickly executed.

Axis Agents in the United States

In the United States, the FBI was also extremely successful in finding Axis agents, and those found almost always ended their days in the electric chair. Even as early as 1941, before the US officially entered the war with Germany and Japan, the American press was busy with vociferous campaigns awakening the people to the dangers of Axis agents in their midst and the scope and potential of an American fifth column. Scores of books and thousands of magazine and newspaper articles sketched portraits of Axis ambitions in the western hemisphere – often drawing to the readers' attention the fact that the American West Coast was a vulnerable and convenient site for Japanese attacks.

In August 1938, Martin Dies was appointed to head a Congressional Committee to investigate the workings of Axis subversive activities in America. The Dies Committee, however, had to struggle against the popular topic of American civil liberties. Dies was accused of being too ready to seize upon an appearance of guilt and to brand many harmless people and some organizations as pro-Axis. As a result his committee met with a great deal of scorn and opposition, but Dies himself seemed to revel in the role of a persecuted crusader and continued with his task undaunted.

During December 1940 he published two reports, the White Paper dealing with Axis activities in the United States and the Red Paper dealing with Communist conspiracies and infiltration into the ranks of American labour. Despite the prior ridicule which Dies had received, the White Paper prompted Americans into calling for immediate action against all organizations linked in any way to Axis policies or ideals. Dies was particularly recognized for his exposure of Dr Manfred Zapp, America's Director of the German Trans-Ocean News Service, who was allegedly closely involved in sending intelligence to Nazi Germany. Dies also received recognition for the work his committee carried out in recognizing the endeavours of Axis commercial intentions in the United States, including the animus of extending patent controls – especially over chemicals. Dies went so far in his report as to call the Federal Bureau of Investigation '... entirely ineffective', and accused the Department of Justice of being inactive in their endeavours to curb the rise of Axis fifth-column activity. The Attorney General, Robert H. Jackson, accordingly made public the relevant findings of the Department of Justice concerning some of the allegations made by the Dies Committee. He announced that his department had been keeping a close watch on Dr Zapp, and had almost completed a legal case against Zapp when the publication of the Dies findings 'made further investigation useless'.

President Roosevelt stepped in to rebuke Dies in a public telegram. A working agreement between the Dies Committee and the FBI was outlined in a letter from the Attorney General emphasizing the restraints under which the Federal Authority should always proceed. Dies made no secret of his intentions to arrange for investigations of certain Axis organizations.

On one occasion the FBI had its own secret agents employed in a German agency. These agents later stated that they had been about to come into possession of original and damning correspondences. Dies, however, gave public notice that he intended raiding the agency. Subsequently all original documents were destroyed, some were transferred to the local German Consulate and fake documents and files were hastily substituted. When the Dies men swooped they found enough evidence to excite the interest of a local journalist, but not enough to warrant a prosecution.

Dies's efforts in spy-hunting encouraged many patriotic citizens, including journalists, to institute their own private man-hunts, many of which ended farcically – and presumably in litigation.

Yet Dies continued his efforts unabated. Taking industry by industry, he promised to unmask the names and affiliations of employers, firms and workers who had any hand in unpatriotic activities.

The Dies Committee, however unpopular or risible it seemed to the general public, did have its advantages. It brought into sharp focus the shortcomings of the US law with special regard to the activities of fifth-columnists. It particularly demonstrated the need for wider Federal powers and the inadequacy of the police to deal effectively with the growing activities of fifth-columnists. The police were largely working under laws designed for a peace time situation, but now that war with the Axis powers was looming, firmer counter-intelligence measures were rapidly becoming necessary. The Department of Justice could not arrest people or groups merely on suspicion, it could act only against individuals on evidence legally admissible before a grand jury. In dealing with sabotage the Attorney General was the victim of the confusing separation of Federal and State powers. Realizing this serious inadequacy, President Roosevelt signed an amendment to the Sabotage Act on 30 November 1940, extending Federal powers under that Act, but even after this amendment the Attorney General was empowered to punish sabotage only against materials and utilities, 'intended for the use of the United States in connection with the national defense'. The wrecking of an aircraft, gun or tank being manufactured for Great Britain, for example, would have been a problem for the local State authority to act upon, and the punishments would often be less rigorous than those of the Federal authorities.

At the beginning of 1941 the US Department of Justice requested the right to tap the telephones of suspects, a right which had been refused just months previously. The right was finally granted. The American people also began to take notice of the remarkable freedom of movement enjoyed by members of the Axis consular staffs, and revelations that many of these staff members were actively involved in espionage activities prompted a publicist, Mrs Dorothy Thompson, to start a one-woman crusade to get the Axis agents expelled. However, there were difficulties in making such a move. There was universal understanding that diplomatic and consular staffs were controlled by international law, and by conventions and courtesies between the two countries exchanging such staff. If one country suspected that diplomatic immunity was being gravely abused, its only real action was that of requesting the home government to withdraw its envoys which could, of course, lead to immense diplomatic and political problems, especially during times of impending conflict when governments such as Spain and Argentina were teetering at the far dark edges of pro-Axis neutrality.

NOTES

1. *The Times*, 17 November 1942.
2. *The Times*, 5 November 1942.
3. *The Times*, 6 November 1942.
4. *The Times*, 28 March 1942.
5. SRS 276. Message of 22 November 1941.
6. Panama declared war on Japan on December 8, 1941. This was followed by declarations of war on Germany and Italy on 12 December.
7. Number 600. Message to Bogota and Caracas. *The Magic Background of Pearl Harbor*, Vol. 4. U.S.A. Department of Defense, page A278.
8. SRS 112. Message: 10 December 1940.
9. SRS 115. Message of 11 December 1940.
10. SRS 113. Message of 17 December 1940.
11. SRS 143. Message dated 17 March 1941.
12. SRS 458. Message of 5 December 1941.
13. No. 243, Vol. 3. *The Magic Background of Pearl Harbor*, 5 August 1941 to 17 October 1941 Dept of Defense, USA.
14. SRS 340. Message of 22 August 1941.
15. SRS 160. Message of 11 August 1941.

16. SRS 161. Message of 12 August, 1941.
17. SRS 133. Message of 16 August 1941.
18. SRS 140. Message of 16 October 1941.
19. SRS 169. Message of 18 August 1941.
20. SRS 192. Message of 6 September 1941.
21. SRS 196. Message of 10 September 1941.
22. SRS 242. Message of 20 September 1941.
23. Falange Espanola, literally the 'Spanish Phalanx', a totalitarian party formed in 1933 by José Antonio Primo de Rivera, who was the son of former Spanish dictator Manual Primo de Rivera, (1870-1930). The Falange was a political party, its doctrine based upon patriarchal nationalism. Like Nazism and Fascism, it attacked the 'social bankruptcy of capitalism' by 'recognizing' the suffering of the workers and peasants.
24. *A Time for Decision*, Sumner Welles, Harper and Brothers, New York, 1941, page 179.
25. Cargoes of oranges to England were also often used by Axis saboteurs who would plant bombs in the orange boxes. By January 1944 the problem had become so intense that the Spanish authorities were made to take action against any possible Axis agents operating out of Spanish ports from which the oranges were dispatched. They were rounded up and forced to leave the ports.
26. The Abwehr. The intelligence department of the German Armed Forces, under the aristocratic Admiral Canaris. The organization consisted of seven specialist groups concentrating on technical, political, military and economic intelligence. They also handled sabotage and counter-espionage.

2 Japanese Spying Operations and *Magic*

BACKGROUND TO JAPANESE ESPIONAGE

The history of Japanese espionage dates from the Middle Ages with the establishment of various secret societies. It has always been a reasonably efficient government and military arm which has trained and operated skilled personnel under some of the most difficult and dangerous circumstances. During the Second World War the secret societies aligned themselves with the Kempei Tai, the notorious Japanese military and secret police.

The Kempei Tai was an immensely powerful organization, and during the war its power was greatly increased by Hideki Tojo's premiership. Tojo became head of the Kempei Tai in the Kanto region in September 1935. The operations of the Kempei Tai can be likened to those of the SS secret police under Hitler's Nazi Germany. Indeed the SS were instrumental in some of the training and supervision of the Kempei Tai during the war years. Communications between the Nazis and the The Black Dragon secret society – one of the most powerful of such societies – were maintained through a German journalist named Don Gato who was based in Tokyo.

The alliance between secret groups, such as the Black Dragon Society, the Dark Ocean Society, the Kempei Tai and the Japanese criminal 'Mafia'-style organization called the Yakuza, is one which has an extended and bloody history.

Secret societies have long been recognized as one of the rather more primitive, though effective, cornerstones of Japanese society. Like many of their Asian counterparts in Hong Kong and Singapore, these societies rely heavily on their clannish brotherhoods for secrecy and survival. They share assets, secrets and guilt. In 1881, the notorious Genyosha, or Dark Ocean Society, was founded by a man who became revered in Japan as the father of such societies. His name was Mitsuru Toyama.

Toyama came to be an extremely powerful man through his secret society. He promoted the use of blackmail and terror, and the ranks of the society formed a paramilitary group of such strength that Toyama could, and did, greatly influence Japanese politics. This society's objective was nationalistic and it promoted itself as existing to guard the rights of the people. However its real motives were rather more sinister. Its *raison d'être* was to expand Japanese influence abroad and to gather secret intelligence from China, Korea, Russia and Manchuria. The Dark Ocean Society, was a terrorist organization and school for spies.

From this point, the growth of such organizations has been quite remarkable. Other secret societies, either allied to the Dark Ocean, or in direct opposition to it, have sprung up in most major centres of Japan. The Yamaguchi-gumi, certainly the largest of these, was formed in 1915. Today it has around 400 affiliated groups with a membership of around 10,000. Other groups include the Sumiyoshi-rengo in Tokyo, the Inagawa-kai in Yokohama, the Ichiwa-kai in Kobe, and many more. From those early years of the founding of the Dark Ocean, such societies under the Yakuza generalization have been influential in formulating Japanese foreign policy, and working towards a powerful military presence throughout the Asian sphere.

The ranks of the Kempei Tai have traditionally been drawn from members of these secret societies. This was a practice which did much to strengthen the alliance between them.

The Japanese in the East Indies and Malaya

An example of early Japanese espionage activities which played a decisive role during the Second World War could be seen in the case of the Dutch Netherlands East Indies. Even before the outbreak of hostilities, the Netherlands East Indies government issued a report which gave a remarkable account of the operations of Japanese espionage in those territories. It was a story of careful planning of the conquest of this important region.

Japanese espionage spread widely in the NEI during and after the First World War, but it was not until 1931 that the first systematic effort in the direction of offensive expansion of espionage was recorded. At this time the NEI was flooded with Japanese goods which often seriously undercut the local products. This success encouraged the Japanese to attempt to gain monopolies in many commercial markets, and the slogan: 'Japanese goods through Japanese hands' was coined and then translated into action by the activities of several Japanese shipping lines, banks, and other commercial organizations. But for the effective measures taken by the Dutch authorities to safeguard national interests, conditions in the NEI would have been seriously disorganized by these Japanese attempts to control commerce. The economic invasion also coincided with an increasing political and military interest in the region.

In January 1933, the Great Asiatic Association (GAA) came into being. Its founders included many leading Japanese politicians, some of whom were former Japanese Prime Ministers and Foreign Ministers. A periodical published by the GAA widely condemned all Western nations for claiming to offer opportunities to struggling nations for trade development while really operating to accomplish a Western stranglehold on commercial development. (Exactly what the Japanese themselves were in fact attempting to do.) Support for credit on the importation of Japanese goods was easily granted to native dealers, the object of this cynical exercise was to create extensive distributing channels which would be dependent on Japanese commercial firms. This economic support was again accompanied by wide-scale agitation against the existing administration. The Indonesian traders were not convinced and the scheme proved a commercial failure, but this did not prevent the Japanese from continuing their intrigue under various guises.

Students, attracted by the cheapness of the education and the financial support promised by the Japanese, were induced to go to Japan. There they found that many of them were coerced into acting as agents for espionage or for anti-Dutch propaganda.

There were widespread propaganda campaigns carried out by the Japanese in the NEI – mostly with little result, and when these poor results were realized, plans were made for the publication of a pro-Japanese newspaper. The publication was financed by the Japanese Bureau of Economic Research – a spy training establishment – and placed under the control of the Japanese Consulate-General in Batavia. A series of embezzlements committed by the newspaper's editor led to an avalanche of unwelcome publicity in the more orthodox press, and the subsequent collapse of the propaganda exercise.

Efforts were made to incite Indonesian politicians against the Dutch authorities, whispering campaigns were instigated with two main themes: Japanese military invincibility and the alleged weakness of the Dutch. In 1939 and 1940, Japanese consular staff began to spread rumours which were based upon local legends and superstitions. One of these was that Java would become independent after a period of prosperous occupation under a 'yellow race'. The fables were expanded and disseminated by Japanese journalists and businessmen. More dangerous were the activities of the Japanese Foreign Office. This office pressed into service Japanese commercial enterprises, fishermen, and individual residents to form a widespread espionage net throughout the NEI territories. Documents seized by the NEI authorities confirmed that these activities were prolific and thoroughly efficient. The documents provided evidence that such noted spies as Keizo Kaneko and others were working directly under the orders of the Japanese government. Also mentioned in the documents were various sinister figures of the secret societies, especially the Black Dragon.

There were more than 4,000 Japanese fishermen in the NEI at this time, many of them kept in contact with the Japanese Naval Station in the Pellew Archipelago. These fishermen were responsible for bullying the islanders into accepting the inevitability of eventual Japanese control, and also of sounding the coastline and making detailed charts. As war drew closer in 1941, British surveillance of these fishing boats increased dramatically, and in November that year, a little more than two weeks prior to the Pearl Harbor attack, Yutaka Ishizawa, the Japanese Consul-General in Batavia sent the following message to Tokyo:

> The surveillance of Japanese fishing boats in the vicinity of Gaspar and Biliton is becoming more and more strict (and) is being reported by the captains of the various vessels reaching port recently. According to their reports, it appears that the ships are stopped at least once or twice a day by flying boats and are subjected to intimidating inspection. Most of these flying boats are tri-motored (with a crew of six or seven). However north-east of Barka, occasionally a four-motored boat is encountered. [It is thought that these are British boats].
>
> Although no warships are encountered in these areas, there are always two or three in the vicinity of Etna, 50 miles north of Batavia; these are patrol boats on duty at night. On the night of the 18th, several of these were recognized.... The fact that our fishing vessels have thus become the objects of strong suspicion and oppression by the government here deserves our attention.[1]

A few days later the Japanese General Staff ordered that all automobile road maps used by the Moto Kurabu (NEI Motor Club) be forwarded aboard the ship *Fuji Maru* to Tokyo.[2]

A grade higher, and far more dangerous, were the various companies ordered by the Japanese government to begin enterprises in the NEI, mostly quite unprofitable, in which the development of mining, forestry, fisheries and agriculture was subordinate to military expansionist aims. A typical example was the Ringyo Kaisha (the Southern Seas Timber Company), itself a subsidiary of the Oriental Development Company which was owned by a Japanese shipping magnate. As early as 1910, the Japanese were taking a keen interest in the forests near the oil-bearing island of Tarakan. Their interest was so obvious that the NEI government closed the area to foreign applicants seeking concessions. Disappointed but undefeated, the Ringyo Kaisha applied for, and was granted, a timber concession farther south at Sangkoelirang Bay. By 1936 this enterprise had lost about 2 million guilders and its methods were so startlingly amateur that in the words of the NEI report, '... there is every reason to doubt whether it was ever intended that the company should be worked on genuine commercial lines. Judging from the names of those who financed the concern, it was more probable that the object was to have a Japanese establishment near the much desired oil-fields no matter what the cost.'

Japanese investigations in the region revealed that a surprisingly large number of middle-class men working for the Dutch administration were homosexuals or bi-sexuals. The Japanese were quick to realize the worth of this knowledge and soon founded a number of male brothels in Java where officials could be first lured and then blackmailed into becoming espionage agents.

Dutch New Guinea was a hotbed of Japanese espionage. The Southern Seas Development Company, heavily subsidized by the Japanese government, could always find funds for economic experiments in the region. Botanical research, for example, covered economic espionage, and the naval commander at Pellew directly controlled all the research company's expensive operations.

Many of these companies did no visible business at all, they were set up for the express purpose of gathering intelligence and carrying out other espionage or propaganda work. Local Japanese associations were brought under consular control. Highly placed Japanese officers would visit the islands under false names, while others, principally members of the Japanese Naval staff, did not conceal their identities.

One of the final steps before aggression was the dispatch of the Kobayashi economic mission to Batavia, in the winter of 1940. Its alleged object was to buy oil, an objective which could easily have been achieved by direct negotiation through regular commercial channels. The real reasons for the visit were fourfold. 1. To give assurances to the NEI government of Japanese policies, stating that the NEI government had no need to arm for war as the Japanese had no military intentions in that direction. 2. To induce the NEI to refrain from preparing to destroy the vital oil-fields. 3. To persuade the NEI government not to cooperate closely with Great Britain and the United States. 4. To demand supplies of raw materials for war industries and to obtain a share in the production of those industries. The mission, not unnaturally, failed.

As tensions mounted during the early months of 1941, the Japanese Ministry in Batavia advised Tokyo that police surveillance and control over Japanese nationals was steadily increasing, and that the ministry planned to destroy all secret documents relating to their schemes to employ locals as espionage agents.

The Netherlands officials were at this time practising censorship of all letters to and from Japan, including letters which should have received diplomatic immunity. In light of this the Japanese authorities decided that all-important written communications should be sent only by military courier. Shortly afterwards these couriers also came under scrutiny, and secret civilian couriers were quickly employed to take their places.

On 24 February 1941, the Japanese Embassy in Bangkok advised the Japanese Foreign Office in Tokyo that they were able to obtain a constant stream of secret documents and messages sent from the Netherlands Ministry in Bangkok, and requested that Tokyo send to Bangkok a Japanese diplomat who spoke the Dutch language so that the documents could be translated. However, the Netherlands Ministry finally realized that their security was being breached in some way, and carried out a secret investigation. They discovered that a native employee had possession of the keys to all the safes, and that he was selling the information to the Japanese. He was immediately arrested.

A second economic mission was sent to the NEI in June 1941. Three of its members were Colonels Maeda and Orga, and Lieutenant Colonel Ishii of the Japanese Army. Officials of the Netherlands Army had been reluctant to admit these three men into the country, knowing that they came not as economic representatives, but as spies. However, the Japanese officers were finally admitted because the NEI government wished to avoid a diplomatic confrontation with Japan. The three officers were closely watched during their visit. They paid less than scant attention to economic matters, but did reconnoitre many of the Netherlands defences and military bases.

During the following months, the Batavian authorities stepped up their counter-espionage and counter-propaganda measures against the Japanese. On 21 August 1941, Batavian police arrested the editors of *To-Indo* and the *Shinarusutan*, two Chinese language newspapers which were being subsidised by Japanese subversive funding. Both newspapers were prevented from printing for a limited period. That same day, Dutch officials announced that a telephone monitoring system was in force and ordered that all telephone calls to and from the islands be made only in Dutch, English or the Malayan languages.[3]

The Japanese Consular authorities in Batavia and elsewhere now redoubled their propaganda and espionage. As 1941 wore on, 6,000 of the 8,000 Japanese living in Java were evacuated, only the fifth-column stayed behind. These people were well known and carefully watched by the NEI counter-intelligence command. On the outbreak of war they were rounded up and interned. This was the end of widespread espionage activities in the NEI.

Six days prior to the Pearl Harbor attack, Yutaka Ishizawa, the Batavian Consul-General advised Tokyo that all his funds were being converted into readily available cash and that secret documents were being destroyed. In a message dated 2 December 1941, Ishizawa stated:

> All copies of wires dispatched or received by this office up to and including the first of this month (including telegraphic communications), have been burned. Henceforth, at the end of each day we will burn all copies of wires received or despatched by this office during that day. Furthermore, please be advised that we will send you an itemized list of everything destroyed, either by a Japanese vessel of by the next courier reaching Batavia.[4]

At least eighteen months before the Japanese invasion of Malaya, the Japanese High Command had infiltrated espionage agents onto the Malay peninsula to report on possible landing sites and the locations of troops and armaments. The reports of these agents were largely responsible for the highly successful Japanese landings in December 1941. One of these agents was an Asian steward named Shawan who worked in the officers' club at the massive Singapore naval base. Shawan's real name was Colonel Tsugunori Kadomatsu, who had been working for Japanese Naval Intelligence since 1930. Kadomatsu's real identity was finally realized when a visitor to the club commented that security within the club was lax and that the steward seemed extremely curious about the conversations of the officers. A plan was devised to trick Kadomatsu and in a loud voice one of the officers mentioned that the British warship *Prince of Wales* was soon to visit the port. Kadomatsu was seen to scribble something onto the edge of a napkin. He was detained and the napkin examined. Kadomatsu had written: 'PW end November'. He was promptly arrested. Other agents working in the Singapore region included Sergeant Fukui, who led a team of highly trained agents with specific instructions to watch the Johore Straits, and Major Asaeda, who disguised himself as a coolie and sent to Tokyo a constant stream of reports from Singapore, Malaya and Thailand.

Another highly placed and extremely successful espionage agent working in the Singapore/Malaya region was a man known only as Colonel Yakematu. Yakematu headed a huge intelligence net which was comprised of almost two hundred Japanese agents. Using this vast network, Yakematu was able to gain precise information about military strengths, arms and supply dumps, the dispositions of troops, possible landing sites, the quality of civil and military administration, food and water supplies, air and sea defences, and many other details so vital to Japan's plans for invasion.

However, such infiltration of Japanese agents has not always been so successful. For example, later in the war, in March 1944, a party of twelve Indian soldiers, Viceroy's commissioned officers and NCOs who had been taken prisoner during the Malay campaigns, were landed by Japanese submarine on the Indian coast. Their orders were to carry out espionage activities and report back to Tokyo. Yet all twelve men gave themselves up to the Indian authorities immediately after landing. They informed the authorities that they had been: 'thoroughly trained in espionage activities, demolition, propaganda and wireless transmission for more than a year before being embarked on the submarine at Penang the previous February'.[5] The submarine put them ashore near Pasni in Kalat State, where they surrendered to the village postmaster. From there they were taken to Delhi for interrogation where they handed over money given to them by the Japanese. By way of reserve funds the Japanese had also supplied them with a few diamonds.

In April 1938, author Jean Marques-Riviere wrote an interesting report on his experiences with the various Japanese espionage nets he had encountered during his travels. It was more remarkable at the time because of the very low degree of general public understanding and knowledge of the existence of such Japanese nets, and his incisive comments concerning Japanese espionage in Malaya – more than two-and-a-half years prior to

the invasion of Singapore – must have raised some incredulous
eyebrows in Whitehall when it was published in the British press.
Marques-Riviere wrote:

> It was at Port Said that I saw them at work for the first time. On
> the quay, a knot of porters, Arabs, Jews and natives rushed to get
> hold of my luggage. Suddenly a little group of Japanese forged
> through the multi-coloured clamorous crowd around me. In
> excellent English they offered me their services and gave me the
> name of a hotel which had already been recommended to me.
> Their politeness was a contrast to the behaviour of the natives.
>
> Though miserably clad, they inspired confidence. I followed
> them. They took my things up to my room while I gave my
> instructions to the manager of the hotel. I went up to my room;
> everything was in order, I paid the porters the agreed price.
>
> Shortly afterwards, when I went to open my suitcases, I saw that
> two locks out of the four had been forced. And the work had been
> done faultlessly.
>
> In Bombay I lived for a long time with Hindu friends, their
> home on one side overlooked the sea, the Indian Ocean with its
> beautiful changing colours, and on the other the heavy Gothic
> monuments of the Law Courts and university. [There was also] ...
> a wide avenue of palm trees. I was soon intrigued by a
> performance which was repeated every morning. A knot of little
> Japanese on bicycles with big packages tied on behind them,
> crossing the avenue going in the direction of the Hindu town, the
> native quarter.
>
> I was told they were hawkers; I was astonished to meet them
> everywhere in the big Anglo-Indian port. An absolute network of
> sellers, one could not take a step in the town without meeting
> them. I understood eventually when a military friend apologised
> for his arriving late as he had to be present at a police council
> which was trying a dozen spies who had been surprised as they
> were photographing certain points on the Bombay coast. I have
> seen these spies everywhere. At Rangoon I learned about the slow
> but sure invasion of the yellow men. The Chinese and Japanese
> then numbered more than 18,000. How were they to be
> distinguished from one another? In this pulsating, poverty-stricken
> mass, how was one to separate the disguised Japanese officer from
> the coolie who lives on a few annas a day?
>
> I saw them in Ceylon, round the Grand Oriental Hotel,
> suggesting excursions to Kelani, to Mount Lavinion or to the
> Dagoba at Kandy. I saw them acting as hotel page boys at Calcutta
> [and] at Mandalay, silent, clean, subservient. If you are wise you
> will trust them with the keys of your room, for this procedure does
> away with the necessity of forcing locks.
>
> Do not think that I am saying that every Japanese one meets is a
> spy, but I know from a very reliable source, a member of the

Intelligence Service, that apart from the professional organization of Japanese agents, every Japanese is by nature ... a spy ...

They are ... [establishing nets] elsewhere too. When I touched at Massawah in the Red Sea, a port buzzing with Italian military activity, just after the conquest of part of Ethiopia, a French friend who lived there told me the fantastic story of three Japanese travellers for the Mitsui firm who held prolonged negotiations with Ras Haylu, perhaps the richest man in the country. They were interested in economic cotton planting of course, but if one could also watch the going and coming of European ships in the Red Sea, this would kill two birds with one stone.

Singapore provides the most concrete evidence of the struggle between Japan and the western empires.... The West thinks itself strong with its guns rearing its barrels above the armoured concrete of the coast fortresses. But the yellow men are really the masters of the town, masters of commerce in which sphere the ... yellow men have become indispensable to the colony. The British may hold the coast, but the roads which cross the Malayan jungle, the tribes of Siam [Thailand] are surveyed, known and weighed by the Japanese agents.... The white men think they will always be powerful, but their adversaries smile and are silent. I have seen [employees] of European firms with luxurious bungalows, they work two hours a day. The rest of their time is spent at the bar, at the club and on the golf course. I have seen Japanese too, energetic, cunning tenacious men of business working to get hold of the market. They live in the native town, it is dirty perhaps, but one has only to cross the street to see them, to buy or to sell. Sometimes, for an important affair, four or five of them will get together, and in twenty-four hours out of their pockets they will pull twenty or thirty thousand pounds.

We struck up an acquaintance with a Japanese while walking around the deck of our ship. He seemed to be a businessman. I had as travelling companion an English civil servant from Delhi.... He noticed my new friend and seemed to be very interested. One day he broke his silence. 'Do you know to whom you are chatting so happily?'

'Yes I answered, pulling his calling card from my pocket. He is a merchant of Tokyo.'

'Whose merchandise is something out of the ordinary,' added my friend quietly. 'He is an agent well known among us, whose work lies in Europe ... We know them well in India, Asia and [now] Europe is being invaded by these Japanese agents, one finds them everywhere. And come a little closer please, for a few words which are somewhat confidential. They are all officers, sometimes actually nobles of ancient Japanese families. You meet them under the filth of the coolie, noting, transmitting, informing, spying.'[6]

Marques-Riviere's observations were remarkably correct, but

not only Asian agents were employed in these endeavours. The fall of Singapore was in no small part attributable to a New Zealand spy named Captain Patrick Stanley Vaughan Heenan, of the 16th Punjab Regiment. Heenan was originally an Irishman, born in Stratford, Northern Ireland in 1910. He was raised in Burma, where his father worked as a mining engineer. He was sent to England for his education, a good steady middle-class schooling at Cheltenham College, where he did well. He also loved to play sports. He joined the Indian Army in 1935 and continued to excel in sports. He became heavyweight boxing champion of India in 1936 and was an aggressive rugby player. His fellow officers described him as a heavy drinker, a loner and generally detested by other members of the regiment. He was also something of a ladies' man, and perhaps this was the reason why he became a Japanese spy. During a holiday in Japan in 1938, he met an attractive young woman and they became lovers. Whether this woman was a plant by Japanese intelligence services is not clear, but because of Heenan's military career, it seems likely. Prior to the fall of Singapore Heenan had been on assignment to the Air Intelligence Liaison Unit. When the Japanese landed in Malaya in December 1941, Heenan was arrested by the British military police as he tried to hide a radio transmitter he had just finished using. He had been passing information to the Japanese regarding the aircraft recognition codes which were changed every twenty-four hours. Official records posted Heenan as missing in action, but the unofficial story is that just prior to the collapse of Singapore, Heenan was being exercised with several other prisoners when he began to taunt his guard stating that within twenty-four hours all the British would be dead and that he, Heenan, would be with his friends once more. The guard allegedly shot him dead. Several hours later Singapore fell.

JAPANESE CODES AND CYPHERS

The enormous espionage system set up world wide by the Japanese prior to and during the Second World War, would have been a formidable organization for the Allies to counter, had it not been for Japanese laxity regarding their secret codes and cyphers.

The modern history of US code-breaking and deciphering of secret military and diplomatic messages really began with a brilliant young man named Herbert Yardley. It was Yardley, who, during the vitally important Washington Naval Conference of 1921/22, first managed to penetrate the Japanese secret code systems. At the time Yardley was a highly respected coding clerk working for the State Department and considered by his peers to be a brilliant expert of cyphers and codes. He had extensive experience as a crypt-analyst and code breaker and was one of the leading such experts then available in the United States.

During the First World War Yardley was promoted to the head of MI8 – then the code-breaking section of the Military Intelligence Division. Shortly after the war, in May 1919, he succeeded in persuading the Department of State and the Department of War into funding an organization designed specifically for cypher and code investigation and attack. Under severe financial pressure following the expense of the Great War, the State Department was incapable of funding the ambitious project in Washington, and a state funded organization called the Black Chamber, was eventually established in New York. The primary concern of this ultra-top secret department was the breaking of Japan's diplomatic codes and cyphers. Even before the Washington Naval Conference began in 1921, Yardley had largely succeeded in breaking most of Japan's diplomatic signals. He stated to his superiors that he would have the codes entirely cracked within twelve months.

For the US government and military, it now became vital that all of Japan's codes be broken as quickly as possible. As the vital Washington Naval Conference loomed, the United States needed a bargaining edge to force military – and specifically naval limitations – on Japan. Yardley's work was completed just in time. America's knowledge of Japan's messages – especially from Washington to Tokyo – enabled the United States to manipulate the arms negotiations and succeed in obtaining strict limitations on naval tonnages. Yardley later wrote a book about his successes, entitled *The American Black Chamber*, more than 40,000 copies of the Japanese edition were sold.

Over the following years the work of American crypt-analysts became far more complex as further more ingenious codes were introduced into diplomatic and military radio traffic.

US authorities were aided in their endeavours by the discovery that the New York headquarters of the Japanese Imperial Railway was being used as a clearing house for Japanese espionage agents. A clandestine operation was mounted which succeeded in obtaining a copy of the Red Book – the complete Japanese 'Number One' secret codes – without the knowledge of the Japanese. This laid the foundation for further work into the complex Japanese cyphers.

In 1925 a secret US radio listening post was set up in Guam –

further enhancing US understanding of Japanese messages, and soon afterwards two others were established in the Philippines and Shanghai. The US Navy also instigated a series of mobile ship's listening stations covering a vast area through the South China Sea.

During the 1930s the Japanese became aware that their codes were not safe and they sought to change and improve their enciphering system. They decided to abandon their ordinary codes for military and diplomatic messages, and changed instead to an *Enigma* machine-encoding system which was perceived as being far more secure. The codes, as a result, became more difficult for the United States to read and further work in deciphering techniques was quickly brought into action.

The *Enigma* system of encoding had been designed and manufactured by the Germans in the 1920s. It was a complex system of layered cyphers which was largely thought to be unbreakable. The Americans themselves had been one of the first countries to purchase a commercially available *Enigma* machine.

In 1931 the Japanese Navy introduced a cyphering machine Type 91, which later became known as the *Red* machine. A few years later this was followed by a new and even more complex encoder called the *J machine*, which the Americans dubbed *Purple*. It was to this *Purple* machine that the Japanese gave their total confidence in the security of their messages during the Second World War, convinced that the seemingly unbreakable *Purple* codes would protect even the most secret of signals.

As diplomatic relations between Japan and the United States soured during the late 1930s, and as the new cryptograms from *Purple* were introduced, a brilliant US War Department crypt-analyst named William F. Friedman, and a team working under Friedman which included three doctors of mathematics, finally managed to crack the *Purple* code. They were aided by the lack of Japanese security measures, specifically by the errors of Japanese officials. After the initial introduction of the *Purple* machine in February 1939, primarily encoding messages from Tokyo and Washington, the use of the machine spread gradually to other Japanese military and diplomatic posts in order of their importance and traffic volume. It had taken four years to replace the *Red* machine with the *Purple* machine, and in many instances both machines were installed and in use at Japanese embassies and consulates during this transition period. Friedman and his team were aided by the Japanese practice of often sending their messages in both *Red* and *Purple* codes. The *Red* had already been thoroughly cracked, and so with the aid of the decoded *Red* messages, many of the *Purple* messages were soon being read by the Americans. Further aid in understanding the *Purple* codes came when an American spy managed to obtain photographs of the machines from various Japanese embassies. These photographs when blown up were then used to make final mathematical calculations on the codes they contained.

By 1941, American command of the *Purple* code was complete, and every Japanese diplomatic or military message was available to US authorities. This intelligence coup was known only to President Roosevelt, a few of his top military advisers, the code-breakers themselves, and several members of the War Department's G2 section, responsible for gathering intelligence.

Most of the decryption work was completed at either OP 20 -G, the Naval listening station based at the Naval Communications Centre in Washington; FRUpac (Fleet Radio Unit Pacific) in Hawaii, or at the listening post CAST in the Philippines. (CAST, comprising a compliment of seventy-five men, was moved by US submarine after the surrender of Corregidor and later located close to the headquarters of the Australian Navy Intelligence Division in Melbourne, Australia. It utilized the only *Purple* decoding machine in the Southern Pacific region. On 15 April 1942, in agreement with the Australian authorities, CAST was incorporated into a new combined intelligence organization, the Central Bureau. Throughout the war the Bureau grew rapidly to a staff of around 4,000 men, and was never far from MacArthur's headquarters, firstly in Australia, later in New Guinea and finally in the Philippines.)

However, in these early years of the war the American Intelligence authorities experienced great difficulties in obtaining staff for the decryption process. Men and women were needed with special talents. Above all, they had to be able to speak fluent Japanese. The Army and Navy installed cramming courses in the language giving students intensive eleven-month and six-month courses.

THE US *MAGIC* SUMMARIES

The *Magic* Summaries were, in fact, daily synopses of all the intelligence garnered from a wide variety of sources, but primarily from the decrypted Japanese diplomatic signals. Later in the war they were renamed the *Magic* Diplomatic Summaries, and were accompanied by special supplements which related directly to the activities of the Japanese Army. The value of

Magic cannot be underestimated. The revealing diplomatic messages did more to supply intelligence to the Allies during the war than a small army of highly successful espionage agents in the field could ever have hoped to achieve. A brilliant example of the double-edged success of the *Magic* decryptions can be seen in the messages which the Japanese Ambassador to Berlin, Hiroshi Oshima, sent back to the Japanese Foreign Office during most of the war. When the Japanese diplomatic code was first cracked, it was believed that the messages would supply a wealth of information specifically about Japanese military and political actions. The Americans never believed that it would also supply very detailed and precise intelligence on the German theatres of war. In Berlin, Oshima held several meetings with Hitler. During these meetings the two men discussed vital details concerning the war and war prospects, including many of Hitler's very secret intentions. Synopses of these meetings were immediately encoded by Oshima's staff and forwarded to the Japanese Foreign Office in Tokyo. The Americans, of course, intercepted the messages and often knew Hitler's intentions before the Japanese government. Later, as the war progressed and as Hitler became more reclusive, Oshima held lengthy discussions with the German Foreign Minister, the autocratic and arrogant Joachim von Ribbentrop. Although von Ribbentrop's influence declined as the war progressed, he was often the recipient of many of Hitler's innermost confidences, these were invariably passed onto Oshima who forwarded them to Tokyo. Thus the Allies were in a position to obtain intelligences from the very highest sources within Germany.

However, the Japanese had become aware that at least some of their codes had been broken – primarily, they thought, the less important secondary codes usually reserved for commercial radio traffic. On 5 May 1941, prior to the attack on Pearl Harbor, Tokyo sent a message to the Japanese Embassy in Washington which stated: 'According to a fairly reliable source of information, it appears almost certain that the United States government is reading your code messages. Please let me know whether you have any suspicion of the above.'

In fact, this message was sourced to the Germans, who had told the Japanese Ambassador in Berlin, Baron Hiroshi Oshima, that German agents in America had discovered that the Japanese codes had been at least partially broken. The Japanese Ambassador in Washington, Admiral Kichisaburo Nomura, held a thorough investigation, and on 20 May he signalled Tokyo and confirmed that some Japanese codes had been broken by the

Americans. But, for unknown reasons, no action was taken by the Japanese to change those codes, they only increased certain code handling procedures. There were, of course, large difficulties inherent in changing codes. Such a move involved the issuing of new code books to every recipient of signals. This was an enormous task involving all diplomatic and army posts, task forces and air and naval commands over a vast area. The Japanese often found that the changing of codes was an almost insurmountable problem, especially when they themselves thought that the codes remained safe. Because of this complacency the Americans were able to continue deciphering Japanese codes and cyphers. But of what real value were the signals? What military or diplomatic profit was gained from these secret signals?

Even before the commencement of hostilities between Japan and America, the United States had been well warned that war was imminent. The decoded messages provided President Roosevelt with prior knowledge of the impending conflict and led to an American seizure of Japan's assets in the United States, an oil embargo on Japan, and prevented the Americans making needless concessions as a price for peace. Through the *Magic* diplomatic messages, America became fully aware that Japan was pursuing aggressive and warlike intent, and that nothing the Americans could do – at least diplomatically – would prevent the eventual outbreak of war. Indeed, the *Magic* messages gave the United States a clear insight into the Janus-like attitude of Japanese diplomacy. During the long and outwardly helpful meetings between the Japanese Ambassador, Admiral Nomura, President Roosevelt, and Secretary of State Cordell Hull, both Roosevelt and Hull were fully aware that, despite Nomura's reassurances, the messages being sent back to Japan by the Ambassador were contrary to the content of actual negotiations. *Magic* supplied a vitally important and accurate perspective of Japan's real policies and intentions of military expansion throughout the so-called Greater East Asian Co-Prosperity Sphere.

During the spring and summer of 1940 the Americans became aware that the Japanese were setting up an unusually large ring of espionage networks in South American capitals. This network was being created on the natural expectancy that once war was declared, the Japanese themselves would be expelled from the United States, and South America would serve as the next best base from which to operate – listening to US radio frequencies, obtaining US newspapers and magazines, and infiltrating agents across the Mexican border. On 14 July a signal from Canton to Tokyo gave an indication to the Americans that war in the Pacific was relatively imminent. The report, quite specific in nature, stated that: 'In the seizure of Singapore, the navy will play the principal part and that the army would need only one division to seize Singapore and two divisions to take the Netherlands Indies.' The message also claimed that airforce bases would be established on the Spratly Islands, Palau, Singora, in Thailand, Portuguese Timor and Indo-China, and that a submarine fleet would be established in the Mandates, Hainan, and Indo-China. The message further stated that using these bases for their forces, the Japanese military would crush all British and American military power in the region.

Indeed, as early as 1940, US authorities were aware that the Japanese diplomatic posts in neutral countries were about to be used as comprehensive espionage network centres. On 14 February, Ambassador Nomura formally presented his credentials to President Roosevelt. However, his arrival in Washington had been preceded more than six weeks earlier by a Japanese diplomatic message dated 25 December 1940 which stated: 'With the appointment of Ambassador Nomura we wish to formulate a definite plan for our propaganda and information gathering work by seeking cooperation of Japanese bank and business officials in the US.' The stage was set, and during the following weeks the New York Consulate sent to Tokyo a list of eighteen Japanese business agencies which were suitable for espionage activities. In Washington, Japanese Embassy officials held a secret meeting with a number of leading Japanese businessmen, at which the possibility of conducting espionage activities was discussed in detail. Shortly afterwards, Japanese Foreign Minister Yosuke Matsuoka gave instructions to proceed with the setting up of the espionage net, '... for the purpose of being prepared for the worst'. His message was also sent to Japanese consulates and legations in many other centres, including New York, New Orleans, Chicago, Portland, Seattle, Los Angeles, San Francisco, and to Mexico and Canada.

Within weeks the *Magic* messages also revealed that in many South American capitals, new Japanese civilian agencies were being hastily set up for espionage and courier services in conjunction with German and Italian agencies. Throughout most of the war, Japanese espionage nets worked closely with the German and Italian intelligence nets in their subversive endeavours – not only in South America, but everywhere else where such nets were formed, primarily in neutral countries. By early May, espionage agents in Seattle and Los Angeles were already sending a steady stream of intelligence reports to Tokyo. These included details of manufacturing, the surveillance of aircraft factories and their outputs, the structure of the labour force, shipping schedules, rail timetables, the degree of contact with Japanese/Americans and their willingness to act as spies or to help in any other way.

One successful and unlikely Japanese agent was Mrs Velavee Dickenson, a frail old woman who owned a small shop in Madison Avenue, New York. US counter-intelligence agents had become aware of Mrs Dickenson's activities through a series of letters which had fallen into the hands of the FBI. She was watched for some time and was observed making contact with a known Japanese agent. She was arrested and subsequently confessed her guilt, claiming that she had become involved in espionage because she was heavily in debt following her late husband's long illness. An examination of a safety deposit box at Mrs Dickenson's bank revealed a sum of $18,000. She was tried and sentenced to ten years' imprisonment.

An example of German/Japanese cooperation regarding espionage can be clearly seen in the case of Pearl Harbor. In June 1943, the Office of US War Information released details about a German/Japanese spy operation which had taken place in Hawaii leading up to the Japanese attack on the US fleet. According to US authorities, Bernard Julius Otto Keuhn was a German agent and a fervent member of the Nazi Party who conspired with several Japanese agents to betray details of the US fleet to the Japanese Military just four days before the attack. The report released by the Office of War Information was based upon details supplied by the FBI.

Keuhn, a former German Navy radio operator who had learned to speak English while a prisoner of war during the First World War, had gone to Honolulu in 1935 – ostensibly for the purpose of studying the Japanese language and to research Hawaii's archaeological sites. Using this cover he was able to move freely around the islands without attracting undue attention to himself. He and his family moved to Pearl Harbor in 1939. Special agents of the FBI learned that on 3 December 1941 Nagao Kita, the Japanese Consul-General in Honolulu, had furnished his Foreign Office with a complete system of signals to be used in the transmission of intelligence information regarding the movements of the American fleet at Pearl Harbor. One such signal was a light in a dormer window of a house in Kalama. Kalama was a comparatively small community at Kai Lua, Obau.

FBI agents arrested Keuhn and his daughter on 8 December 1941. Keuhn's wife was arrested shortly afterwards. On 30 December, 1941 Keuhn signed a statement admitting that he had prepared the system of signals for Kita, which Kita had dispatched to Tokyo in a message on 3 December.

The FBI stated that on or about 25 October 1941, US$14,000 in cash had been delivered to Keuhn by Tadasi Morimura, the Fourth Secretary to the Japanese Consulate. This man was also known as Ito Morimura, but whose real name seems to have been Takeo Yoshikawa, the alleged head of all Japanese espionage in Hawaii. In 1920, Keuhn had married Friedel Birk, who had had two children by a previous marriage, one of these was alleged to have been an assistant to the German Minister for Propaganda, Josef Goebbels. Her daughter Ruth, ran the women's hairdressing shop, which Mrs Keuhn later admitted was really opened to obtain intelligence information from the gossip of soldiers' and sailors' wives. Between 14 May 1936 and 7 February 1939, more than US$70,000 was deposited to the Keuhn's credit in a Honolulu bank. The money came through the Rotterdam Bank Association. In 1940 the dormer window was constructed in the Keuhn's Kalama home and Mrs Keuhn bought a pair of eighteen-power binoculars, so powerful that they could not be used without a rest.

Bernard Keuhn was tried before the Military Commission of Honolulu for violations of the US Security Code. He was found guilty on 21 February 1942 and sentenced to be shot. On 26 October 1942 his sentence was commuted to fifty years' hard labour. Keuhn subsequently cooperated with US counter-intelligence authorities and made a series of statements concerning German and Japanese intelligence. Because of this cooperation he was released from prison in 1946. His wife and daughter were deported.

One of the leading protagonists in the Keuhn affair was the head of Japanese intelligence in Hawaii, Takeo Yoshikawa, who ostensibly worked under the Japanese Consul-General Nagao Kita. In fact Yoshikawa was Japan's leading spy in the region and he reported directly to Tokyo. Described as being a colourful and likeable character with a penchant for women, Yoshikawa was extremely successful in his espionage activities. He would disguise himself as a labourer to gain access to restricted areas, he was gifted with an easy manner and glib tongue and easily extracted information from sailors, soldiers and bar-girls. A proficient photographer, he catalogued the area's defences on film and forwarded his efforts to Tokyo. After the attack on Pearl

Harbor he quickly destroyed all his code books and any other incriminating evidence, and was interned as a diplomat of an enemy power by the US authorities. He was subsequently released during an exchange of such diplomats and returned to Tokyo where he continued to work for Japanese Naval Intelligence. American authorities never suspected that they had detained – and then released – one of Japan's most brilliant and successful spies.

Time magazine of 5 January 1942, also published that the Consul-General of Japan was one of the leading espionage controllers then operating in the region. The publication claimed that espionage activities were arranged by the Consul-General through the consular police, whose chief purpose was to organize the Ronin cellular organizations of young people who had been educated in the US. These included former teachers. The financing of the consular police and the Ronin was directly under the control of the Consul-General.

Japanese Army intelligence was also heavily involved in the Pearl Harbor region. They operated a vast organization of fifth-columnists, mainly shop-keepers and other small businessmen, all of whom were financed by the Japanese Tourist Bureau. Japanese Navy Intelligence was also prevalent in the region, operating in similar fashion but with the advantage of having truck drivers delivering fresh fruits, vegetables and other items to American ships in the harbour. These agents could calculate the likely operations of a ship from the amounts and types of stores they loaded.

The Americans were, of course, aware of the increase in Japanese agents at Pearl Harbor and their general methods of operation. Reading decrypted messages US authorities became aware that on 14 September 1941, the Japanese Foreign Minister instructed his agents that in future all reports from Hawaii and Pearl Harbor waters were to be divided into five designated areas.

Area A. Waters between Ford Island and the arsenal.
Area B. Waters adjacent to the Island, south and west of Ford Island.
Area C. East Loch.
Area D. Middle Loch.
Area E. West Loch and the communicating water routes.

The Japanese Foreign Minister also ordered precise details of all shipping movements, what ships were anchored and which ships were at wharves or in docks. On 29 September 1941 the agents were instructed to use a special code when referring to ship's details. KS meant that the ship was at the repair dock. FV meant the ship was moored near Ford Island, FG meant the ship was moored alongside Ford Island.[7]

It was clear from these precise requirements that the Japanese were planning something very special for Pearl Harbor.

Six days prior to the attack, US authorities received another subliminal warning in the form of a message sent from Tokyo to its embassies and consulates in Havana, Ottawa, Vancouver, Panama, Los Angeles, Honolulu, Seattle and Portland, which stated:

> Strictly secret. Take great pains that this does not leak out.
> You are to take the following measures immediately:
> With the exception of one copy of the O and L code, you are to burn all telegraphic codes.... As soon as you have completed this operation, wire the one word, Haruna. Burn all secret documents and the work sheets on this message. Be especially careful not to arouse the suspicion of those on the outside. Confidential documents are all to be given the same handling. The above is preparatory to an emergency situation and is for your information alone. Remain calm.[8]

Three days later, several key Japanese personnel in the United States, including Taro Terasaki, the head of Japanese intelligence-gathering in the US, were ordered home. However Ambassador Nomura in Washington quickly disputed the decision to return Terasaki, and in a message of 5 December Saburo Kurusu, Aide to Nomura, sent the following message to Tokyo:

> I feel confident that you are fully aware of the importance of the intelligence set-up in view of the present condition of the Japanese-US negotiations. I would like very much to have Terasaki, who would be exceedingly difficult to replace, because of certain circumstances, remain here until we are definitely enlightened as to the end of the negotiations. I beg of you, as a personal favour to me, to make an effort along these lines.[9]

US Code Security

But, paradoxically, the United States too had serious problems with the security of their codes, as was clearly illustrated in the case of the American spy named Tyler Kent. Kent was a twenty-three-year-old diplomat stationed at the US Embassy in London in 1939. Highly intelligent, a talented linguist, and an all-round sportsman, his career seemed promising. He was working as a cypher clerk at the embassy, a sensitive post as all important messages to and from the embassy passed over his desk. Unfortunately, Kent was an idealist and a pacifist and he believed the Nazi propaganda that the Jews had caused the war. He was soon marked by Axis agents as a possible convert and shortly afterwards he was introduced to an attractive young woman named Anna Wolkoff, the daughter of a Tsarist Russian admiral who, after leaving Soviet Russia, settled in Great Britain. Wolkoff and Kent became good friends and eventually lovers. Finally, she suggested to him that he should do some work for an anti-Jewish agency. Kent foolishly agreed. Within days large amounts of highly secret messages were being delivered to Wolkoff. Later Kent began to photograph sensitive documents, sending them in the diplomatic bag to Anna's German friends. During the winter of 1939-40, Kent managed to copy more than 1,500 reports and messages passing between Washington and London. These reports included vital information concerning oil supplies, war materials, the build-up of forces, the availability of military hardware, statistics of US economic and military aid and much more. Kent also passed over the secret diplomatic code.

The flow of information might have continued almost indefinitely, and would certainly have affected the length of the war and possibly even its outcome. However, Kent became lazy and rather than processing the photographs himself, he stupidly gave them to a commercial photographer to develop. The photographer, realizing the importance of the documents, alerted the British authorities. Kent was arrested, tried by the British and sentenced to seven years imprisonment, Anna Wolkoff received ten years. Kent was released in 1945, and upon his return to the United States he proclaimed his innocence and unsuccessfully attempted to sue the American State Department for wrongful dismissal.

After the war, captured German documents testified to the value of Kent's information – and the problems caused by the case were enormous. The revelation that the US diplomatic code was being read by Axis powers meant that it had to be immediately changed. This, at the time when the Germans were advancing through France and Dunkirk was being evacuated. As a result of the intrigue, US embassies were virtually blacked out for between two to six weeks – the time it took to provide all the various embassies and consulates with new code books from Washington.

Japanese successes in reading US codes was also significantly advanced at this stage. As far back as 1919, a Polish Army officer named Captain Kowalefsky – an expert on cyphers and codes – was recruited to revise all Japanese cyphers. Kowalefsky was later installed as the head of the Communications Department of the Japanese Naval General Staff – with a specific portfolio. He was to work on breaking the American diplomatic codes. Based in the Navy Ministry building in Tokyo, Kowalefsky was singularly successful in his task. His work was later carried on by a brilliant naval officer named Hideya Morikawa, the nephew of the Japanese Naval Chief of Staff. How successful this section was in breaking the almost never ending succession of US diplomatic codes is not certain, but many US diplomatic messages were certainly read, adding greatly to the volume of Japanese intelligence. The Japanese Navy worked closely with the Japanese Foreign Ministry's Anpo Kenkyu, the special section designed to work specifically on cryptographical analysis.

The Importance of Magic

Meanwhile, the *Magic* messages were confirming American belief that Japanese espionage activities were expanding, not only into South America, but world wide. G2 and the US State Department became ever more increasingly aware of the importance of the messages and the fact that Japanese embassies and consulates throughout the world were either preparing for, or actively engaged in, espionage on a large scale. Through these messages the United States was forewarned of the attack on Pearl Harbor. The Americans knew that Japanese diplomats acting as spies had sent details of all harbour installations back to Tokyo so that Admiral Yamamoto could plan his attack. A measure of the scope of importance the United States placed upon the *Magic* and other diplomatic and military messages can be seen in a top-secret letter carried by US Army Colonel Carter Clarke from Army Chief of Staff General George Marshall, to the Governor of New York, Thomas E. Dewey, in September 1944, when the war was at its height. Dewey had become aware that the War Office had received certain indications from deciphered Japanese codes which gave warning that an attack on Pearl Harbor was imminent in December 1941. Dewey, the Republican candidate nominated to run for the presidency, intended to reveal that Roosevelt's administration had been forewarned of the attack through the Japanese messages, but General Marshall was determined to stop him. If the Japanese had become aware that their most secret *Purple* code had been broken, the war could have dragged on for many years at the cost of tens of thousands of lives. (General Marshall's own estimates of an American landing on Japanese soil, made in 1944, were that at least 250,000 men would die, and that the toll could have gone as high as 1 million.) Marshall's letter in part stated:

TOP SECRET

For Mr Dewey's eyes only. 27 September 1944.
My Dear Governor,
... The most vital evidence in the Pearl Harbor matter consists of our intercepts of the Japanese diplomatic communications. Over a period of years our cryptograph people analysed the character of the machine the Japanese were using for encoding their diplomatic messages. Based on this a corresponding machine was built by us which deciphers their messages, therefore we possess a wealth of information regarding their moves in the Pacific which in turn was furnished to the State Department, rather than, as is popularly supposed, the State Department providing us with the information.... The point to the present dilemma is that we have gone ahead with this business of deciphering their codes.... our main basis of information regarding Hitler's intentions in Europe is obtained from Baron Oshima's [Japanese Ambassador to Germany] messages from Berlin, reporting his interviews with Hitler and other officials to the Japanese government.... To explain further the critical nature of this set-up, which will be wiped out almost in an instant if the least suspicion were aroused regarding it, the battle of the Coral Sea was based upon deciphered messages and therefore our few ships were in the right place at the right time. Further, we were able to concentrate our limited forces to meet their naval advance on Midway, when otherwise we almost certainly would have been some 3000 miles out of place. We had full information of the strength of their forces in that advance, and also of the small force which was directed against the Aleutians, which finally landed troops at Attu and Kiska.

Operations in the Pacific are largely guided by the information we obtain of Japanese deployments. We know their strength in various garrisons, the rations and other stores continuing available to them, and what is of vast importance, we check their troop movements and the movements of their convoys. The heavy losses reported from time to time which they sustain by reason of our submarine action largely result from the fact that we know the sailing dates and routes of their convoys, and can notify our submarines to lie in wait at the proper points. The current raids by Admiral Halsey's carrier forces on Japanese shipping in Manila Bay and elsewhere, are largely based in timing on the known movements of Japanese convoys, two of which were caught, as anticipated, in his destructive attacks.

You understand from the foregoing the utterly tragic

consequences if present political debates regarding Pearl Harbor disclose to the enemy – German or Jap – any suspicion of the vital sources of information we possess.... The conduct of General Eisenhower's campaign and of all operations in the Pacific are closely related in conception and timing to the information we secretly obtain through these intercepted codes. They contribute greatly to the victory, and tremendously to the saving in American lives, both in the conduct of the current operations, and in looking towards the early termination of the war.[10]

This letter placed Dewey in a serious dilemma. Was Roosevelt using Marshall as a means of staving off charges and an inquiry into the Pearl Harbor disaster? Dewey confidentially consulted with his closest advisers and they came to the conclusion that it must be true. Dewey knew Marshall to be an 'utterly truthful and honourable man',[11] and that he would not be involved in anything so underhanded. It is to Dewey's credit that he did nothing further to publicize the events surrounding Pearl Harbor, even though the publication of such details at that time would almost certainly have landed him in the White House. News of the letter and its ramifications were not made public until 1945, when the editor of *Life* magazine, John Chamberlain – quoting Dewey as his source – gave some of the details.[12]

GERMAN/JAPANESE COOPERATION

Even before the beginning of the war, Germany was sending agents to Japan in efforts to increase Japan's knowledge of espionage activities.

The Times had made a careful study of German/Japanese espionage activities, and claimed that a large percentage of the 3,000 or so Germans then resident in Tokyo were there on some kind of work related to espionage or in an advisory capacity. The newspaper claimed that the first wedge of fifth-column activities in Japan was against non-Nazi Germans. In one case a German economist, Dr Kurt Singer, was expelled from Hamburg University because he was a Jew. He was later appointed to Tokyo Imperial University as Professor of Economics. However the renewal of his contract was refused by the Japanese Department of Education, allegedly at the request of General Ott, because of Singer's refusal to aid the fifth-columnists to train agents. Singer found a humbler post as teacher of German in a provincial university. Once again the fifth column advisers found him and he was forced to leave Japan. His post was taken by a member of the *Auslandsorganisation*.

In 1934, a German named Hans Binkenstein arrived in Japan with a scholarship for language study. The Japanese Society of International Cultural Relations had awarded him a three-year fellowship. Shortly before it expired he was told by the German Embassy that unless he placed his exceptional linguistic talents at the disposal of the fifth-columnists, he would obtain no further employment. He left Japan shortly afterwards.

One of the most notorious reactionaries in Japan at this time was Seigo Nakano, the leader of a fascist party whose members included some of the worst gangsters in the underworld of Japanese politics. Nakano visited Berlin sometime at the end of the 1930s and was impressed to find that Germany was interested in training Japanese spies. Upon his return to Tokyo he and his organization were instrumental in the anti-British demonstrations which took place in 1939 and 1940, and when war was declared his secretary was given a position in the German Embassy. Nakano became a go-between through whom the Japanese fifth-columnists and the Germans worked.

Prior to the attack on Pearl Harbor, one of the most efficient groups of Japanese spy rings operating in the United States comprised Inao Ohtani, a Doctor Furusawa and the owner of a number of nightclubs operating on the American west coast named Commander Itaru Tachibana. It was this spy ring which attempted to recruit a former US Navy yeoman named Al Blake. Blake, a staunch American patriot, informed American counter-intelligence that he had been approached by Toraichi Kono, the former valet to film star Charlie Chaplin. Kono was working with Tachibana in establishing a spy network along the west coast. Blake was instructed by US counter-intelligence to go along with the Japanese plan and soon found himself in Hawaii where he was to obtain intelligence information. The information was actually fed to him by counter-intelligence operatives. Tachibana and Kono were later arrested by the FBI.

THE AXIS AND SPAIN

The American military authorities became aware early in the conflict that several Japanese embassies and consulates around the world were being aided in their activities of intelligence gathering by the embassies of Spain, and to a certain degree, Portugal and Chile, although at this stage the actual espionage networks which were to operate through these embassies were in their embryonic stages. Head of the embassy in Madrid at the time was Japanese Minister Yakichiro Suma, who was later to be greatly responsible for setting up and operating the *TO* spy network and for infiltrating agents into the US and South America. On 9 April 1942, Suma sent the following report to his superiors at the Japanese Foreign Office in Tokyo. The source of the report is not known but it was assumed by G2 that it had come from a freelance espionage agent operating out of London.

Today the 9th I have obtained by a certain method an exact copy of a highly secret message from British Foreign Minister Eden to British Ambassador to Madrid Hoare, containing the outline of the views and opinions on the war situation of the highest war council in the United States. This secret message was brought from the United States to Britain by US Army Chief of Staff Marshall, and Harry Hopkins who have just come to London. I am forwarding the text to you by separate message.[13]

The views referred to in Suma's message were as follows:

1. Japan's main objective can be surmised; first, a junction between Japan and Germany, i.e. Japan's operation in near future is Indian Ocean and not Australia; Japan first trying to reach Burma oil-fields and to capture Akyab in Burma and next move of Japan will be bombing of industrial regions near Calcutta and concentrating Japanese Naval forces near Andaman Isles, land on Indian coast in Bengal Gulf.

2. The oil strategy will be followed with a view to the desirability of eventual separation of British and American sea powers.

3. Axis [Germany in particular] principal operations can be surmised; first, a new offensive against Egypt and the Suez led by the Axis forces under Rommel. [This cannot be minimized, considering enormous war materials transported during these three months.]

4. The corresponding German drive not only against the oil-fields of the Caucasus but also against Syria, Iraq and Persia.[14]

From such messages, it quickly became clear that Madrid was about to begin participating in passing information of some importance to Japan, although as yet the Americans were still in ignorance of the *TO* network which had yet to be formalized. Within weeks however, the extent to which the Spanish intended to collaborate with the Japanese began to become known through a secret message sent by Yakichiro Suma, concerning the arrangements being made for the introduction of a spy network which was being organized in conjunction with Spanish Foreign Minister Ramon Suner.

Suma sent:

Spain's Collaboration with Axis
in Intelligence in America and England.

Madrid to Tokyo April 15, 1942.
Regarding my number 305. [Not yet declassified by US authorities.]

1. Since I last reported on the matter, Foreign Minister Suner has been making arrangements to send the agents to the United States as soon as possible and had made arrangements to appoint them as staff of the information bureau in the San Francisco Spanish Consul General's office, and in the Spanish Embassy in Washington; a request for the diplomatic visa for them had already been applied for through the United States Consul in Spain and they (are) now awaiting orders from the United States on this matter.

It was just at this time that the ... attitude of the United States toward all such matters became very rigid and the United States started to take a great interest in the activities of Spanish diplomats and people in the Americas. Finally, a short time ago, the US Embassy here made a request of the Spanish government that in the future, would Spain please refrain from sending over to America more than a certain number of couriers, and due to conditions they would not be able to accept any new diplomatic appointments.

As I heard all this from a person connected with the matter, at my interview with Foreign Minister Suner, I went right to the point and asked him about the matter. He replied that he really felt very responsible about the whole thing.... However if the Spanish Foreign Office could help in any way towards the ultimate victory of the Axis, they would be very glad to do so....

I therefore showed him the Spanish translation of your message 052 [deleted by US censors] which I have had made just in case it was needed. [I also included some parts regarding Britain] and said that the Japanese government was interested in obtaining the above type of information and had been planning to even organize a special organ for collecting this information. [This organ was ultimately to become the *TO* network.]

I then said that couldn't the Spanish Foreign Minister secretly ask his diplomats stationed in Britain and the United States to gather information regarding these points. To this the Foreign Minister said that, as I already knew, all countries were being especially alert recently about just such information leaking out, so that he was not at all sure that he could obtain information which would be what we wanted, but he would be very glad to take the responsibility of trying anyway, and took my list of requests.

As conditions turned out as above, the four persons [agents], who have been awaiting their chance to operate here, were each given a sizeable gift of appreciation by me, and our relations for the time being were broken off. As for ——— [person's name deleted by US censors] as he had his connections which enable him to obtain the information from the German intelligence network in England on conditions in England, I plan to continue to keep up my connection with him. I hope all of the above meets with your approval.[15]

Alarm bells now began to ring at the State Department in Washington, and a careful check was made on the messages being sent or relayed through the Madrid Embassy. For the following few weeks most of the messages were routine, but on 2 May Suma forwarded another 'strictly secret bulletin' in which he stated that the Allies were considering a trans-Arctic route for eleven-hour bomber flights which could be used to attack Tokyo, and that estimates were being made of arms requirements, including long distance bombers manned with RAF airmen, or those from Empire air-camps in Canada.[16]

There followed several reports concerning troop movements, and the infiltration of 'radio equipped' British agents into Norway, and also the report of 'rumours' that US troops were being landed at various locations on the African continent,[17] rumours which must have caused some disbelief in Tokyo. However, far more accurate reports concerning the morale of the American people, were soon to follow. On 4 May Suma forwarded to Tokyo:

There are innumerable rumours to the effect that labourers in arms factories are demanding salary increases and better treatment and lack zeal in improving products and in turning out material of excellent quality. According to intelligences which I have obtained, the workers in a certain factory in the state of Michigan, in order to express their opposition to Roosevelt's policy, resolved intentionally not to bring the arms they produced up to the expected standard.

Competent military officials, as soon as they discovered it, threatened the penalty of death if this was established as fact.... However, lately some of the workers in this plant were moved to another plant at the hands of troops.

Concerning the education of the personnel of flying units, strict secrecy is being maintained. It is even forbidden that members of the units use the words 'fly', 'war', 'go', and 'because'. However, the amount of liquor that these units consume is attracting attention. In any case, in various states, particularly in Missouri, a large number of training schools for airmen exist and they are training pilots on a large scale. Also among the youths who are conscripted, a very great many express the preference of being inducted into the airforce. This I think is quite in line with the rugged adventurous spirit of this country. I hear it said that the United States has trained or is now training a total of a million men of most excellent quality who are ready to face any enemy. The other day for example, I had a conversation with an air officer and he said: 'Of course our pilots have had no experience in actual warfare, but do we have to worry? No, not much. When Germany entered this war it was one thing, but now that she has had a few rounds with the enemy, she has had to change her tune – now the war reports sound somewhat different. German parachute troops were quite effective against the English and French forces, but in the war in the east, accompanying a broadening of the battle area, their effectiveness has been virtually lost.'

I replied, 'Well then you Americans won't have to train any such troops.' But he answered, 'Well, not only are we in a position to train American parachute troops on a vast scale, but we have got a great air arm to back them up with.'[18]

On 11 May the *Magic* Summaries stated that Suma had obtained Spanish Ambassador Gardenas' (in Washington) report to Spanish Foreign Minister Suner (in Madrid) by a 'certain method'. The report, also on US conditions, was forwarded immediately to Tokyo.

Gardenas finds it widely divergent, with some people doubting whether the US should have entered the war, quite a few believing that the US will not win, and about 70 per cent being against war in general. While the latter feeling does not greatly impede the actual conduct of the war, Gardenas thinks it has caused the US leaders to believe that the public is not yet willing to make maximum sacrifices and hence the leaders have hesitated to call for them. Some blame Roosevelt for the lack of spirit, claiming that he kept the likelihood of war from the people, and instead led them to believe that the best thing to do was to remain neutral. While there are those who defend Roosevelt, Gardenas does not think there are very many who are prepared to sacrifice everything. Moreover the people's dislike of British imperialism is comparable to their dislike of Nazism. Some even think Hitler greater than Roosevelt, because of Hitler's ability to accomplish objectives. US politicians are strangely quiet. Roosevelt's production figures seem like a dream to the outside world, but quite possible to Americans. If the US is allowed to keep on for another three years, there is real danger that it may attack the whole of Europe 'without mercy or humanity'. Japanese victories in the Pacific are not causing as much stir as Gardenas expected. All reports of losses are met calmly. This has greatly impressed Gardenas, who believes that he should re-judge the US.

At the bottom of this report, US analysts had noted:

Note that on 15 April 1942, the Japanese Minister in Madrid reported a conversation with Suner, during which Suner said that he would try to have his ministers in Britain and the US gather certain types of information requested by the Japanese, although he was not sure that the desired information would be obtained.[19]

Shortly afterwards, in messages sent to Tokyo from Hiroshi Oshima, the Japanese Ambassador in Berlin, it was revealed that the Japanese were once again aware that their codes were not secure. In reports from Berlin to Tokyo and Vichy on 7 May and 11 respectively, Oshima reported his belief that the Germans were reading some of the Japanese codes. He based this upon evidence secured by Japanese intelligence in Berlin, and also on the fact that the Germans had been admonishing the Japanese as to the security of their codes. Oshima was uncertain which codes were being read, but believed that the machine code – *Purple* – was safe, and that the less complex and less important commercial or abbreviation codes may have been broken or partially broken. He recommended that all commercial messages between Germany and Japan be sent by means of a commercial attaché's code (which was believed to have been far more secure) and that commercial request messages be suspended. In reply, Tokyo disapproved of allowing private firms to use secret codes fearing there would be difficulty 'in control of the German firms' ... Tokyo said that it would compile a new code for commercial request messages and that a total revision of the Japanese codes was being completed. They added that it would be impossible to put the new codes into practice speedily, because of transportation difficulties (in getting new code books to code recipients, etc.).

It also appeared that the Germans in Vichy had offered the Japanese copies of US telegrams sent between Washington and Vichy. Tokyo politely declined this offer, as the Japanese themselves could intercept these telegrams to a degree in Tokyo, and that if Berlin should send them to Tokyo, enciphered in the Japanese codes, they would still be of only limited use and would endanger the security of the Japanese codes. (Presumably because Germany and the US would have copies of the original telegrams.)[20]

The value of some of the reports coming out of Madrid were certainly open to question, especially at this early stage of the war, and before the *TO* network was effectively up and running. On 10 May Suma forwarded to Tokyo a report on Allied movements which was so inaccurate that it is difficult to understand where his information could have come from. He was purchasing information at this stage from a wide variety of freelance agents, and clearly the worth of these agents was open to question.

1. The War Department has just decided to invade Turkey and is hastening secret preparations. I heard this directly from one who participated.

2. I heard the following from C—— one of the Welshmen mentioned in my 23b. He is correspondent for a certain newspaper and he is engaged in an independence movement for his country. It is a little late but I send it nevertheless. I have just heard from naval circles that the navy is preparing to land on Madagascar, the Reunions and Cameroon, in the face of the enemy. These islands will be used as bases for convoys to India and subsequently as bases for strategy.

The troops to be used in this action are principally those stationed in South Africa and Syria. In view of the gravity of the coming action, it has become urgent to seize completely as many places on the African continent as possible.[21]

Other reports however were certainly more accurate, as with his message of 18 May detailing the arrival in Britain of shipping.

a. Londonderry. One-2000 ship, one-2500 ton ship, three-unknown tonnage.

b. Belfast. One-4000 ton ship with troops, three ships (total tonnage 10,000 with equipment)

c. Harrenpoint. Six ships loaded with troops. Three ships loaded with equipment, the above ships are to join a British convoy and proceed to Cape Town. An auxiliary force from the West Coast of Africa is scheduled to arrive in Cape Town at the same time.

d. Military supplies and airplanes are due to arrive in England and particularly in Scotland.[22]

With the rapid build-up of Japanese and German submarine packs, the value of such reports to the enemy was inestimable. On 7 June 1942, Suma sent:

A convoy of 15 ships left the ports of Sunderland and Hull headed for Archangel. They were protected by one aircraft carrier (7 cruisers), and a number of destroyers. Judging by the strength of the escort, this must be a very important convoy.

It was reported that the Great West Road Gas Company, in the vicinity of Hounslow [A Middlesex suburb of London] was sending large quantities of asphyxiating gas to Berwick, Scotland. However, upon investigation, it was ascertained that said gas was being sent from Chester to Liverpool. The intelligence agent there was prevented from going and had to ascertain this indirectly.

One damaged ship has entered Newcastle for repairs. As soon as the name is ascertained it will be wired.

In military quarters there is optimism over the new developments on the Libyan front. This is a test of strength of British-American forces versus German-Italian forces. It is reported that large stores of military supplies are being piled up in Egypt, of which the Germans and Italians are ignorant and that the battle line is strengthening day by day.

It is also said that since Japan has turned her attention to the prosecution of the war in China, the Japanese navy has relaxed its vigilance in the Indian Ocean and that United States military aid to India is proceeding smoothly.[23]

OPERATIONS PROBLEMS

It was also apparent to the US intelligence services that spy networks such as those being set up by the Japanese could only operate with large amounts of cash at their disposal, and that in itself presented enormous difficulties as currencies were severely restricted and no belligerent nation could legitimately obtain the currencies of an enemy. The difficulties of cash transactions for espionage purposes was to plague all the Japanese diplomatic missions throughout the war. In the initial months of the *TO* network operations, its operatives were functioning with only limited financial resources, mainly drawing funds from whatever still remained available since before the beginning of hostilities. Spanish and Japanese officials were also reluctant to be seen carrying large amounts of American or British currencies, as they perceived that this would have betrayed to the Allies the fact that they were operating as financial couriers for spy networks.

On 13 June 1942, US intelligence operatives were informed through a communication from Santiago to Tokyo, that one of the reasons why the Japanese Minister to Chile (Yamagata) was visiting Argentina may have been secretly to arrange for the dispersal of United States dollars held in Chile. Yamagata stated that it was 'undesirable' for him personally to carry US money on such a trip, '... because of the danger of being observed with it.' From this and other communications, the US were aware of '... a large amount,' and a 'considerable sum,' of US dollars held by the Italian Embassy in Chile, which indicated that Japanese diplomats were involved in plans to dispose of the money. Previous communications over several months had indicated that there were substantial transactions in dollars (running up at least as high as $200,000) between the Japanese and Italian Embassies in Santiago and Buenos Aires.[24] Two days later, the Japanese Ambassador in Buenos Aires sent the following message to Tokyo:

> Since it is now possible here to buy exchange in United States dollar currency, please dispatch to this office secretly, as soon as possible, the funds which you have to be transferred. [Explanation is not available] Make arrangements to turn the funds over to the Spanish Ambassador in Brazil and have them dispatched here by a safe method as soon as possible. Please let me know how you are going to do it.[25]

The Mikimoto Pearls

The following day, in response to a communication from a European representative of Mikimoto (Tokyo dealers in cultured pearls), stressing the wonderful business opportunities that existed in Paris and Lisbon, the Japanese Foreign Office transmitted a 'strictly secret' message to Vichy, to the effect that Mikimoto approved the suggestions and had prepared to send 20,000 sets of pearls 'mainly from 10 yen to 50 yen', though there were some that were more expensive, as well as an assortment of unset pearls. As we shall see, these pearls were often used as payment to agents in the field.[26] Several days later US authorities were informed through a secret message sent from Shui Tomii, the Japanese Minister in Buenos Aires, to the Japanese Foreign Office, that some of the Japanese 'military people' in Buenos Aires, 'have recently been making large purchases of diamonds'.[27]

The true reason for the dispatch of pearls was only revealed to G2 over the following months. On 3 December that year (1942), the *Magic* Summaries gave details concerning the scraps of information the US War Department had received through the secret messages. The summary stated:

> Last Spring this branch was supplied with an abstract of a badly garbled Japanese message from Vichy to Tokyo dated April 18, which indicated that the Paris representative of Mikimoto ... was

planning to send a lot of pearls to Lisbon by courier. The pearls, said to be worth about one million yen, were to be forwarded from Lisbon to England where they were to be sold pursuant to some arrangement previously worked out. The message stated that considerable risk would be involved but that if the first attempt succeeded, it would probably be repeated. Further study of the message has now indicated that its author was proposing to establish a regular route for smuggling pearls into England for sale there, the proceeds to be used, at least at the outset, to obtain technical, military, naval and aeronautical magazines not available in Lisbon. On June 3rd, the Mikimoto representative in Paris, one Ando, sent a message to Tokyo via the Japanese Embassy in Vichy, stating that he had gone to Lisbon to investigate the question of foreign trade, and had found that it had possibilities if he could only get sufficient 'merchandise' in Europe, there was no limit to what he could do and that he wished his home office to send him half a million yen worth of merchandise immediately. It seems clear that 'merchandise' means pearls and that subsequent events proceeded as follows. A lot of pearls – value not disclosed – were sealed in a folder and placed in a Spanish diplomatic pouch which left Tokyo on a diplomatic exchange ship. The ship arrived at Lourenço Marques on July 22nd, and the pouch was put on the *Gripsholm* [steamer] which arrived in this country on August 25th. It appears however that the pearls were not in the folder when it reached Japanese hands. Tokyo, apparently concerned over the matter, instructed Ambassador Mitani in Vichy to have Minister Suma in Madrid check into the matter with the Spanish Foreign Office. On November 6th, Mitani reported to Tokyo as follows: 'The Spanish Foreign Office enquired of the Spanish Ambassador in Washington in regard to the matter of the first shipment. Ando would like them to arrive by Christmas or the New Year for convenience of sale. Please arrange to send a second shipment at once'.

In November Minister Suma sent a message to Tokyo containing the following statement:

The commodities in question which were sent by way of the exchange ship from the Spanish Ambassador in Tokyo via the United States have not arrived. It seems probable that they were seized by the British or American officials. I asked an official in the Spanish Foreign Office to take this matter up immediately with the Spanish Ambassador in Washington, however this official said that since its contents might have a deleterious effect upon Spain as a representative of third powers, and destroy faith in her government, it was too dangerous a thing to trust even to a code message which might be read and that they were going to have a Spanish diplomat who is soon going to his post in Cuba via

Washington investigate the question. I judged from the statement
of this official that the commodities were seized, but I do not feel
that he is giving us a frank report of the situation.[28]

Evidently, Suma himself was not aware of what the folder had
contained, as in another part of his message he asked Tokyo to
inform him of the 'contents and nature of the things in question'.
But what really happened to the pearls? Subsequent messages
gave no indication other than official speculation, and G2
concluded that there were several possibilities. The first of these
was that the pearls had been removed (or stolen) by US
authorities at New Orleans, the ship's first US port of call,
although G2 was quickly informed that not all the Japanese
folders had been opened during normal customs inspection and
that no pearls were found. The second possibility was that the
pearls had been removed by 'persons unknown' during a call into
Port of Spain, Trinidad, or that the Spanish couriers at some
point took the pearls for themselves. In fact the State
Department was responsible for the removal of the pearls at New
Orleans.

More detailed information was supplied several days later from
the contents of another top-secret communication from the
Japanese Foreign Minister in Tokyo to Ambassador Suma in
Madrid. In his request for information regarding the content of
the shipment, Suma had stated very strongly that he was entitled
to know the exact contents of the folder. The Japanese Foreign
Minister replied:

> The contents of the folder were pearls that we were sending over
> for a special scheme of ours.... They were addressed to Ando in
> Lisbon. To the Spaniards we have explained that the packet only
> contained official business. Until we get an official explanation of
> this matter from you, we do not want to believe that the contents
> have been seized. Furthermore, for the time being we are keeping
> it a secret from the Mikimoto Company that the pearls were
> probably stolen by the Americans. We would like to have you
> keep this in mind.[29]

Suma was furious when he discovered that he had not been
informed of the scheme or of the contents of the folder. In a
heated message to his superior in Tokyo he quickly replied: 'In
view of Spain's delicate international position and considering the
danger involved from the point of view of her representing the
interests of other nations, this happening was most regrettable, so
don't let anything like this happen again.'[30]

The 'special scheme' referred to by the Foreign Minister was, of course, to use the proceeds of the sale of the pearls to purchase intelligence and to pay espionage agents in the field. The incident led to heated words between Suma and Spanish Ambassador Gardenas when he arrived from Washington for a visit to Madrid several months later. Gardenas fumed:

Before we discuss anything further, I want to tell you what has been most unpleasant. It is that trouble about the pearls. Some time ago the [US] State Department delivered to the Spanish Embassy in Washington two packets of pearls valued at 40,000 yen [US$10,000], and using very unpleasant language, dropped me a sly hint. The language used was hard to take and I did not like the affair a bit. I want you to know, sir, that those pearls are now in a safe at the [Spanish] Embassy and you may be sure that I am going to keep them there until after the war. Ever since that incident, nearly every one of our diplomatic pouches has been opened. You can see how embarrassed I was. I was surprised to see the Japanese government do such a thing – really surprised![31]

Additional portions of this conversation surfaced later, during which Gardenas is alleged to have said:

Spain's representation of Japanese interests has made us the object of all kinds of contempt and is costing the Spanish Embassy in Washington its popularity. Americans feel more animosity towards Japan than they do toward Germany. While they were stirred up by Pearl Harbor, their reaction to the execution of American aviators [flyers captured after bombing runs over Japan] has been far more profound. This execution, if I may speak frankly, shows a failure on the part of Japan to understand the American psychology. This one thing makes it forever impossible to negotiate a settlement with Japan ...[32]

Three days after reporting this conversation to Tokyo, Suma forwarded another message stating:

When I was talking to Ambassador Gardenas the other day about the pearls and other matters, twice his eyes narrowed and he said musingly, ponderingly and in a soft, half-questioning voice: 'It is strange how quickly the United States finds out about matters such as these. I wonder if Japanese codes are safe.'[33]

On 26 May after receiving this disturbing message, Japanese Foreign Minister Shigemitsu replied: 'I have studied the matter from a number of angles, but I cannot believe that it is the result of their having solved our codes.'[34]

With regard to Ando's request for a second shipment of pearls, the Japanese forwarded another pouch aboard the German steamer *Rhakotis*. The pearls were personally entrusted to the captain of the ship. The vessel left Yokohama in late September, but, as we shall see, even this attempt was to end in disaster.

The dispatch of pearls as payment for espionage activities was to continue for some time – and these pearls regularly disappeared. Two pouches of pearls were sent by the Japanese to Buenos Aires to help pay for the services of the *TO* network in the United States. The pearls were supposed to be carried by a *TO* agent from Buenos Aires to New Orleans, and then on to the Spanish Ambassador in Washington who was to arrange for their sale. However, the pearls were never sold by the ambassador because they apparently never arrived in Washington. The Japanese were incensed, and blamed the Spanish agents for the loss of the pearls. During a trip back to Spain, the ambassador firmly laid the blame with a group of Argentineans who were supposed to act as go-betweens for the transaction. What became of the pearls was never resolved.

NOTES

1. SRS 1092. Message of 22 November 1941.
2. SRS 1098. Message of 21 November 1941.
3. SRS 613. Message of 21 August 1941.
4. SRS 1102. Message of 2 December 1941.
5. *The Times*, 24 May 1944.
6. *Maryborough Chronicle*, 2 April 1938.
7. SRS 150. Message of 24 September 1941.
8. SRS 433. Message of 2 December 1941.
9. SRS 460. Message of 5 December 1941.
10. File SRH 043. Statement for Record of Participation of Brigadier General Carter W. Clarke, GSC, in the Transmittal of Letters from General George C. Marshall to Governor Thomas E. Dewey, the Latter Part of September 1944. Modern Military Section, National Archives, Washington DC.
11. *The Times*, 22 September 1945.
12. *Life*, 21 September 1945.
13. SRS 573, 16 April 1942.
14. SRS 573, *ibid*.
15. SRS 586, 30 April 1942.
16. SRS 590, 4 May, 1942.
17. SRS 591, 22 April 1942.
18. SRS 593, 7 May 1942.
19. SRS 597, 11 May 1942.
20. SRS 601, 15 May 1942.
21. SRS 601, *ibid*.
22. SRS 605, 18 May 1942.

23. SRS 628, 13 June 1942.
24. SRS 628, *ibid*.
25. SRS 629, 15 June 1942.
26. SRS 631, 17 June 1942.
27. SRS 634, 20 June 1942.
28. SRS 795, 3 December 1942.
29. SRS 979, 5 December 1942.
30. SRS 807, 15 December 1942.
31. SRS 973, 22 May 1943.
32. SRS 984, 2 June 1943.
33. SRS 984, *ibid*.
34. SRS 984, *ibid*.

3   The *TO* Network

Many of the reports sent by Suma were not well received in Tokyo, and Foreign Minister Shigenori Togo himself, at least in these early years, was wary of their accuracy. Togo wisely questioned and requested verification of some of Suma's more outlandish reports – reports such as Suma having obtained an exact copy of a top-secret message that General Marshall was transporting to London; that on 10 May England had decided to invade Turkey; that native chiefs in French West Africa had made 'impressive preparations' against US and British attack; that another raid on Tokyo would soon be carried out, 'using British and American pilots', and that the United States was feeling 'acute' concern about the spread of Communist propaganda in Iran. This feeling of incredulity was attested to in a diplomatic communication sent by Togo to Suma in June 1942:

> You do not know how grateful I am for your efforts in sending me continually very precious intelligence which you have gathered in strict secrecy. Now judging from the phraseology and contents of these messages however, there are often certain things which we find hard to believe, that is, things which do not necessarily seem to be factual. Therefore, since everything you send us is of the highest importance, will you in so far as possible send us the proof of the messages.[1]

The reports sent by Suma quickly became more accurate – and supposedly more effective. He began concentrating on more general espionage activities such as troop and convoy movements, reports which could be readily obtained through simple observation by spies at the various ports and military barracks. On 7 July 1942, under the heading of 'American Intelligence' he sent:

> Reports from Boston and Portland are in agreement with the report issued confidentially by Navy Department officials to the effect that a convoy of 43 ships was to leave for Ireland yesterday,

but the facts are that yesterday a convoy of 35 ships left at about noon and another of 9 ships at about 4 o'clock.

On the same day between 2 and 5 o'clock, 19 ships sailed from Boston and 9 ships from Portland.

According to reports from San Francisco, a convoy of 5 ships arrived at Oakland from Australia. Judging from the escort of this convoy, we believe they must have left a rather large number of ships in another port on the way back. The ships assigned to the escort were one airplane carrier, 5 cruisers and 20 destroyers. Every ship of the escort left going north.

According to dispatches gathered in Washington, special transport planes are under construction for use in establishing air connections with Hawaii, Australia and Aleutian Islands. The United States regards the Aleutians as of primary importance in supplying the Soviet.[2]

And so the simple and now relatively accurate reports continued, reports such as indications that Spanish authorities had been carrying on conversations with Suma, with a view to the purchase of rubber and tin in exchange for Spanish products, and that the Spanish were giving serious study to the possibility of establishing Spanish-Japanese commerce with the Philippines as a relay point. And then, on 17 July, the *Magic* Summaries mentioned for the first time a comprehensive reference to the *TO* network of agents. The following is a transcription of that report, and the flurry of *Magic* Summaries which quickly followed. On 14 July 1942, Suma received from New York a message from one of his agents there: '*TO* Intelligence. Extremely Urgent. A convoy of 45 ships assembled from various places left San Francisco this morning bound for Australia, carrying tanks and troops.'

When this message had been decoded, a member of G2 appended his own brief report on what was then known of *TO* intelligence:

> The evidence in our files is believed to establish that *TO* Intelligence is intelligence collected by a Spanish spy ring operating under (Spanish) Foreign Minister Suner. Further light is thrown on Spanish operations in this respect by another Suma communication, reported below.
>
> The Navy Department informs us that no convoy for Australia left San Francisco on July 14, but has given us information as to recent sailings from West Coast ports which might have led an intelligence agent to the conclusion expressed in the above report. At the request of the Navy Department, we are omitting the details from this Summary.
>
> The Navy Department has undertaken to check all sources in New York from which the communication might have gone out to

Madrid on July 14, in an effort to identify the sender of the message which Suma relayed to Tokyo.

As reported in previous summaries, it has been suspected that a certain class of intelligence reports which purportedly originate in New York and Washington and which are forwarded by the Japanese from Madrid to Tokyo are originally collected by a Spanish intelligence net and given to the Japanese in Madrid. These suspicions are confirmed by a Japanese communication of July 11 in which Ambassador Suma says:

'In connection with the matter of the spy net in the United States, I have since prevailed upon the chief of the agency [not otherwise identified] and through the good offices of Foreign Minister Suner, after numerous complications, am now in strictest secrecy in touch with the chief of the Phalangist branches in New York and Washington. We are communicating through the telegrams and mail of the Spanish Embassy and Consulate-General.'

Suma also says that each of 2 Madrid newspapers intends to send a special correspondent to the United States soon to carry on espionage; that the Spanish Military Attaché in Washington will soon be replaced and that it is planned to substitute for him, 'a certain general with whom the chief of the agency has been in touch for some time'. Suma expects good results if the latter plan succeeds. He concludes:

'The foregoing items are all so secret that I send only sketches and the definite statements I am keeping entirely secret.'[3]

The following day came another report:

Ambassador Suma has sent to Tokyo two more '*TO*' intelligence reports [believed to be gathered by Spanish agents], the substance of which is as follows:

New York, July 15:
A convoy of approximately 20 ships, which is scheduled to go to Australia, is to have special protection against torpedoes and mines.

According to the stories of members of the convoy's crew, the escort ships have flexible nets which are dropped to intercept torpedoes, and which have shown excellent results in actual tests.

According to confidential remarks of an American officer who recently returned from Australia, fortifications and trenches have been built throughout Australia. If the Japanese cannot land in Australia and New Zealand soon, they will never be able to do so, and all points in both places likely to be chosen for landing have already been strongly fortified. The officer describes the defences between Cooktown and Cairns, stating that there is a strip of land-mines a mile from the coast which can be detonated in sections from an encampment in the rear; that behind the mined area, there are anti-tank defences; that behind these there is another mine-field with barbed-wire entanglements; and that still farther back are trenches, machines guns, pillboxes, and reinforced gun emplacements. It is thought that the Allies have also set up gas throwers to be used 'in the event of a gas attack'.[4]

On 24 July, US Intelligence compiled a brief report based upon their very limited knowledge of the activities of the *TO* network, which stated:

When *TO* Intelligence Reports arrive in Madrid, they are distributed immediately to Ambassador Suma, the German Special Affairs Agency and Foreign Minister Suner. Suma and the German Agency receive the reports promptly but Suner sometimes does not, because he is so busy that he is not always accessible to the Chief of the Espionage Agency [presumably Spanish] who is required to hand these reports to Suner in person.

The German Special Affairs Agency is basically a military intelligence agency. Its primary purpose is to obtain information that will facilitate the operations of submarines and airplanes, viz., information about convoy movements and the weather. It has a staff in England which has constantly been transmitting such information to Germany. The Chief of the Agency is ostensibly a member of the German Embassy staff, but actually he reports only to the Department of National Defence and the German Ambassador has no authority over him and does not receive his reports.

C——— formerly ——— [deleted by US censors] of the Spanish Embassy in London, who established the Spanish espionage net in England, and returned to Spain shortly before January 4 of this year, has been continuing his 'plots' since his return. He has been in contact with the German Special Affairs Agency for about two years.[5]

Other reports on the known activities of the network included the information that Suma had informed Tokyo that certain of the communications generated from the intelligence net operating in England were written in a German secret ink which neither the Spanish nor the Japanese could read, and that they had to be sent to Germany where the ink was once again made visible. On 27 July Ambassador Suma sent the following to his counterpart, Ambassador Hiroshi Oshima in Berlin:

In connection with my spying activities in America I would like to obtain some of the special secret ink used by the German Defence Bureau together with instructions as to its use. I would be much obliged if it would be possible to turn this over to Secretary Miura, who plans to arrive in Berlin from Paris on August 3rd or 4th.[6]

And so Suma continued with his spying activities without being in the least aware that his every message was being carefully monitored. On 30 July he sent:

> Ever since the Germans began to display such splendid successes on the Eastern Front, the inbred capacity of the British for argument is running wild. In other words, these people are shot through with bureaucracy, a fact which ruins their whole character. Why? An office head will give certain orders for tomorrow's propaganda, and by that afternoon they become utterly impracticable. On a given day the Air Department will rant and brag that England will only have to show her full might to make the whole world situation change completely. The next day, however, they will whine that the German Army, using its experience in this war, will blast England at any moment.
>
> This is having a terrible effect on British morale. Of course, I would not say that British morale is gone, but as for that high British spirit that we used to hear so much about, well, now it just does not exist.

And on 16 August the *Magic* Summaries had some delight in reporting to senior US military officials:

> On August 13 Ambassador Suma sent to Tokyo, Berlin and Rome the following intelligence given to him by the, 'Chief of our *TO* intelligence net':
> We have had difficulty in reading our telegrams from England, so things are not clear, but Churchill's attendance at the Gorki Conference is certain, and he expects to stop off at Cairo on the way home'.

This message was followed by a US translator's note which stated:

> The Chief difficulty may account for the fact, noted in previous Summaries, that some of Suma's *TO* items have appeared to be unintelligible, inaccurate or incredible or, to use Togo's characterization, 'hard to believe'.[7]

It was not until 21 August that the US military authorities learned anything substantial about the physical make-up of the network, when Suma sent to Tokyo a two-part message which dealt specifically with the activities of the network in the United States. The first part of the report stated:

The *TO* intelligence net has smuggled three agents into the United States. One of them is in New York, one in Washington and the third in San Francisco, and they are in very close touch with each other and lately have been, 'hitting the mark rather well'. (Note: Previous messages indicate that these three men have been in the United States at least since January. [US intelligence note.])

Two 'special correspondents' will sail for the United States shortly, one between the last of August and the middle of September, and the other at the end of September ... the Spanish government is trying to send as its Military Attaché to Washington a man who will act as a spy, and the matter is, 'proceeding beautifully ...' The chief of the *TO* intelligence agency has had one of his most trusted subordinates pass himself off as a member of the Communist Party and [has made] arrangements with the US Military Attaché in Madrid to give him secret passage to the United States so that he may enrol in a force of Spanish communists which the United States is said to be organizing. The person in question is now in Lisbon awaiting a ship.

The second part of the message commenced by incorrectly quoting the 'Chief of the Agency'. In fact, the message was quoting Suma.

Now, in order to perfect this espionage work, just as in England, we shall have to smuggle a minimum of 20 spies into the United States.... As you know, the espionage net in England was founded by Germany regardless of expense, with the co-operation of the Spanish government. It has been functioning for three years, since the beginning of the war. Through the good offices of (Spanish) Foreign Minister Suner, we are using it free of charge. As a matter of principle, Germany is paying operating and salary expenses for the agency's work in England. All we do is send some of these spies special bonuses, so to speak, when they do fine work. However, when it comes to the United States, we will have to pay it all. The expenses for getting it started and operating expenses from then on will be our burden. These agents ... will be in the direst danger of their lives; and from the very nature of their work they will require very large amounts of money. So please see that this is taken care of.

When we first started out on this undertaking, you sent some money; 30,000 paper dollars of which is still left. When we embark on the adventure in the United States, we may need as much money instantly, so please send 400,000 yen to the Yokohama Specie Bank in Berlin to be placed on our account there (if possible in Swiss francs – otherwise in German Marks). I hope you will do this by return wire.

In response to this admission by Suma that he was planning a huge espionage network in the United States, several days later the *Magic* Summaries finally delivered a substantial – although belated – report on the activities and operational structure of the *TO* network; and while the report was far from complete, it at last gave US military and intelligence chiefs an overview of the espionage forces being gathered against them through the Spanish embassies.

The report stated:

MEMORANDUM:

Subject: *TO* Intelligence Reports.
1. The Intelligence Net in the British Isles.
Early in January 1942, the Spanish Foreign Minister Serrano Suner arranged for the Japanese Minister in Madrid [Suma] to receive intelligence reports produced by an espionage net operating in the British Isles and having a 'Chief' in Madrid. In a message of 8 January, the meaning of which has just become clear through a complete de-cryption and translation, Suma forwarded one such report to Tokyo, stating: 'I hereafter designate these intelligences as *TO*.'

Since January, as indicated in previous Summaries, Minister Suma has forwarded to Tokyo many *TO* reports containing information about British military and political affairs. That the term *TO* (meaning 'East') has continued to signify information coming from the intelligence net mentioned above is indicated by (a), a *TO* report of May 10 mentioning as a source one of the members of the net; and (b), an August 13 communication reporting that the 'Chief of our *TO* intelligence net' is having difficulty reading telegrams from England.

From time to time Suma has informed Tokyo of details concerning the organization and operation of the net, which he has learned through his Spanish contacts. A summary of such information follows.

The prime movers in setting up the net were the Germans, whose main objective was to gather information about the movements of convoys and weather reports to facilitate the activities of submarines and airplanes. The actual organization of the net however was undertaken by ——— [deleted by US censors], a member of the Falangist party and a protégé of Suner sent to London for the express purpose of organizing the net. The Spanish Ambassador to Britain was party to the plan. It seems that [the agent] succeeded in getting together a group of spies composed of 5 Welshmen, 2 Irishmen, 11 Scotchmen, 2 Spaniards and possibly one other man.

The Germans financed the enterprise and supplied the agents

with short-wave sets and secret inks. The agents were also to have the use of the short-wave equipment of Spanish ships if necessary. They received all communications at a central headquarters, but transmitted from various places, moving their transmitting equipment from day to day by automobile.

Apparently some reports are sent directly to Germany by short-wave. Others, however, are sent to Madrid via the Spanish Embassy in London.

They are received in Madrid by the 'Chief' who passes the readable ones onto Foreign Minister Suner, and Minister Suma as well as the 'German Special Affairs Agency', a military intelligence unit headed by a man who is nominally attached to the German Embassy but actually reports directly to Berlin. Suma says, however, that neither he nor the Spaniards know the proper re-agent to bring out the secret ink messages, and those have to be sent along to Berlin to be read.

It is not clear that the Germans realize that the Spanish authorities have been making the *TO* reports available to Suma.

2. *Early plans to establish an intelligence net in the United States.*

Early in January, after he had arranged to get the *TO* reports coming from England, Suma told Suner that he would like to make similar arrangements to get information from the United States. Suma said that he had three agents in the United States, but that neither their reports nor those of the Spanish Ambassador contain any important information. A few days later Suma and one of Suner's representatives agreed on a plan to send 2 espionage agents to the United States (and at the same time one to Dakar and one to Australia). These agents were to be given diplomatic status, and those coming to the United States were to be installed, respectively, at the Spanish Consulate-General in San Francisco and the Embassy in Washington. All four were to be equipped with short-wave sets, secret inks and special codes. Funds were to be supplied to the US agents 'by clipper mail'.

However, according to Suner, some sort of incident occurred involving ——— [name deleted by US censors] which gave the Allies an opportunity to charge Spain with complicity in Axis espionage activities, whereupon Suner said the United States started to take great interest in (the) activities of Spanish diplomats in the Americas, and the State Department informed Spain that only a limited number of couriers could be sent to this country, and that no new Spanish diplomatic appointments to the United States would be accepted. The plan to dispatch agents to the United States (and also the plan for Dakar and Australia) were thereupon abandoned, and the four agents were discharged with, '... sizeable gifts of appreciation'.

The first available *TO* report labelled as coming from the United States was dated 14 June and headed: 'telegram, 12 June, from

Washington.' Thereafter as noted in previous Summaries, numerous *TO* reports have been received with either Washington or New York datelines. They have contained a wide variety of information on political and military subjects. Their headings and contents have indicated that one or more agents has forwarded several reports from a person whom he calls: '... my colleague in California'. The latter reports have included information about ship sailings from Los Angeles, San Francisco and Santa Cruz. One of them, designated as extremely urgent, was headed 'New York 14 July'. It referred to a convoy leaving San Francisco '... this morning', and was forwarded by Suma to Tokyo on the same day.

For a time we had no evidence, except the identity of headings, that the *TO* reports coming from the United States were produced by an agency similar to that operating in England.

As reported in the July 17 Summary however, Suma advised Tokyo on July 11 that: 'through the good offices of Foreign Minister Suner' and by 'prevailing upon the chief of the *TO* Agency', he had finally succeeded in getting in touch, in strictest secrecy, with the chief of the Falangist branches in New York and Washington.

Suma stated: 'We are communicating through the telegrams and mail of the Spanish Embassy and Consulate-General'.

(Suma) went on to tell of plans (a), to send two special news correspondents to the United States for espionage purposes, both of whom were 'reliable men' and were in contact with the 'Chief', and (b), to send to the United States as Spanish Military Attaché 'a certain general with whom the Chief of the Agency has been in touch for quite a while'.[8]

It was now becoming increasingly clear that the three operatives already established in the United States were highly competent spies capable of supplying a wealth of details. Just two days after the comprehensive *Magic* Summary detailing the activities of the *TO* network, Ambassador Suma sent a damaging message to Tokyo, Berlin and Rome:

I have a report that landing forces have left a certain Pacific port, probably Los Angeles, bound for Australia. In this force are included 12,000 picked parachute troops. Each of them is equipped with a light rifle and a flame thrower.

I have also learned from the same source that liaison between New Zealand and the continent by military planes is functioning excellently, and that soon the same sort of service will be opened to other distant points in the Pacific.

A convoy bearing American troops and specially built tanks has arrived at Aden, doubtless to be used in the great battle of Egypt which is expected to start ere long. The number of men shipped on this convoy was approximately 40,000

On the 24th, a convoy made up of 24 petroleum ships sailed from New York for Panama. Upon leaving they were escorted by one lone destroyer, but at the port of Dover they are to be met by two heavy cruisers and several destroyers.

On the 22nd and 23rd respectively, convoys of 43 ships and 19 ships docked in New York. The former came from the South Pacific and the latter from England.

Two convoys left New Orleans for Brazil bearing airplane parts, and I have confidential information to the effect that the United States, preparing for swift development in this war, is now establishing a large system of aerial bases in Brazil.[9]

On 31 August Suma forwarded a vital message to Tokyo which informed the Japanese of the American intention to concentrate their forces in the Pacific region. While the outline of the report was vague and even incorrect in some instances, the essential content was accurate and this gave Japan clear warning of what she might expect in the Pacific, and therefore the future prosecution of the war.

A certain powerful individual has informed me that the American War Department has decided upon plans for the occupation of the Pacific and preparations are already complete. The objective is to occupy the Aleutians, Timor, Java, and other islands that have been lost. The bases of operations for this action will be New Zealand and Australia and the Coral Sea, and soldiers and material and airplanes in great numbers are already placed in position. The main type of airplanes to be used in this engagement are Flying Fortresses and attack planes. On the other hand, in this battle, the United States plans to concentrate her full naval power in the region described. Thus, while the Pacific will be taken care of, the Atlantic will be left wide open. Great Britain condemns this, but it appears that the United States will pay no heed but proceed to the fight as planned.[10]

And so the Japanese espionage communications continued over the following few weeks, informing Tokyo and Berlin about the loss of British confidence after the raid on Dieppe, and that an unescorted convoy was en route to Malta, via Gibraltar, with a vital supply of fuel which had to get through at any cost.

In Great Britain, frantic efforts were being made to protect the convoys from espionage activities as the toll in sunken ships steadily mounted. In October 1942, during a spirited debate in the House of Lords, allegations were made by the Earl of Cork that security measures on the docks were abysmal, and that it was a simple task for Axis agents to find out when convoys were leaving, how many ships were in the convoys, what they carried and where they were heading. The Earl stated that he had received a considerable number of letters from concerned citizens claiming to have seen the cargoes of ships clearly stencilled on the crates as the crates were being transported through towns to the various docks. One letter claimed that at Liverpool, the Liverpool Overhead Railway was a superb advantage ground from which almost everything that happened in the docks could be observed. The author of the letter had seen cargoes being loaded for Malta, Murmansk and Archangel. It was principally to these ports that the convoys were being subjected to attacks by the German submarines.

Another letter to the Earl was from the manager of a large engineering firm in northern England who wrote to state that his only son, an engineering officer in the Merchant Navy, home on a visit during July 1942, had seen cases being loaded into his ship clearly marked with the destination Malta. Several of his fellow engineering officers had discussed the question of refusing to sail in the ship as a protest against what they regarded as culpable carelessness. The officer managed to persuade his colleagues to make the journey, primarily because of the desperate situation of the soldiers then fighting in Malta. Before sailing they stated that when they returned they would require a full investigation of the affair. In a farewell letter to his father, dated 18 July 1942, the engineering officer wrote: '... Jerry will be watching for us in full force, it will be a miracle if we return, this is probably our last farewell ...' The ship did not return, she was lost with more than one hundred of her crew, including all her officers.[11]

Shortly afterwards the Spanish Foreign Minister, Ramon Suner – the man who had aided Suma in setting up the *TO* agency, resigned from his governmental position after a heated disagreement with General Franco. The argument concerned the execution of a Falangist who had been tried and convicted of an assassination attempt on the Spanish Minister for War. Suner was quickly replaced by Foreign Minister Gomez Jordana. It seemed for a while that Suma had lost an important ally in the Spanish government, and also a vital source of information. However, this was disproved when Jordana supplied Suma with a report allegedly quoting the American Secretary of State, Cordell Hull, during a supposed meeting with Spanish Ambassador Gardenas which – according to Gardenas – had been recorded in secret by a shorthand secretary hidden by the Ambassador in an adjacent room at the Spanish Embassy in Washington. Gardenas stated: 'If you want to get the most reliable opinions of the [US] government, you have to look at the Secretary of State; so on the

5th I invited him to dine at the embassy. After dinner, he opened up and we had quite a tête-à-tête.'

This alleged tête-à-tête (which never took place) would have been instructional had it been true. According to Gardenas, Hull spoke openly of some key policies such as continued US military support to the Russians, the losses of aircraft off the Netherlands Frisian Islands, the fact that long-range bombing of German cities was preferable to establishing a second front, the success with which the Americans viewed their air-raid policy, the high morale of the Australian people after the Battle of the Coral Sea – the number of American ships lost or damaged during that engagement, and much more. It is difficult to imagine that the Japanese military and government minds in Tokyo would have swallowed such a story. The idea of the US Secretary of State speaking so openly to the representative of a country known to favour the Axis powers was so obviously nonsensical.

On 4 October, Spanish Foreign Minister Gomez Jordana further indicated that he was prepared to allow the *TO* net to continue its work under Spanish guidance and help – although with care that security would not be breached. He summoned the head of the *TO* network to his office and stated:

> As regards the matter of the intelligence net, I have known about it in general since my assumption of office, and I have no intention of making any change in the policy of Spanish cooperation with the Axis. Ex-Foreign Minister Suner's way of doing things was too brash and occasionally caused trouble. Therefore, on the surface, I shall maintain in future the strictest possible neutrality. I want you to carry on as if I knew nothing at all about the existence of this intelligence net.
>
> There is no objection to the use of the Foreign Office codes and pouches as before. But in case anything happens, I ask you frankly and explicitly to take the greatest care not to compromise Spain's neutral position in any way.[12]

Several days later Suma conveyed to Tokyo a report which claimed that the Americans were building a submarine aircraft carrier capable of carrying six airplanes and also that, according to information supplied by one of his spies, New Zealand was being deliberately neglected by the Allies in favour of Australia. The report concluded that New Zealand was short of tanks, weapons and ammunition, and that anti-tank guns were especially needed.

Indications that the *TO* network was expanding came to G2 on 16 October with a detailed report prepared for US military chiefs concerning the smuggling of a spy into Vancouver. The beginning of the report is mostly censored, but continues:

> Suma immediately set about secretly investigating him (the proposed spy) to determine whether he would be willing to work for the Axis. Apparently satisfied with the results of his investigation, Suma had the head of the spy ring get in touch with ... [the proposed agent] and on October 15, the latter told Suma that [the agent] had consented. Apparently however [the agent] believes that he is working either for Spain alone or for Spain and Germany, rather than for the Japanese, for Suma reports that the head of the spy ring has not told [the agent] that he is to be acting as a [Japanese] agent, and is making it appear that he is to be the head of the spy ring in Vancouver. Suma adds: 'Now the only way to make certain of his cooperation and faithfulness is after all by money, therefore in the near future we intend to scrape together a large sum of money and hand it over to him. He leaves the Spanish ship *Marques de Comillas* about the 10th of January and expects to reach Vancouver about the latter part of February going via Havana, Washington, New York and Montreal. Accordingly, if there are any special details you wish to know about Vancouver, Alaska or the Aleutians, aside from the regular routine information, please get in touch with the army and navy and let me know in plenty of time.'

From other messages G2 became aware that two large newspapers in Madrid were sending 'special correspondents' to the United States, and that both correspondents had agreed to act as espionage agents. The first of these agents was to sail sometime between 1 and 15 September, and the other at the end of that month. Suma also added at the end of his 22 October message that: 'I have just established connection with a reliable gentleman who is leaving by clipper plane on the 8th of next month. He is going to Mexico, Peru, Colombia, Ecuador and Guatemala. I have asked him to help us establish the espionage net in all of these places.'[13]

The American War Department was already sceptical about the quality of some of the information being channelled through the *TO* network. For example, following the alleged meeting between Secretary of State Cordell Hull and Ambassador Gardenas, the State Department later informed G2 that no such meeting had ever taken place. Hull had never accepted an invitation to dinner nor had he even spoken to the Ambassador since Gardenas had formally presented his credentials. Further proof of the inaccuracy of the information emanating from the various *TO* agents came in a message dated 17 October to Tokyo,

Berlin and Rome which claimed inaccurately, among other things, that the US were preparing a large-scale second front in South Africa or Northern France, that a considerable offensive against Japan was planned, that a new chemical bomb was under construction, that the US authorities had prohibited all persons listening to Japanese radio broadcasts, that anyone doing so was 'picked up and punished without further ado', and that no reports put out by the Japanese were allowed to be printed in the US. G2 also checked the accuracy of ships' movements against the alleged movements reported by *TO* agents, and discovered significant discrepancies. For example *TO* agents reported that on 19 October 29 ships sailed from New York, in fact on 18 and 19 October, 30 ships had sailed. *TO* reported that their cargoes consisted principally of bombers. In fact, there were no bombers aboard, only aircraft parts and some Kittyhawks and Lightnings. *TO* agents stated that the destination of the ships was Egypt, when in fact the ships were destined for various ports including Egypt, South Africa, Brazil, the Caribbean Islands, Panama, Australia and England. On 25 November, G2 reported:

As pointed out in previous Summaries, some of the *TO* reports have proved highly inaccurate, and certain of them are thought to have been fabricated in their entirety. However [some] appear to be sufficiently near the truth to justify discarding the possibility that all of the *TO* reports are the product of someone's imagination. It now seems likely that one or more Axis agents are preparing reports in the United States, supplementing actual information with a liberal amount of guess-work and forwarding them to Madrid. In connection with the above, the following November 17 report from Japanese Minister Suma, discussing the *TO* net in England, seems of interest:

'Lately communication with London has been severed. I investigated and found that some days ago the British government made representations to the Spanish government that it is strongly suspected that Spain is furnishing the Axis with intelligence by diplomatic pouch and by diplomatic code; and that Spain should consider this a strong protest. In reply, the Spanish government denied it most vigorously, declaring that there is absolutely no basis for such a speculation. Since then, Spanish Ambassador Alba [the Duke of Alba] in London, has in all probability been refusing to send the communications to our spy agency here. [In Madrid]. On the day before yesterday, the head of the ring in Great Britain also issued a warning that a frightening situation[14] has developed and that the ring had better lie low for a while.'[15]

SPANISH/JAPANESE RELATIONS

One of the few differences of opinion, a difference which caused
considerable consternation to Suma and the head of *TO*, was the
concern of some Spanish officials over the treatment by Japanese
authorities of Catholics and Spanish nationals in the Philippines
and elsewhere. The diplomatic friction caused by these incidents
was important, for it threatened the very existence of the *TO*
network and the continued goodwill of Spanish espionage
cooperation. This ill treatment of Spanish nationals led to several
very strongly worded diplomatic notes of protest being given by
the Spanish government to the Japanese government through
Minister Suma. Some Philippines churches had been closed. The
Japanese, with their usual degree of thoroughness and brutality
had arrested so-called agitators and incarcerated them in the
ancient bastion of Fort Santiago, which had been taken over as a
headquarters, prison and 'interrogation centre' by the notorious
Kempei Tai. According to contemporary reports in the US,
British and Spanish press, two Spanish Catholic priests,
Monsignor Olano, the aged Bishop of Guam, and his secretary,
Father Jauregui, had been placed into a concentration camp with
500 American prisoners of war, and afterwards transported by
sea in foul conditions to Shokoku.[16] These reports, made public
by the Buenos Aires 'Efe' news agency, shocked the
predominantly Catholic South American and Spanish public. In
October 1942 the Spanish government delivered a protest note to
the Japanese Embassy in Madrid complaining of the treatment of
Catholics and Spanish nationals. In addition to this, the Japanese
had decreed that thenceforth the Spanish language was to be
banned in the Philippines – the only languages permitted were to
be Japanese and Tagalog (the most widely spoken of the many
Filipino dialects). The only exception to the rule was that Spanish
(and, to a certain degree, English) could still be used in courts of
law, as the laws were generally those of Spain and therefore had
been drawn up in Spanish. The Spanish note complained that
Spanish subjects in the Philippines were 'vitriolic' on the subject,
and that they had complained of the many inconveniences which
the Japanese had caused, such as the suppression of the
transmission of funds by churches and industrialists. The note in
part read:

> The government of this country is deeply incensed over this,
> because of the amity supposed to exist between Tokyo and

Madrid. The outlawing of the Spanish language is a thing which the Spanish government cannot endure. The customs of the Filipinos sprang from Spain, and the majority of them appreciate deeply their ties with the Spaniards. It is beyond the government's comprehension why the Japanese would preclude the language of a friend and permit the use of the tongue of an enemy like the United States. Therefore the Spanish government herewith demands that the Japanese government rescind this ruling and permit the use of Spanish along with Japanese and Tagalog everywhere throughout the islands. It is further hoped that no other such incidents will, in any case, occur.[17]

Concerned over the possible consequences of the note, especially to his continued good relations with the Spanish Foreign Minister and the activities of his espionage net, Suma forwarded an urgent message to his superiors in Tokyo.

Seldom in this country is there seen anything in writing more strongly phrased than this Spanish note. It is a strong reproach against our conduct which took them utterly by surprise in view of the very many kindnesses they have shown us all along. I think Spain must have made every preparation before driving this final nail.

Well, we do not have Suner any more; we have a new Foreign Minister to deal with who has his *carte blanche*, and if we do not act to suit him, not only will he stop helping us in representing enemy interests, but he will also cease permitting his country to help us in espionage. Please think this over very carefully and lean over backwards to do as I suggest. I will keep you advised all along.[18]

In a later Summary Suma added:

I told you last year that in the Philippines action Japan should be very careful to respect Spain's position and to do nothing to harm her culture there. I think that the same advice is still pertinent, so will you please consider it seriously.[19]

Japanese Foreign Minister Tani replied:

... Spanish is being tolerated in the court-rooms and therefore there is no justification for Spain's present misunderstanding. In any case, no matter how we decide this issue, there is nothing Spain can do with all her protesting. Tell her that Spanish is being used in the court-rooms and that we are not in the slightest degree attempting to weed out Spanish culture.[20]

In fact, this obstinacy on Tani's part was to later have serious consequences on Japan's abilities to carry out espionage activities from the Japanese Ministry in Spain.

NOTES

1. SRS 643, 29 June 1942.
2. SRS 647, 9 July 1942.
3. SRS 655, 17 July 1942.
4. SRS 656, 18 July 1942.
5. SRS 662, 24 July 1942.
6. SRS 667, 29 July 1942.
7. SRS 685, 16 August 1942.
8. SRS 697, 28 August 1942.
9. SRS 699, 30 August 1942.
10. SRS 702, 2 September 1942.
11. *The Times*, 15 October 1942.
12. SRS 740, 9 October 1942.
13. SRS 758, 27 October 1942.
14. There seems to be no record of what the 'frightening situation' was.
15. SRS 787, 25 November 1942.
16. *The Times*, 14 February 1944.
17. SRS 977, 26 May 1943.
18. SRS 769, 7 November 1942.
19. SRS 773, 11 November 1942.
20. SRS 977, 26 May 1943.

4 The Crucial Year

The first half of 1942 was an exceptionally successful period for the Japanese. After the bombing of Pearl Harbor and subsequent successes in taking Singapore, Manila and Hong Kong, the invasion of Burma and the signing of a new military pact with Germany and Italy in January that year, the Japanese people generally, and especially the military, were flushed with their successes and felt that nothing could stop them with their plans for the Co-Prosperity Sphere. Their successes were highlighted by the sinking of British navy ships *Dorsetshire*, *Cornwall*, *Hermes* and *Holyhock*, and the sinking of USS *Lexington* during the Coral Sea battle in May. The Axis powers seemed impregnable – despite some of the set-backs Hitler was experiencing on the Russian Front. However, by the end of the year, the situation had changed somewhat, and the tide of the war was already turning – much to the consternation of the various Japanese diplomats stationed around the world. This feeling of impending gloom was amply demonstrated in a secret message, also decoded by the Americans, which was sent by Japanese Minister Okubo from the Budapest Legation to Tokyo in December that year. Okubo lamented the fact that, as the year drew to a close, the military situation was very different from the one which had taken place during the first few months of the year, at least up until August. He stated:

This summer we all thought that the German drive on the Eastern Front would be successful. The German troops were not worn out and we felt sure that the Reich would get vast military resources, [from the captured territories] and make it impossible for Russia to revive. We thought that the fight Hitler was putting up was most effective and would produce a great change in the world. How we rejoiced then, thinking that Moscow would fall, that Stalingrad would be occupied and that the Germans would get a strong hold along the Volga and Don, making it impossible for her to hold out indefinitely. It seemed then that Russia's striking power was gone for lack of food and oil, and that next year, if she struck back at all, it would be very weakly. We thought that England and the United States, seeing how Russia was holding out, would postpone their second front in Europe until it was too late. Ah...how well those U-boats were doing. Rommel invaded Egypt and we were practically sure of an Axis victory. Certain small countries were absolutely convinced that the hour had come when they would be bereft of their independence because of a German victory. Moreover, aside from carrying out more air raids and spreading disruptive propaganda throughout Europe, England and the United States seemed absolutely unable to cope with the situation.

But then the picture began to turn and change. September came, and aside from the siege of Stalingrad and the action in the Caucasus, the German forces came to a virtual standstill.... In September Rommel's drive failed, Italy's morale stagnated, and the President of the United States proclaimed the Italians in America were free. England began, on the one hand, a rousing campaign through propaganda and intrigue to eradicate Italy from the camp of her foes, and on the other hand began to bomb Italy. Slowly it dawned upon us that the occupation of Liberia by American troops and their designs on Dakar were, in the main, to get bases for a concerted attack against Italy...But now behold the Eastern Front. The Red Army has smashed the Italian and Roumanian forces, and whether they will succeed or not, are plunging towards Rostov.... This is a possibility which we cannot but view with fear and trembling. In short, these two theatres of war are powerful; in their portents of what the ultimate outcome of the war will be.[1]

THE POSITION OF SPAIN AND PORTUGAL

Both Spain and Portugal were now strongly defending their neutrality but, in the face of mounting international pressure from the Axis governments, they were teetering on the edge of abandoning this neutrality and joining with the Axis powers. Spain was concerned that the Allies would attempt to establish a second front by landing on Spanish shores, and General Franco strongly stated that should this happen he would defend Spain with every means at his disposal. He requested that Germany and Italy sell Spain tanks, aircraft and anti-aircraft guns in large quantities, but neither Italy nor Germany was in a position to supply such aid.

Japanese diplomats in both these countries found themselves in a particularly delicate position. Forced to maintain a semblance of impartiality in order to appease the neutral status of their hosts, they were also forced to instigate, wherever possible, policies and whisper campaigns to further promote a move by the Spanish and Portuguese governments towards a deeper commitment to Axis policies.

An example of the delicacy of the situation can be seen in the case of Rogerio de Magalhaes Peixoto de Menezes, an aristocratic Portuguese diplomat turned spy, who arrived to take up his position at the Portuguese Embassy in London in July 1942. He brought with him various items of spying equipment, including a code and invisible ink. He had been instructed to send his messages back to the Portuguese Foreign Office via the diplomatic pouch. However, his efforts at spying were never very good. He managed to send clippings from newspapers and magazines, and the synopses of gossip he had heard at social gatherings. He also admitted sending details of the anti-aircraft defences of London, some war shipments to Turkey and had made reports on the possible developments in Greece. He had received £50 from an Axis agent in Lisbon before leaving to take up his post in London, and had been paid at a rate of £25 per month. The money had arrived regularly in a sealed envelope via the diplomatic pouch. Finally, however, he became lazy and started to send messages via the ordinary post to Axis letter-drop boxes, these boxes were known to British counter-intelligence. The letters were traced to their sender and Menezes was arrested on 22 August 1942. Like all other spies, he was convicted under the Treachery Act of 1940 and sentenced at the Old Bailey to death by hanging. He appealed the sentence but was rejected. His mother sent a long and heart-searching appeal for clemency to King George, and another to Winston Churchill. Whether these appeals were effective or not is a moot point, Menezes was reprieved by the Home Secretary in May 1943 – thirteen days after his appeal had been rejected – his sentence commuted to a term of imprisonment, but only because the British government feared that the execution of a Portuguese diplomat would lead to such a diplomatic rift that Portugal would be forced to break off relations, thus moving closer to the Axis camp.

CONTINUED OPERATION OF THE *TO* NETWORK

Meanwhile, Japanese Minister Yakichiro Suma in Madrid continued to build up the *TO* network. On 22 October 1942 he informed Tokyo that another special press correspondent working for a large Madrid newspaper was due to leave for Washington early the following month with specific instructions to become a member of the *TO* net. What Suma did not know was that this unnamed spy had distinct pro US sympathies, and shortly after being recruited by the Japanese, this man arrived at the American Embassy in Madrid and gave detailed information concerning his mission to US Ambassador Hayes. The correspondent said that he had been supplied by the Japanese with a complex word code for use in plain text press dispatches and he also had a formula for making his own invisible ink. He gave Hayes copies of both. He also gave the Ambassador a list of names of American columnists whose articles he had been instructed to forward to Madrid. The list was identical with a list set forth in a message dated 30 October 1942 from the Japanese Foreign Office to Suma, outlining what the Japanese wished the special correspondents to do in the United States. The informer also said that he had been instructed to forward some of his reports to the Spanish Foreign Office, via diplomatic pouch from the Spanish Embassy in Washington, that several officials in the Foreign Office in Madrid were members of the espionage organization, and that he could expect to have US currency forwarded to him from Spain in the diplomatic pouch. He was also instructed that Ambassador Gardenas, the Spanish Ambassador to the US, was not to be informed of the real nature of his mission.

Both Suma in Madrid and Morishima in Lisbon worked together in gathering intelligence information during the entire war. These men collaborated in intelligence gathering within their respective spheres, often sending information either to Hiroshi Oshima, the Japanese Ambassador in Berlin, nominally their superior, or directly to Tokyo, or both. In many instances Morishima's intelligence was vastly superior to that gained by Suma through his *TO* network, and his observations of the political and military scene were often keenly accurate. In December 1942 Morishima had a lengthy meeting with Nicholas Franco, Spanish Ambassador to Portugal and brother of General Franco. Nicholas Franco made some penetrating comments about the possibility of an Allied invasion of Spain or Portugal. Morishima later reported to Tokyo that according to Franco, before the United States and Britain had invaded North Africa, the United States had spent 'great sums of money in Morocco', and that such expenditure on espionage, psychological and subversive activities should have been a warning of what was to come.[2]

On 23 December 1942, Suma sent a two part message to Tokyo regarding some of the successes he was having in placing agents into the United States. He wrote:

> Two espionage agents apparently arrived safely in America two days ago. They are posing as special newspaper correspondents for in no other way could they have obtained American visas, but they really are our agents. They have been instructed to send daily dispatches to Madrid, and by use of code words to include in these dispatches secret information.
>
> Spanish consuls in the United States will send special communications to Madrid by weaving them into their regular business communications.
>
> Other agents in America – those on the west coast and in the eastern cities – are hampered from lack of funds. Though we should be careful in supplying them with funds, it is very important to have on hand in Washington a sum of money which can be drawn upon at will in cases of urgency. We therefore should have the Military Attaché take with him to Washington a considerable sum of money when he leaves for his post. Accordingly, please send me 1 million yen [Approximately $US250,000]. This money will be used for general expenses of all agents (including the costs of daily dispatches) and for the purchase of exceedingly important documents.[3]

The Military Attaché referred to by Suma in this message was possibly the Spanish Consul who was soon to arrive at New Orleans. Immediately he landed the consul was seized by US officials. He and the two hermetically sealed containers he was carrying were taken into custody. The containers were addressed to the Spanish Ambassador in the United States. The Spanish Consul resisted arrest but it did him little good. However, as a result of the speedy intervention of the Spanish Ambassador in Washington, the containers were returned unopened to the consul and he was reluctantly released.

This message, quickly decoded by the Americans, was the first evidence to confirm a report sent to G2 by Ambassador Hayes on 6 November that *TO* intelligence agents were about to begin sending messages from the United States in a cypher concealed in plain text as news copy. One of the two agents mentioned in Suma's message was the man who presented himself to the Spanish Embassy in Washington, and who had been turned into a double agent. The other was almost certainly the man Suma had previously referred to as the 'reliable gentleman' who had arrived in the United States after a tour of the Latin American countries. Upon receipt of this latest message from Suma to Tokyo, US counter-intelligence and the FBI were notified, and it was considered within these circles that as there was then so much evidence available concerning the *TO* intelligence network, that the apprehension of some or all of its agents could be carried out. However, this was quickly decided against as it was thought that to arrest the men would be confirmation that the US counter-intelligence agencies were reading Japanese codes.

On 6 January, Foreign Minister Tani in Tokyo replied to Suma's plea for more funds stating:

> We have considered your request for one million yen and I am wiring you half that amount at once. However so that the enemy will not have the slightest suspicion, I will send it to our minister in Berne. Please get in touch with him and make the necessary arrangements.[4]

Tani went on to point out that the use of plain text dispatches involved great danger, and suggested that the 'correspondents' stop sending information in that form. Tani requested Suma to look for another method of sending such secret information, stating that perhaps intelligence could be forwarded to Madrid via a new military attaché. Tani also requested that intelligence should emphasize the potential and actual US production of aircraft, tanks and other armaments, the disposition of all American land, sea and air forces, in particular the disposition of all overseas troops and all strategic movements.[5]

A later message from Tani,[6] added a number of other items to the list of matters the Japanese Foreign Minister wanted investigated. These included the strength and numerical designation of each overseas unit, the numbers and sizes of convoys bound overseas – especially those destined for Australia, the South Pacific or India – the state of air transport between America and China, India and Russia, land transport between the United States and Alaska, the military strength and its whereabouts in Alaska, shipping and ship schedules and the use of troops belonging to various Latin American countries. One can only imagine what this request did for Suma. He was already complaining that he and his staff were overworked and underpaid, and this almost impossible list of intelligence needs would have taxed even the most efficient of espionage operations.

The new military attaché referred to in Tani's message was actually an unnamed Spanish general who was due to be appointed to the United States in February, and whose specific role was to be to take charge of all *TO* espionage activities in the United States.

Shortly afterwards, and possibly a result of Suma's earlier

message requesting additional funds, Suma received the following fascinating message from Tokyo:

> Please tell the government to which you are accredited the following, and ask them to keep it strictly secret. Wire me back what they say.
> When we evacuated our Embassy in Washington last 5 January, we left $500,000 in cash in a large safe in the treasurer's office in the Chancellery there. According to the exchange agreement, we could not take much cash with us, but our main reason for leaving it was that we foresaw the impossibility of sending any more money back to the United States. We wished to keep it in reserve for the Spanish government to use it in representing our interests. Therefore we desire that the Spanish Ambassador, as soon as it is needed, go and get this reserve money.[7]

The message then went on to give the combinations of the safe and of the smaller safe concealed inside, in which the money was supposed to be found. To this rather startling report, G2 had appended a note voicing their own reservations about the authenticity of the message.

> Although the Japanese continue to give evidence of their complete confidence in their cryptographic system in which the above message was sent, it is possible that the message was intended as a plant, to determine whether we are reading that system. It has some of the earmarks of a plant, viz., it gives startling information likely to induce a particular course of action, which would be taken very promptly and be of such a nature that the enemy would almost certainly learn about it.
> Whether or not intended as a plant, the message is calculated to work out as one, since almost any action taken in response to it is likely to come to the attention of the enemy and may lead him to the conclusion that we are reading his most vital diplomatic correspondence.[8]

According to the State Department, the Spanish Embassy and the Swiss Legation then occupied the building of the Japanese Embassy, and the Spanish actually occupied the former Japanese Treasurer's office. No action was taken to confiscate the funds and they were presumably used to pay the *TO* net, although there is no official confirmation of this.

As the *TO* network grew, so the messages to Tokyo intensified. On 8 January, Suma advised Tokyo that the construction of important defences and strategic points along Spain's coastline was under way. Quoting the head of the *TO* net, Suma stated that 4,700 labourers were being used for the work and that an additional 2,000 men were to be employed before the end of the month. He added that three regiments had recently arrived in Spanish Morocco and that, according to information from the Spanish Foreign Office, the United States had informally requested that conversations be begun with a view to putting Tangier (also a hotbed of political and military intrigue and a base for spies from most major powers), under international control. Spain however turned down the suggestion.[9] In fact it was known to the US authorities at this time that there were at least twelve 'clandestine circuits' operating from Spanish Morocco. On the same day, sandwiched between more general and quite legitimate diplomatic messages, Suma also forwarded another *TO* intelligence message:

From Washington, January 7

According to reports from San Francisco, two convoys have recently sailed in the direction of the Aleutians. For three days ships were constantly leaving and were assembled at a pre-arranged position where they were formed into convoys.... Thirty-three ships were observed sailing out in the day-time and a large number must have gone out in the night. It is persistently rumoured that some great happening is due to occur simultaneously in the Far East and in Europe.[10]

Shortly afterwards, Minister Morishima, the Japanese representative to Portugal, forwarded a detailed report concerning 'conditions in England'.

The people in general feel that the Allied forces everywhere have changed from the defensive to the offensive and that the dawn of victory is already at hand. Although they do not as yet see clearly the path to victory, they have a rather vague idea that increased production of airplanes will give them mastery of the air; that there will be an internal collapse in Europe, and that after completing the European war they will direct all their efforts towards the Far East. They think that production of war materials should reach its peak in the spring of 1943 and that victory will come in 1944 when these materials are utilized on the battlefields. The one point to which we should pay attention is the fact that the unquestioning conviction of final victory is prevalent.[11]

In response to a request from the Japanese Foreign Minister in Tokyo regarding the costs of living in various European countries Suma took the opportunity not only to supply the necessary information but also to bemoan the fact that because of his added duties in collecting and correlating his secret reports, he and his staff were experiencing various difficulties, stating:

> Lately, because of sickness among our staff members, there has been an alarming increase in absences from work. This is chiefly due to colds caused by the difficulty in getting fuel, malnutrition due to the shortage of food and to our excessive work every night on secret reports.

Suma concluded his report by suggesting that one of his previous requests for more funds might well be considered.[12]

G2 became aware that a general strengthening and streamlining of Japanese intelligence services was being planned when they read a message from Japanese Ambassador Oshima, in Berlin, to Tokyo, requesting permission to hold a conference in Berlin from 10 to 28 January. The conference was to be attended by most of the Japanese intelligence officers then stationed in Europe. Tokyo quickly approved the conference. From the decoded messages US authorities even knew the subjects to be discussed, these included the general situation in Europe and Africa, the establishment of an espionage net to gather further information in America and England and the founding of an 'agency' to study from every angle British and American military power. The delegates to the conference were also to discuss methods to strengthen liaison among officials in charge of intelligence, particularly the exchange and evaluation of information and a means to bring intelligence personnel up to full strength.[13]

On 9 January an unnamed member of Suma's staff held discussions with the head of the *TO* network regarding the circulation of counterfeit money by Germany – a method used by the Germans in an attempt to destroy the British economy. The head of the *TO* net was quoted as saying:

> The Germans themselves have told me that in their activity in London, they are circulating a vast number of British pound and American dollar notes. Lately the German government – up to the same trick – has printed about two million Spanish pesetas and is circulating it throughout Spain. The German agent tipped me off and I have been using some of it myself.
>
> Now of course such methods are perfectly all right if they are used to upset an enemy nation's economy, but for an Axis country to treat its friend in this manner is a low down dirty trick.[14]

On 24 January 1943, G2 gave a detailed outline of all the information they then held concerning the setting up, operations and personnel of the *TO* net.

Three days after Pearl Harbor, the Japanese Foreign Office sent out a circular to its representatives in various parts of the world pointing out that, 'With the outbreak of the war against England and the United States, the position played by our organization [the Japanese diplomatic corps], is of increasing importance'. Each representative was asked to reply to the following questions:

a. What authoritative information will the government to which you are accredited give us?

b. What information is available from secret connections with nationals of that government?

Minister Suma at Madrid replied on December 13 1941 that 'to ask Spain to gather information of benefit to us would be a rather delicate matter since Spain is neutral, but I believe that it could be managed if handled in the right way'.

The matter seems to have been handled 'in the right way', for on January 9, 1942, Suma advised Tokyo that 'the man who is responsible for our information here' had called upon him at the request of Foreign Minister Serrano Suner, 'to help Japan out by planning the means of gathering intelligence reports from the United States'. From Suma's statements in earlier messages and from information obtained from other sources [the report from US Ambassador Hayes at Madrid and another report from the FBI in London], it is now certain that Suma was referring to —— [name deleted by US censors], a former Press Attaché to the Spanish Embassy in London, and that [this man] is the head of the *TO* net in Madrid.

In a later message Suma describes [the *TO* head] as 'a cavalier – one who will do anything on earth for his friends and those he likes; of strong character but rather quixotic and hot-headed'.

Agents who have entered the United States.

At this time at least six *TO* agents have entered the United States and a seventh agent is to leave Spain for this country next month.

A. The three original agents.

Three *TO* agents apparently have been in the United States for more than a year. On January 7 1942 Serrano Suner remarked to Suma: 'Although we have dispatched three men to the United States, we have not had any important communications from them'. On August 21, 1942, Suma reported that [the head of *TO*] had told him: 'Up to now, the three spies whom we have been able to smuggle into the United States, one in New York, one in Washington and one in San Francisco, are in very close touch with each other despite the distances that separate them ...'

The only evidence in Secret Service Bureau materials as to the identity of these three agents is as follows:

1. On October 10, 1942, one of the agents reported from Washington that, 'my colleague in New York has just been jailed in Baltimore'. [On October 8 the FBI arrested six men on charges

of attempting to export platinum without a licence. The six men were the captain and crew members of the Spanish ship *Motomar* which was in Baltimore, and four individuals who were arrested in New York and jailed in Baltimore having waived extradition proceedings.]

An October 17 *TO* report from Washington stated that, '... my New York colleague is still in jail. It seems that he was apprehended because of a letter sent from Cuba.'

2. Information in *TO* reports has been attributed to the following sources. 'A major in the office of ... Air Branch', 'a certain Army officer', 'a US officer who recently returned from Australia', 'an Army man in the Air Force Headquarters', 'a certain Jewish officer in the Aviation Department', 'my informant in the air corps'; 'a certain officer of the Air Defence Command'; 'my friend in the Navy Department and the one I have in the War Department'; 'a certain officer in the War Department'; 'an instructor at the Merchant Marine School in New London', 'the manager of a Scranton munitions factory', 'and a supervisor of floating piers in New York who arrived in Washington October 20'.

In addition to the foregoing information, reports from US Ambassador Hayes in Madrid have contained some data which may be of assistance in identifying one or more of the three agents in question. Some time prior to October 21 1942, one ———— [name deleted by US censors] came to Mr Hayes and told him that he was being sent to the United States, ostensibly as a press correspondent and that he was to participate in the activities of an intelligence net operating here.... The part of his story which seems pertinent here is as follows:

1. [The agent] was to carry with him a letter intended for one...[name deleted by US censor], at 500 West 144th Street, New York N.Y., whom [the agent] described as an employee of the Chilean Consulate General in New York. The letter was signed by one 'Pepe' whose identity is unknown, and directed [the Chilean] to place himself at the disposal of [the agent], evidently for the purpose of helping him in gathering information or transmitting it to Spain. [The agent] received the impression that [the Chilean] was in charge of secret radio communications between the United States and Spain, the messages being routed via Columbia. However [the agent's] impression was somewhat inconsistent with the letter he was to carry, since the letter indicated that although [the Chilean] had given evidence of his willingness to cooperate on one prior occasion, he had not yet been assigned any missions.

2. As one means of communicating information to Madrid, [the agent] was given codes which he was to conceal in plain text press dispatches. For some time a Spanish press correspondent in New York named ———— [name deleted by US censors] has been sending plain text dispatches to Madrid, averaging in excess of 500 words

per day, at a daily cost of approximately $50. His dispatches are long and rambling and frequently seem to be devoid of news value. [The agent] was also instructed that when he forwarded letters by Spanish diplomatic pouch, he could address them to [name deleted by US censors], Pouch Section of the Ministry of Foreign Affairs ...

On October 22, 1942, Suma advised Tokyo that a reliable gentleman was leaving Spain by clipper early in November to go to Mexico, Peru, Colombia, Ecuador and Guatemala, and that he had agreed to help establish an espionage net in all of those places. On December 4, Suma reported that the gentleman in question had gone to Mexico City via Washington, and had been, '... in touch with Washington people from Mexico City'. A *TO* report appears to have been sent from Mexico City to Washington on December 9, 1942 and to have been forwarded from Washington to Madrid the same day.

On July 11, 1942, Suma advised Tokyo that two leading Madrid newspapers were sending a special correspondent to the United States very soon, that both were, '... reliable men in touch with the head of the agency', and that both would be acting as spies....

On July 11, 1942, Suma advised Tokyo that: 'before long a Spanish Military Attaché will be sent to Washington, and it is being plotted to send a certain general with whom the chief of the [*TO*] agency has been in touch for quite a while'.

On January 6, 1943, in reply to an unavailable message from Suma, [Japanese] Foreign Minister Tani stated: 'The securing of Major-General Kasutehon to head our agency in the United States will bring tremendous results. Please give him your constant assistance since this will greatly increase our effectiveness in collecting information from the United States'.

To date the State Department does not know of any request by Spain to fill the vacant office of Military Attaché in Washington. It is making a discreet inquiry of our Madrid Embassy.

The first available *TO* message purporting to have been sent from the United States was headed June 12 from Washington, and was forwarded by Suma to Tokyo on June 14, 1942. Since then some 80 such reports have been received from the Secret Service Branch. This branch has checked the accuracy of most of them. Usually they are either vague or quite inaccurate. Only occasionally has a report been partially correct and of some importance. The impression is obtained from the reports that they are bread and butter stuff for the senders, and for the Spanish residents also, and that where facts are lacking the writers draw on their own imaginations....

In smuggling money into the United States [the agent] was instructed to enlist the help of one 'Ramos', who was said to be the second radio telegraph operator on the (cargo ship) *Marques de Comillas*. However, there is as yet no evidence that Senor Ramos' assistance to the net has included transmitting messages by the ship's radio.

Upon reaching Madrid, the reports are delivered to [the head of the *TO* net], who distributes them to Suma and almost certainly to the German Special Affairs Agency, a German intelligence organization in Madrid, which, according to Suma, has devoted itself primarily to obtaining information on the movements of convoys and weather reports.

Serrano Suner also received the reports while he was Spanish Foreign Minister. Apparently Suner's successor, Count Jordana, does not receive them, since Suma reported that shortly after assuming office Jordana told [the head of *TO*]: 'I have known generally about the intelligence net since assuming office. I want you to carry on as if I knew nothing at all about its existence.'

The only evidence on hand as to the method by which funds are supplied to the *TO* agents is as follows. In January 1942 Suma advised Tokyo that: 'We can supply the agents in North America with funds by clipper mail'. On January 9 of this year Suma sent a message to Tokyo discussing the problem of getting funds into the United States ... [The agent] told Ambassador Hayes that he expected to receive US currency from Spain via diplomatic pouch. He also said that he had been instructed to deliver francs[15] to 'Ramos' the second radio operator on the ship on which he was to travel, *Marquis de Comillas*, who would change them into dollars in Cuba and smuggle the dollars into the United States at New Orleans.... On December 23, 1942, Suma reported that he had received word from the agents in the United States that because of lack of funds their activities do not come up to expectations.... In response Foreign Minister Suma sent him 500,000 yen. Not satisfied with this Suma sent the message to Tokyo in which he stated that he wished to send the money by the new Military Attaché ... Suma added: 'I would like to send him a lump sum to cover the expenses of the United States agents for about a year – this I believe to be absolutely necessary. So, if possible, please see if you can't scrape the rest of the money together by the end of this month and send it to me'.

If the Military Attaché [General Kasutehon] arrives in this country with the dollar equivalent of a million yen, or even 500,000 yen (the latter figure would be approximately $US125,000), it seems reasonable to expect an increase in the activities of the *TO* net. Both the FBI and counter-intelligence have been notified of all information received to date.[16]

The name given as Kasutehon was almost certainly the Japanese version of a Spanish name, probably Castillon or Castajon. In fact, this officer was never appointed as Military Attaché because the Americans '... suddenly picked all sorts of holes in that man and declared that they would not accept him.'[17]

Concerned that the Spanish General would be aiding in increasing the output of *TO* intelligence, the State Department flatly refused to allow him into the country on diplomatic grounds. Suma quickly arranged to send instead, 'a telegraphic expert next month by boat. The expert is to serve as a spy.'[18] Suma did receive his $500,000 yen but Japanese Foreign Minister Tani pointedly refused to send any more, indicating that the Japanese Foreign Office could not spare any more money at that time. However, he did inform Suma that he had asked the army and navy to contribute funds towards the running of the *TO* net, and that both had agreed to do so in principle. Even so, no further funds were immediately forthcoming.

Despite the difficulties of getting funds through to the *TO* agents, and the American opinion that the agents themselves were not of a particularly high calibre, some accurate information was now flowing through. On 16 January a *TO* agent in Washington advised Suma accurately, that a drive would soon begin in North Africa – even giving the approximate dates, between the 17th and 22nd of that month. Highly damaging intelligence also continued to come from various parts of the United States. On 28 January Suma forwarded to Tokyo the details of a *TO* report stating that sixty-five ships of large capacity were then being loaded with freight destined for North Africa, and that the sailing dates would be sometime between 29 January and 3 February. According to G2 records, the *TO* report was 100 per cent accurate.

Meanwhile, in Lisbon, Japanese Minister Morito Morishima was also having some successes. Quoting a mysterious informant, known only as a British aristocrat named Sir L.O., Morishima stated that this person – 'an influential Englishman performing espionage for the Portuguese Ambassador', had told the Ambassador certain details of the American/British Casablanca Conference, including a plan to carry out large scale bombing of Italy, a landing expedition against Italy and a landing by British and American troops in Southern France.[19]

Suma also received interesting information regarding the infiltration of Allied fifth columnists into Japanese-held territories. On 30 January he informed Tokyo that because of the very great difficulties in infiltrating spies into the Japanese occupied territories, about fifty Australians, Hindus and Filipinos were receiving special training in espionage activities. Suma claimed that it would be their task to proceed to Japanese lines in various occupied countries, give themselves up to the Japanese, and then engage in undercover work after escaping into Japanese-occupied zones. Suma advised Tokyo that the special

Morito Morishima, the Japanese Minister to Portugal during the Second World War. Morishima was also head of all Japanese intelligence operations in Portugal

The Japanese Minister to Spain during the Second World War, Yakichiro Suma, co-ordinated all Japanese intelligence activities from Madrid and was instrumental in forming the *TO* Intelligence Net in the US

Ramon Suner, the Spanish Foreign Minister who allowed the *TO* net to
function in Spain

Count Gómez Jordana, Spanish Foreign Minister and Suner's successor, knew of all the Japanese espionage activities and, while he would not be associated with them, he secretly aided the Japanese in building their spy nets

training was taking place in a small bungalow near the Naval Meteorological Observatory in Washington.[20]

JAPANESE INTELLIGENCE PLANS

On 26 January 1943, the conference of Japanese intelligence officers opened in Berlin. It was attended by seventeen 'councillors, secretaries and clerks', of whom seven were from the Japanese Embassy in Berlin, the remainder coming from Sweden, Spain, Portugal, Switzerland, Turkey, Bulgaria, Italy, Vichy, Paris and the Vatican City. The conference had been called by the Japanese Ambassador to Berlin, Hiroshi Oshima, who suggested that subjects on the agenda should include, the situation in Europe, establishing means to procure further information about the United States and Britain, strengthening liaison between intelligence officials and the means to bring intelligence personnel to full strength. A message from the Japanese Embassy in Rome to the Foreign Ministry in Tokyo suggested two additional points, the study of Soviet military power and the setting up in Europe of a centre for spreading propaganda. Other additional subjects suggested by Tokyo included the study of methods of establishing radio stations in Europe to monitor US domestic broadcasts, methods of procuring intelligence gathered by the countries to which the various Japanese officials were accredited, and methods of getting more intelligence from the United States through neutral countries.

It was decided at the conference that plans should be made to study US and British military power from sources (such as diplomatic sources) in neutral countries, and also through reports circulating among civilians, that is, to keep a strict listening watch in public places. The conference recommended that agents should develop informal contacts with members of the various governments, keep in direct and indirect touch with newspaper correspondents who travelled back and forth between neutral countries and England and the United States, and, if possible, instigate a system to bribe them. They should purchase existing news agencies in Spain and Switzerland or set up new ones. These agencies would act as normal news gathering organizations, just like the British or US agencies legitimately employed on such activities, but the Japanese would also gather intelligence at the same time. Such agencies were perfect covers for espionage, as those employed by the agencies could quite openly ask even the most penetrating questions without arousing undue suspicion.

Funding of these projects tended to be a problem, and Suma

related how he was having great difficulties in getting money from Tokyo and then arranging to have it smuggled to his operatives in the United States. The conference decided that such funding should not come from 'secret funds of high officials' (this is possibly a reference to the various secret societies who often backed such espionage activities), but a lump sum was to be sent to Oshima in Berlin as a secret intelligence fund.

It was also decided to set up facilities in Europe for monitoring domestic American radio broadcasts. Such broadcasts were then made on the medium wave and according to German specialists, could be clearly received in many European countries, although it was envisaged that there would be difficulties in obtaining the personnel and necessary equipment for this operation. In fact, despite Oshima's statements at the conference regarding the advice of the Germans, the American broadcast authorities believed it unlikely that US domestic broadcasts could be heard in Europe. However, it was probable that a monitoring station situated somewhere in southern Europe could pick up a fair amount of such broadcasts during the period 8 p.m. to 12 p.m. Eastern War Time, which would be the most valuable for intelligence purposes.

With regard to the study of Soviet strength, it was decided to station in Germany, Turkey, Bulgaria, Sweden and Finland accredited intelligence agents who were thoroughly familiar with Russian conditions. Such agents were already employed in Germany, Bulgaria and Turkey, and the Japanese delegates at the conference considered that it would be a simple matter to provide personnel in other places from the large number of vice consuls, research experts and students of the Russian language then in Europe. These intelligence officers would meet occasionally, compare the results of their studies and report everything of importance to Tokyo.

It was decided that the 'front line' for intelligence gathering should be diplomatic offices in Turkey, Portugal and Spain, and that only the best agents should be placed into these offices. It was also decided to place a Consulate-General at Tangier, as the gathering of intelligence from North Africa was considered to be of the utmost importance. The North African theatre was certainly a problem to the Axis powers at this time. On 23 January the 8th Army had entered Tripoli. Secretary Obayashi of the Madrid Ministry was recommended for the Tangier position. An intelligence agency was to be established in Istanbul as quickly as possible, and the Paris Consulate was recommended to be strengthened in order to study the North African problem and to broadcast propaganda.

It was also recommended that the Spanish Legation should be upgraded by the Spanish authorities to an embassy, in this way a great deal more high level diplomatic and military information could be coming across Suma's desk – information which could have vital intelligence purposes.[21] At the conference, moves were also made to infiltrate more agents into enemy countries – agents already in place in several countries in the Near and Middle East and in India were proving extremely successful. The conference delegates thought that the Japanese should be making more use of electrical communication devices, such as short-wave radio sets. Oshima made the point that the use of such short-wave sets was becoming common among the intelligence-gathering operations of other countries – indeed, such communications systems were then widely in use by the Germans, who had installed a complex system of clandestine stations throughout Europe and the Balkans. The conference delegates recommended that high-speed receivers were to be installed in Berlin, Madrid and Sofia and a plan was formed to supply agents in the field with portable transceivers.[22]

Shortly after the end of the conference, the story of the mysterious Mikimoto pearls once again received some attention in Japanese diplomatic circles. On 14 February the *Magic* Summary stated:

> As previously noted, the Japanese have been endeavouring for several months to send some pearls from Japan to Europe in order to sell them in England and use the proceeds to further their intelligence-gathering activities. The first shipment was concealed in a Spanish diplomatic pouch which left Tokyo on a diplomatic exchange ship last summer, but the pearls mysteriously disappeared while the pouch was en route to Madrid. Thereafter a second shipment was entrusted to the captain of the *Rhakotis*, a German blockade-runner which left Yokohama in September.
>
> On January 1, the *Rhakotis* was intercepted about 400 miles west of Bordeaux, and was scuttled by her crew. The Japanese however have not yet abandoned their efforts to devise a means of delivering pearls to their representatives in Europe.
>
> In a February 4 communication, Ambassador Oshima stated that he had talked with a representative of the Japanese Embassy in France, who, 'wants to continue with these schemes and needs some pearls just as soon as he can get them'. In a February 11 report, Oshima again alluded to the pearls stating: 'If possible I would like for you to put one batch of them in a suitcase and send them along with Ambassador Hidaka and his entourage.' [Hidaka was the new Japanese Ambassador to Italy – he planned to leave

Tokyo on February 15, travelling through Russia on the Siberian railroad.][23]

There followed a number of *TO* reports, varying in importance and accuracy, including one item of highly classified information. Suma sent:

According to a secret report [US] Army Ordnance has approved the manufacture of a new powder which is 50 per cent more powerful than any other known powder. Its formula is very secret, but it has a basis of ammonium nitrate. It will be used principally in aerial bombardment.[24]

In fact, about a year previously, US Army Ordnance had obtained from the British a new kind of extremely destructive explosive, named RDX, and its manufacture in large quantities was almost immediately commenced. Ballistic mortar tests had shown that RDX was indeed around 50 per cent more powerful than the standard TNT. However, despite intelligence coups such as this, both Suma in Madrid and Morishima in Lisbon continued to be cheated into paying for intelligence of only limited value and sometimes of no value at all. On 15 February, Suma informed Tokyo that the Allies would be carrying out an invasion of Europe, commencing on the 1st or 3rd of April, and that Allied troops would land from the Mediterranean and on the coast of France. At around the same time Morishima was making what he termed *Fuji* intelligence reports. Many of these reports were considered to be of no value to the Japanese by the listening US authorities. The intelligence contained within these reports was allegedly solicited from a member of the Portuguese government who was selling the information to Morishima, but as G2 stated for the State Department: 'As in the case of some of the information Minister Suma buys in Madrid, this material of Morishima's is of dubious authenticity.'[25]

SPAIN'S COOPERATION WITH THE AXIS

Further evidence of Spanish involvement in assisting the Axis powers wherever possible came at the beginning of March 1943, when it was discovered through diplomatic message intercepts that various commodities badly required by Germany were being purchased in Argentina and shipped secretly aboard Spanish ships bound for Spain, where the cargoes were unloaded and taken overland to Germany. From the fragmented messages it was not clear exactly what quantities or commodities had been purchased, or which of those commodities had actually reached Germany. However, it was clear that the Germans had succeeded in buying caffeine, industrial diamonds, insulin, liver extract, hypophysene and campolon concentrate. These items were shipped aboard Spanish ships with the help of sympathetic Spanish crew members, and were not listed on the ships' manifests. The items were unloaded in Spain with the connivance of Spanish customs officers. An August 1942 communication to Buenos Aires from the German Embassy in Lisbon had also suggested that materials may have been shipped under the guise of legitimate shipments to firms in Spain and Portugal. The particular communication stated that a Lisbon firm had agreed to order a hundred cases of corned beef for shipment from Buenos Aires to Lisbon on a Spanish ship, the beef was then to be shipped to Germany upon arrival in Portugal.

On at least one occasion, a Spanish ship was used to send materials from Germany to Argentina – apparently for use in connection with clandestine radio activities. According to a German communication of 15 December 1942, a shipment of filament material for radio tubes was dispatched to Buenos Aires in the custody of the Chief Steward of the Spanish ship *Cabo le Hornos*.

How high the level of cooperation went within the Spanish Customs Department can be gauged from a secret communication from the German Embassy in Madrid to the German Embassy in Buenos Aires which referred to, 'the suggestion of the General Director of Customs that camouflaged shipments be sent by trunk'. The message explained that the taking ashore of unmanifested boxes, cans etc. was impossible in Spain without a large number of persons knowing about it, whereas trunks only passed one or two inspection points.[26] Later secret communications confirmed that the transport of such goods on Spanish ships was continuing, despite surveillance from US and British authorities.

British and American naval superiority was having a marked effect on the prices of many commodities inside Germany. For example shoes, with an authorized price of 15.97 marks, were selling on the black market for 150 marks. Black tea was authorized at 12 marks, yet actually sold for the quite amazing price of 800 marks, and coffee with a fixed price of 7.60 marks was only obtainable through the black market for 260 marks. According to a report sent to Tokyo by Ambassador Oshima in Berlin, distribution of commodities was under very strict control in comparison with other countries, liquor and clothing were unobtainable.[27] In light of such shortages, the traffic of goods through Spanish ports continued unabated.

Suma also reported to Tokyo that since the crew of the scuttled German battleship *Graf Spee* had been interned three years previously, 120 of the crew members had escaped and many of them were reported to have returned to Europe aboard neutral ships – principally Spanish vessels. US authorities suspected that the crews of these ships were cooperating in the escapes, and on 3 January 1943 the US Military Attaché in Buenos Aires reported that according to British intelligence sources, two *Graf Spee* crew members had escaped as stowaways aboard the Spanish ship *Monte Naranco*. Earlier German messages confirmed that such escapes had been happening with the aid of Spanish nationals. One message sent from Madrid to Buenos Aires stated: 'Jose Luis Agnar, proprietor of the Naviarre Aznar Ship Company Bilbao, has instructions from the head of the Spanish Shipping Bureau in the Commerce Ministry to favour taking along *Graf Spee* members.'[28] Later it was discovered that a large shipment of goods from Argentina was planned, including 1,000 tons of dried milk, cholesterin, liver extract, caffeine, quinine, Beryl, Tonka beans and insulin. This was the largest known smuggling operation into Spain to that date.[29]

TANGIER

The attempts by the Japanese to have a consulate established at Tangier met with only stony refusal on the part of the Spanish, who claimed that to have the Japanese establish a diplomatic office in Spanish Morocco – directly across the straits from the British Naval base in Gibraltar – would constitute a breach of their neutrality and, despite Suma's repeated attempts to change their mind, the Spanish remained adamant. On 30 January, Japanese Ambassador Mitani in Vichy again brought up the proposal outlined at the Japanese intelligence conference that a 'suitable man like Shokise Obayashi', who was then based with Suma in Madrid, be sent to Tangier so that he could get in touch with other military agents working the region and so send additional details of Allied movements in the Mediterranean and in North Africa. In an attempt to circumvent the Spanish attitude to establishing a formal diplomatic post in Tangier, Suma suggested that, as relations between the United States and Spain 'have to some extent calmed down', he believed it would have been appropriate for Obayashi to make the journey to Tangier in advance of establishing an official diplomatic post. Suma suggested that Obayashi be allowed to occupy the official Japanese apartment in Tangier.[30] In fact, Obayashi was finally allowed to take up his position on 2 April and immediately requested 10,000 pesetas ($US900) for the purchase of a short-wave radio set. He also stated that his operating expenses – including telegraphic and automobile maintenance for the month of April – would be 3,000 pesetas ($US270).

Obayashi's first intelligence message to Suma stated:

> Recently the number of Anglo-American convoys passing through the Straits of Gibraltar has increased. Several of those heading into the Mediterranean – especially in the early part of April – numbered more than 400 ships. They were carrying great quantities of equipment for landing operations.[31]

Sometime after this report, another agent, Lieutenant Colonel Kiyoshi Hasebe – formerly Assistant Military Attaché at the Madrid Legation – was sent to the Tangier office (or apartment). Hasebe was presumably a more experienced intelligence officer. At the end of June 1943, Hasebe was recalled to Tokyo (via Madrid) and Obayashi was once again instructed to take charge of espionage activities in the Tangier area. At the time Suma advised Tokyo:

> As Tangier is our only [intelligence] post in Africa, it would seem to be very valuable in obtaining military information concerning the enemy and also for getting reports on measures they are taking in Africa and on the extent to which America is using African resources, etc. If the circumstances permit, we intend to leave Obayashi there, but as I have repeatedly told you, there is no guarantee that communication between the Iberian Peninsula and Africa may not be cut off with the opening of the Anglo-American Mediterranean campaign. Should that happen, we shall take the proper measures to evacuate Obayashi.[32]

In fact, Hasebe's return to Japan was postponed shortly afterwards. He returned from Madrid and the Tangier office maintained its staff of two agents.[33]

THE VANCOUVER NET

A message from Suma to Tokyo on 4 March, confirmed that Suma had managed to infiltrate one of his *TO* agents into Vancouver. Previous messages had confirmed that the agent was to investigate, among other things, US military, naval, and air strengths in Alaska. The 4 March communication stated that the agent had sent his first intelligence report which claimed that every night a large number of vessels went through the Strait. All of them were loaded with arms and soldiers for the Aleutians, and as there were many sailors in the region the agent felt sure the Japanese could employ some of them as spies.[34]

EUROPEAN INTELLIGENCE BUDGETS

Soon afterwards G2 gleaned a rich crop of information concerning the estimated intelligence budgets of the various Japanese embassies, ministries and consulates through Europe. The information was forthcoming after a message from Japanese Foreign Minister Tani requested his diplomatic posts to furnish him with plans for espionage and propaganda for 1943. From these plans and budgets G2 and the US State Department were able to gauge the amount of intelligence activities they could expect from the Japanese during the following year and also have a rough idea where those intelligence agents would be operating.

Chargé Kase in Italy expected to spend a modest 100,000 lire ($5,000) to secure information about the Allies. Kase stated that he could not get information directly, but that he could sometimes obtain it from members of the Italian government. Kase said that he also expected to spend around 410,000 lire ($US20,000) getting information about Italy. In doing this he planned to employ informers to maintain contact with Italian press correspondents and intelligence officials of other embassies and legations and to obtain copies of messages from communications agencies. However, in light of subsequent events and the invasion of Sicily, which was about to occur, Kase's espionage plans were already hopelessly outdated.

Ambassador Oshima sent a detailed message to Tani, which unfortunately was too garbled to be translated in full. However, it was ascertained from what little of the message could be read that Oshima was budgeting 672,000 marks ($US270,000) for intelligence gathering and propaganda work during 1943.

In Hungary, Minister Okubo's description of his intelligence operations was not entirely clear, but it appeared that he had agents both abroad and inside Hungary itself, and that some of these were persons connected with the Hungarian government. Others included newspaper reporters in various countries, and a Hungarian semi-official correspondent on an important newspaper. Okubo also hired people to monitor radio programmes. He estimated that these activities – together with travelling and communications expenses – would cost him around 75,000 pengos ($US15,000) for the year.

In Turkey, Ambassador Kurihara expected to spend 50,000 yen ($US12,000) on such activities. These would include the employment of secret agents – both on a regular and occasional basis – procurement of newspapers and magazines, and communications between Ankara and Istanbul. Kurihara stated that he intended to increase his efforts to obtain from the Turkish government (which had its own highly efficient secret service) all possible information about Russia and to obtain information about England, the United States, Poland and other countries in the possession of Russia and her allies. He was also contriving to gather intelligence from people in the Caucasus and Central Asia. Kurihara estimated that these activities would cost another 50,000 yen. He planned to spend a third of that sum in enlarging his espionage activities in Iran and Iraq, working in cooperation with the Germans and Italians. He also repeated a previous plea for the installation of short-wave radio equipment. Finally, Kurihara stated that he would need a further 130,000 yen ($US30,000) for espionage in India. Part of this money was to finance his existing organization there. Some of the money was to be used in sending additional spies into India, including, 'one more Spaniard'. Kurihara also suggested that disruptive subversive intelligence could be fed to the Allies at Istanbul – then, like Madrid, Lisbon and Tangier – a centre of intelligence gathering for both Allied and Axis powers.

Portugal
In Portugal, Minister Morito Morishima and his staff claimed that they would continue to analyse English, American and Portuguese newspapers and magazines, and forward important journals to Tokyo. They would also listen to radio broadcasts, keep in touch with foreign envoys in Lisbon, obtain *Fuji* intelligence and secure information from spies already sent abroad. Morishima estimated that he would spend 2,000 contos ($US80,000) on those projects during 1943. This was only an estimate, and depended largely on the availability of foreign currencies. There was, of course, no currency exchange between belligerent countries during the war, and even between neutrals foreign exchange was limited – especially in Portugal and Spain.

Morishima also claimed that he hoped to send a man to the United States in similar fashion to Suma's agents. He estimated this would cost 400,000 yen ($US93,000). This is the first indication the Americans received that there was to be another Japanese spy ring installed in the United States. Up until this time, Suma was the only Japanese diplomat in Europe known to have sent agents into America. Whether Morishima managed to infiltrate another agent at this time is not clear, but both he and Suma later worked closely with German operations to have agents landed in South America.

In addition to this, Morishima planned to bribe several Portuguese police officers for information – estimated cost, 600,000 yen ($US140,000).[35]

Morishima was also working – at least in a loose fashion – with Nazi espionage activities operating out of the Portuguese colony of Lourenço Marques. Since the outbreak of war in 1939, the German Consulate in Lourenço Marques had played an increasingly important role in espionage activities throughout Mozambique and the Union of South Africa. Between 1939 and 1943, the German consular staff had been enlarged from a consul and one secretary, to a consul-general (Paul Trompke) a vice-consul (Luitpold Werz) two chancellors and around twelve other employees. In January 1943 the Nazi Party organization in Lourenço Marques was raised from a temporary operating group (Stutzpunkt) to a permanent group (Ortsgruppe). The activities of this consulate included organizing and controlling an espionage net operating throughout Mozambique and the Union of South Africa, directing subversive activities and sabotage in the Union, and assisting with propaganda campaigns directed against the Union. The principal means of communication between the consulate at Lourenço Marques and Germany were coded messages sent to Lisbon via the Portuguese commercial radio circuit. Some of the information concerned ship movements from Mozambique, especially Beira, and other movements from Durban, Port Elizabeth and Cape Town. The Germans also collected a considerable amount of military intelligence on such subjects as troop movements, military and naval fortifications, the construction of docks and the manufacture of munitions in South Africa. At least some of this information was made available to Morishima in Lisbon – but not all. In August 1942, realizing the very high value of the intelligence being gathered by the Germans in Lourenço Marques, Morishima asked his German colleagues if Trompke's reports could be made available to him, explaining that he understood Trompke was 'an expert, and must have some powerful information'. However, his request was flatly refused, the only reason being that Trompke's telegrams had to be forwarded directly to Berlin. Later, however, the Germans relented, and a certain amount of this very valuable information was forwarded to Morishima.

Confirmation of this general information was a report dated 17 October 1942 from the US Military Attaché in Pretoria which stated:

> There are several hundred German and Italian nationals resident in Lourenço Marques, regular residents, crews of interned vessels, refugees from British territory, etc., and probably every one of the Germans at least, and many of the Italians can be regarded as an actual or potential fifth columnist. This is undoubtedly the headquarters for all Axis undercover activities in this part of the world. It has been definitely established that the German and Italian Consulates together are spending an average of £10,000 per month, and it is almost a certainty that the greater part of this sum is going to the Union of South Africa where the Nazis have many agents among the members of the Ossewa Brandwag and among the disloyal Dutch elements.[36]

The Ossewa Brandwag (Sentinels of the Ox wagon) was a violent anti-British, pro-Axis Afrikaner organization which had been seeking to overthrow the government of the Union of South Africa by force, and to compel secession of the Union from the British Empire. The Ossewa Brandwag had a secret cadre of storm troopers, some of whom had been convicted for high treason. It also ran its own extremely vicious Gestapo organization. Its membership at this time was at least 75,000.

Yet the effectiveness of some of Morishima's intelligence – and especially some of his sources – was still open to question. As we have seen, he intended – like all of his colleagues – to purchase much of his information from casual informants and spies. After checking some of his reports sent during the first three months of 1943, the Japanese Foreign Office began to believe that Morishima and those working with him in intelligence gathering were victims of a hoax, and that someone in the Portuguese Foreign Office had not only succeeded in selling the Japanese false information, but had managed to sell the same information to both the Japanese Military Attaché and to the Minister, Morito Morishima, without either of them knowing that the other was getting it. Morishima had been sending, under the heading of *Fuji* Intelligence, what purported to be copies of messages between the Portuguese Foreign Office and various Portuguese diplomatic posts throughout the world. Morishima was quite proud of his efforts, however some of the information was almost certainly not authentic, and much had already been sent to Tokyo via the Military Attaché. On 9 March 1943, Morishima sent the following message to Tokyo:

> Secretary Komine [Morishima's subordinate in Lisbon], gets these *Fuji* Intelligences from an old friend of his who is a Portuguese government official. They work on a mutual understanding that we both will be perfectly circumspect. We get decoded messages just as they are, with no changes at all – even the numbers of the messages are on them. I am sure that you need not worry about our falling into traps of the enemy. You know this is a very crowded city and there are a lot of enemy agents and we are all very careful that we leave no tracks behind us. Not even my Military and Naval Attachés know that we are getting these intelligences.[37]

Among the items produced by the 'old friend' of Secretary Komine – and forwarded by Morishima to Tokyo on 5 March – was a lengthy set of instructions relating to Portuguese/Japanese negotiations over Timor and Macao, which was supposed to have been sent by Portuguese Premier Salazar to the Portuguese Minister in Tokyo on 2 March. The instructions concluded with a request that the Portuguese Minister discuss the situation with the Japanese government. This provided the Japanese with an excellent opportunity to check the accuracy of the *Fuji* reports and on 25 March, Japanese Foreign Minister Tani sent the following message to Morishima:

> In order for the Army, the Navy, and the Foreign Office to cooperate in the prosecution of the war, we have found it necessary to exchange secret intelligences which are received. As a matter of fact we have allowed top Army and Navy officials to obtain a very small number of our intelligences, among them some *Fuji* Intelligences. Well, we have found that your Military Attaché during March sent in two or three messages identical with yours, which he said he got from some official in the Portuguese Foreign Office. Now note that he got these without any contact with you. Among the intelligences forwarded by the Attaché is one from the Portuguese Foreign Office to the Minister in Tokyo which is almost identical with the one you sent to me on March 5. Now if the source of intelligence in both instances is the same, we must take heed lest we be taken in. However, among these *Fuji* Intelligences there are quite a number which are, it seems to me, of great value to us. Please try to make sure that there is nothing suspicious about them and that they are continued, but we can't forget this instance. What I would suggest is that you get together with the Military Attaché and that both of you see that you are not

being taken in by someone. The Army is so advising your Attaché.[38]

Yet despite this type of blunder, Morishima was certainly capable of providing the Japanese Foreign Office with some detailed, accurate and very precise information. A later communication to Tokyo, dated March 1943, was a report on the tonnage of shipping available to the Allies. It was a classical piece of patient intelligence gathering.

PRESSURES INCREASE

In Madrid, the Philippines problem continued to be a cause of great concern for Suma and his relations with the Spanish authorities, especially so because of the disruption which might have been caused to his espionage activities. Treatment of Spanish nationals in the former Spanish colony – especially of priests – raised strong protests from the Spanish government. When the Japanese Army first occupied the Philippines it became necessary for them to make use of several Spanish schools and other Spanish buildings – often for the use of the Kempei Tai as interrogation centres or for barracks. The Japanese claimed that it was difficult for them to make distinctions between such property and enemy property, which was, of course, simply confiscated. The Japanese claimed that where it had become necessary to retain possession of Spanish property, a 'fair price' had been paid. There were practical difficulties however. Many of the Spanish properties were under the joint ownership of Spaniards and enemy nationals – Spanish men with American wives, etc., or business partnerships between Spanish nationals and nationals of Allied powers. In Spain, Suma was under almost constant pressure to do something to help alleviate the problem. Repatriation of Spaniards had been considered for some time but in view of the overpowering strength of the Americans in the Pacific and the dangers involved in transportation, the Japanese could see no practicable method of carrying it out. The condition of Spanish nationals in the Philippines was also a major stumbling block in Suma's attempts to have the Japanese Ministry in Madrid elevated to an embassy. Such promotion (as well as promoting Suma himself from Minister to Ambassador) would have meant more prestige in Spain and many more opportunities to glean intelligence information from a widening group of diplomatic associates at higher levels of confidence. After listening to

Spanish Foreign Minister Jordana's many complaints regarding treatment of Spanish nationals in the Philippines Suma replied:

> The Japanese government also realizes that matters in the Philippines will have to be arranged to make for more friendship between our two countries, and, in spite of these terrible war conditions, we are doing our best. Do you mean that if we do not satisfy you completely ... you will not consent to the elevation of the Ministry to an Embassy?

Jordana replied:

> Let us not quibble. As long as my people are dissatisfied over the way the Japanese are handling matters in the Philippines, try as I will, it will be impossible for me to do anything. The Japanese will have to stop doing things that make my position harder than ever if they expect me to do anything for them. I will appreciate it if you will inform Tokyo of my very frank opinions and ask them to understand my own position.[39]

On 6 April came the first indication that the American counter-intelligence agency was doing something to disrupt *TO* intelligence reports. On that day Serrano Suner, the former Spanish Foreign Minister, and the head of the *TO* net were walking together in El Retiro park, Madrid, when they were suddenly attacked by two men. Both Suner and the *TO* head managed to escape with their lives, the two men who had attacked them were apprehended by police and thoroughly 'interrogated'. During this interrogation the men revealed that they had been employed by a member of the American Embassy to assassinate Suner and the *TO* head. The Spanish government kept the entire incident a closely guarded secret while conducting a thorough investigation. Details of that investigation have never been released.

Shortly afterwards Suma reported to Tokyo that he had despatched another *TO* operator to the United States. The operator was a personal friend of the head of the *TO* net who up until that time had been working as a civilian research official in the Guatemalan Ministry in Madrid. The agent sailed from Cadiz for Buenos Aires on 8 April in the Spanish ship *Cabo de Hornos*. He was actually a French national who had managed to obtain a Guatemalan diplomatic passport. From Buenos Aires the agent was to go to Guatemala, where he was to persuade the Guatemalan Foreign Minister and other high officials to get them to arrange for him to be sent to San Francisco or Los Angeles. Suma advised Tokyo that the agent could be expected to be closely watched by British and American officials while en route, so he could not carry much money with him, just enough for necessities. Suma stated that when the agent arrived in South America however, the Japanese Embassy in Buenos Aires would let him have $5,000 to tide him over until he could get in touch with other agents in the United States. Suma concluded his message to Tani:

> The *Cabo de Hornos* is due at Buenos Aires between May 1 and 6. When the agent gets off the ship we must be awfully careful. It has already been arranged that he is not to go straight to the embassy, so our Ambassador had better make arrangements for some Argentinian in whom he has implicit confidence, to meet the agent. We must be very careful that we Japanese are not implicated in any way.[40]

Despite the increase in *TO* operatives, much of the information coming out of the US continued to be inaccurate. For example, Suma sent a report to Tokyo on 23 April detailing an estimate of US shipbuilding capacity for 1943. Suma's figure for the first quarter came to 1,900,000 tons, when construction for that period was actually 2,805,000.[41] On the other hand, some of the material Suma was accumulating about the Northern African campaigns was extremely accurate, despite the fact that he had no full-time specialist espionage agents operating in that theatre. For example on 11 May 1943 he forwarded to Tokyo a lengthy report describing details of US ship movements in the harbour at Oran – one of the Allied landing ports. The message accurately gave the names of sixty ships, their tonnages and cargoes. The ships had all arrived at the port during a six-day period in mid-April. Suma told the Japanese Foreign Minister Memoru Shigemitsu (who had recently replaced Tani) that the report had been compiled by the Spanish Consul at Oran and that Suma himself had obtained it through a communications clerk at the Spanish Foreign Office in Madrid.[42]

By now, of course, Tunis had fallen – much to the consternation of the Japanese who believed that Hitler should have made peace with the Soviets after the previous disastrous year for the Germans on the Eastern Front. This would have allowed Hitler to concentrate instead on fighting the Americans and British in other war theatres thus taking the pressure away from the Japanese.

On 17 May, the Japanese Foreign Minister sent the following message to all Japanese embassies and ministries in Europe:

I wish to thank all of you for the reports you have sent in since the fall of Tunis concerning military moves, Soviet, American and British strategy, propaganda and the consequent reverberations in the various nations.

Now, in view of the growing seriousness of the situation, I want you to send me as quickly as possible more and more reports on those subjects.

As soon as the second front appears imminent, will you all please get in touch with one another and decide who shall stay where in order to keep in touch with the situation, how communications are to be kept up, what offices are to be closed etc.[43]

On the following day Shigemitsu sent a further circular:

I know that you must be considering quite thoroughly what to do with your communications material in case of a sudden explosion in Europe. I herewith instruct you to standby to carry out instructions. If worse comes to worst, destroy your codes and cipher machines and take every other measure necessary to the maintenance of telegraphic security. Make every preparation beforehand. Please instruct your clerks not to leave anything on hand that might cause us grief in the future.'[44]

NOTES

1. SRS 826, 3 January 1943.
2. SRS 829, 6 January 1943.
3. SRS 831, 8 January 1943.
4. SRS 838, 15 January 1943.
5. SRS 838, *ibid.*
6. SRS 843, 20 January 1943.
7. SRS 832, 9 January 1943.
8. SRS 832, *ibid.*
9. SRS 835, 12 January 1943.
10. SRS 835, *ibid.*
11. SRS 836, 13 January 1943.
12. SRS 837, 14 January 1943.
13. SRS 837, *ibid.*
14. SRS 840, 17 January 1943.
15. Swiss francs. The message dealing with funds to be supplied to Suma for the use of the *TO* net indicated that the procedure was to exchange Japanese yen for Swiss francs in Berne, which were then made available to Suma.
16. SRS 847, 24 January 1943.
17. Suma to Tokyo, SRS 869, 7 February 1943.
18. SRS 869, *ibid.*
19. SRS 866, 4 February 1943.
20. SRS 871, 9 February 1943

21. SRS 874, 12 February 1943.
22. SRS 878, 16 February 1943.
23. SRS 876, 14 February 1943.
24. SRS 878, 16 February 1943.
25. SRS 885, 23 February 1943.
26. SRS 899, 9 March 1943
27. SRS 972, 21 May 1943.
28. SRS 972, *ibid.*
29. SRS 1016, 4 July 1943.
30. SRS 900, 10 March 1943.
31. SRS 961, 10 May 1943.
32. SRS 1019, 8 July 1943.
33. SRS 1037, 26 July 1943.
34. SRS 901 11 March 1943.
35. SRS 906, 16 March 1943.
36. SRS 923, 2 April 1943.
37. SRS 924, 3 April 1943.
38. SRS 924, *ibid.*
39. SRS 977, 26 May 1943.
40. SRS 944, 23 April 1943.
41. SRS 959, 8 May 1943.
42. SRS 972, 21 May 1943.
43. SRS 972, *ibid.*
44. SRS 972, *ibid.*

5   Japanese Spy Nets Under Pressure

By mid-1943 the tides of war were turning in favour of the Allies. Tunis was under Allied control after an Allied invasion of North Africa, Attu in the Aleutians – previously held by the Japanese – had fallen. Admiral Yamamoto, the man who had commanded the attack on Pearl Harbour, had been assassinated by the United States military, twelve Japanese ships had been sunk during the Battle of the Bismarck Sea, there had been an unsuccessful attempt on Hitler's life, RAF Lancasters had managed to breach the formerly almost impregnable Mohne and Eder dams, and also had dropped 2,000 tons of bombs on Dortmund. In the battle of the Atlantic the German submarine packs were finding it increasingly more difficult to locate and destroy Allied shipping, mainly because of advances in anti-submarine warfare and also because of efficient convoy control and protection. Concerned that sinkings were decreasing, the German High Command sent several messages to its espionage operatives in Lisbon in May and June, requesting specific information concerning British submarine locating devices (ASDIC). *TO* operators, on 30 June, informed Suma that the Americans were remodelling their Liberty Class ships, and that once the modifications were complete the ships would be almost impregnable to submarine attack. The agents stated that helicopters would also be mounted and launched from large platforms 11 yards square on the stern hatches of the ships. This was remarkable news indeed. Helicopters were a relatively new addition to modern warfare and using them in an anti-submarine role was nothing short of inspired. Tokyo wanted to get added information, and on 5 July the Japanese Foreign Minister instructed Oshima in Berlin to find out more:

> Is there any relationship between the foregoing facts and the recent decline in the amount of enemy tonnage sunk by the Germans. Will you send me as far as you can an explanation of the intelligence the Germans possess on the actual details of these

various enemy defence measures and of the counter measures being taken by the Germans, Also let me know what are the prospects of the submarine war from now on.[1]

On 6 July, Ambassador Oshima replied:

The Naval Attaché here has already sent a telegram regarding the decrease in the amount of enemy tonnage sunk by Germany. Therefore I wish you would find out the details from the Navy, but the following is what we have been able to find out here. On 13th of June when I had a conversation with Admiral Doenitz, I took occasion to enquire about this matter. The Admiral replied: 'The enemy has begun to use a new direction finder, and they have attached auxiliary aircraft carriers to their convoys; as a result the losses in German submarines have become very great and we Germans have had to stop the use of submarine wolf-packs. At present we are investigating what counter-measures can be taken to render these direction finders ineffective, as well as what changes we wish to make in our methods of attack'.[2]

Knowledge of radar technology and frequencies was also high on the list of items the Japanese wanted to know a great deal more about and, in April, Tokyo was able to supply the Germans with details concerning the British radar used for long distance alarms and short-range firing, and also for the American SCR-271 long-distance radar – although some of the information was technically inaccurate.[3]

INTELLIGENCE PROBLEMS

On 10 June 1943, Argentina issued a decree further suspending the use of coded communications. This caused some consternation in Tokyo, as much of its US intelligence came through Latin American countries. On 12 June Foreign Minister Shigemitsu advised his ministers in Madrid and Lisbon, that in view of the Argentinian decree they should do their best to gather information concerning the political situation in Argentina and the other Latin American countries. On 23 June, Suma reported that he had been in touch with the Lisbon Legation and that a programme had been mapped out for covering Latin American intelligence 'with particular emphasis on Brazil and Argentina'.[4] Suma went through the usual list of methods he and Morishima planned to use, including monitoring of newspapers and radio broadcasts, adding that another two operatives would be employed on this task. He said that contacts would be established with visiting influential people and officials arriving in Madrid from Latin America and that efforts would be made to gather what was termed *Kita* intelligence from the Ministry in Portugal. Kita intelligence was Spanish diplomatic communications derived from paid informants within the Spanish government – either from the Spanish Foreign Office or from other communications centres.

Upon hearing these proposals, Foreign Minister Shigemitsu instructed Suma to put the plan into effect at once, adding: 'The importance of collecting intelligence isn't confined to Brazil and Argentina. Countries like Chile, Peru, and Mexico which are situated on the Pacific Coast, are not to be overlooked'.[5]

Immediately after the complete ban on coded communications was imposed in Argentina, Japan was searching for ways to evade it, and a number of evasive measures were quickly attempted. Shortly after the Argentine announcement, the Japanese Legation in Madrid asked the Spanish Foreign Office if it would bring pressure on Argentina to reconsider. Jordana, the Spanish Foreign Minister, replied that he had decided informally not to interfere – for diplomacy's sake – Suma asked him to reconsider but Jordana was adamant. A secret radio transmitter was then installed at the Japanese Legation in Madrid and Suma attempted to use the transmitter to contact the Japanese Ambassador in Argentina. The Buenos Aires Embassy had a receiver but no transmitter – unfortunately for Suma, his attempts were unsuccessful. The Americans however were convinced that some success had been achieved in sending coded messages direct from Tokyo to the embassy in Buenos Aires. These were concealed in general intelligence reports. A report from Chungking indicated that Tokyo may have been concealing the messages in Domei news broadcasts. The German Embassy in Argentina continued to receive coded radio messages broadcast from Berlin. There was also radio surveillance evidence to suggest that the German Foreign Office had received at least six coded radio communications from a clandestine transmitter situated at their embassy in Buenos Aires.

Because of this radio code suspension, on 23 June, Suma was directed by Tokyo to supplement his other sources of intelligence about America by arranging to place correspondents [agents] of the Spanish newspapers *Ya*, *ABC*, and *El Alcazar* in Mexico, Guatemala, Panama, Peru, Chile, Argentina, Brazil, Colombia and Venezuela. In reply to this directive, on 13 July, Suma stated:

In order not to compromise security by division of too much intelligence work, the problem has been put to the head of the *TO* net in Madrid. Through his good offices arrangements have already been made to send correspondents of *El Alcazar*, *ABC* and *Información* [another Spanish newspaper] to Latin America. The *El Alcazar* representative is an able young correspondent – [apparently the other representatives had not been chosen as at July 13]. All three correspondents will leave for Buenos Aires during the latter part of July. As to where the correspondents will ultimately be stationed, *ABC* and *Información* favour sending men either to Buenos Aires or Rio de Janeiro, New York or Washington. They balk at sending men to any other South American cities because it would look suspicious to everybody. For the time being therefore, correspondents will probably be sent only to Buenos Aires, Rio de Janeiro and Santiago. If anyone is to go to North America, it would be better to send him to Los Angeles or San Francisco, since there are already special correspondents [agents of the *TO* net] who cover New York and Washington. However the newspapers don't want to send men to the West Coast. All correspondents will have means for sending not only special dispatches, but also secret communications to Madrid. Furthermore they will be able to send important newspapers and magazines to the Madrid headquarters of the *Hispanidad* Society. The latter arrangements will be easy to carry out because the staff on *El Alcazar* actually controls the *Hispanidad* Society.

As for financing the enterprise, not one of the newspapers has a single flat dime to spare for these correspondents – they are all broke; therefore we will have to bear the entire expense.[6]

The *Hispanidad* Society referred to in Suma's message was an organization dedicated to the re-establishment of unity between Spain and Spanish-speaking Latin American countries.

Further messages pursued the same line of intelligence gathering. A 22 June message from Tokyo to the Japanese Embassy in Istanbul mentioned a delegation of Turkish reporters who were due to be sent to England and America, and instructed the Japanese Ambassador to approach the men and to do his best to arrange to get information from them about the Allies, paying particular attention to news from Central and South America.

The following day, Japanese Foreign Minister Shigemitsu sent a very surprising and urgent reply to Suma's demands for financing – surprising because it was the Japanese Foreign Office which had made the initial demand for further espionage activities to be instigated throughout South America. Shigemitsu stated:

I have just read your telegram. You must think that we are made of money. As a matter of fact we haven't any money at all to throw away. I too would like to carry out some such plan as you mention, but if we were to do it in the way you suggest, then you would find yourself greatly hampered by lack of funds in much of your other [espionage] work. Therefore I would say that the *El Alcazar* correspondent [the one Suma had described as 'an able young correspondent'], would be enough to send. Just let him find some Spaniards in Buenos Aires, Rio, etc. who could for the time being serve as correspondents.[7]

SPANISH POLITICAL ATTITUDES

Spanish Foreign Minister Jordana's reluctance to assist the Japanese in any way, especially over the very public issue of communications, is perhaps quite understandable. As we have seen, the tide of the war was definitely turning against the Axis powers, and it was at about this time that the Spanish began to believe that they had perhaps backed the wrong horse. Within Spain itself, rapid changes in attitude were taking place, changes brought about not only by the events of the war, but also because of concerted clandestine and diplomatic efforts on behalf of the British and American governments. Suma was noting these changes with some trepidation, and on 7 July, he forwarded a top-secret report to Tokyo outlining the shifting Spanish attitudes and explaining that the old rift caused by the Spanish American War was healing. He stated:

US Ambassador Hayes, a Roman Catholic, is constantly spreading propaganda that the Germans are persecuting the Catholics, trying to make it appear that the United Nations are going to be the deliverers of the faithful. I would say that by now the Catholic Church is lock, stock and barrel in the hands of the United States. The United States now has practical control over the *Hispanidad* Society, which, by fostering the principle of Pan Americanism, in encouraging the study of Spanish culture in America; they are using it for their own purposes. In Spain itself the United States has recently established a *Home of America*, copying the *British Institute*. This is just another means to win over the moneyed people here, the classes with power.

The Americans are spending a huge monthly amount in Spain, some $US1.8 million. Among other things they employ people who are busy trying to find out what I and my people are doing, using thugs to investigate my Legation to get all the intelligence they can out of it.

Since the war broke out, American capital has been flooding the country. Furthermore, now that the United Nations are doing better, Spain is getting more Navicerts and her exports from South America amount to two or three times more than they did last year.

Not long ago the American Congress pointed out that Germany had considerable interests in Spanish aviation. This brought about a transfer of German aviation interests in the country – at least ostensibly to Spain – consequently Spain can now get from the United States not only gasoline, but also railway and electrical equipment and technical assistance. The United States will probably take Germany's place in the field of air development in Spain.[8]

All periodicals and newspapers are publishing a great deal of American propaganda. There are many speeches by important men declaiming against German persecution of the Catholic Church. Anti-Japanese pamphlets are distributed everywhere.... Axis films have practically vanished from the screen. More than 90 per cent of the pictures are now American. What a contrast to last year!

Suma went on to state that the British were making headway by similar methods and that England and the United States were actually competing – although not in an unfriendly manner – in changing Spanish political thinking. He mentioned British efforts to spread propaganda, particularly by cultural activity, to re-establish the Spanish monarchy, and to work on the religious feelings of the Spaniards. He pointed out that Britain was in an excellent position to keep Spain supplied, and that because the Mediterranean was held by the Allies, it was possible for Spain to obtain Egyptian cotton and Caucasian oil through Cairo, and wheat from French Morocco. Suma concluded his report by stating that he feared Spain would become 'a slave to Washington and London', but added: 'Franco is aware of the trend and will fight it. As long as he is head of the state it will be all right.'[9]

In a second message on the subject of Spain's rapidly changing attitudes, dated 9 July, Suma described a conversation he had had with the local German Ambassador whom Suma quoted as saying:

Recently the attitude of the Spanish towards Germany has been most disconcerting. At the same time that German capital is being squeezed out of the Spanish aviation company, plans are revealed for American capital to take its place. Furthermore we have applied for permission to be affiliated in a new telephone project, but obstacles are placed in the way. Both here and in Morocco our men are being more and more restricted in their movements. For the last four weeks Foreign Minister Jordana has avoided meeting me.[10]

Shortly afterwards, Suma advised Tokyo that, because of this shift in political thinking and public attitudes, there was a marked increase in the activities of Spanish Communist elements. Suma added: 'At the present time the Spanish government is conducting a secret investigation to determine the strength of communist groups within the country and the extent of their tie-up with elements outside the country.'[11]

The delicate relations with Argentina, its cultural links with Spain, and the role Japan was playing through its espionage activities in both those countries was indeed a dangerous game of international politics, subterfuge, clandestine diplomatic manoeuvres and double dealing. Japan was doing everything in its power at this time to maintain diplomatic relations with Argentina. Had relations been severed, the highly successful Argentinian base for espionage activities would have had to be closed down. This hazardous game was best demonstrated in a top-secret conversation between Shui Tomii, the Japanese Ambassador based in Buenos Aires and Argentine President Ramirez, which took place on 12 July 1943. The transcript of this conversation is as follows:

Tomii: In a recent speech you expressed a desire to cooperate with all nations. Do you intend to cooperate with the American nations while maintaining your present relations with Japan and other Axis nations?

Ramirez: Cooperation with the nations of the Americas is based upon our foreign policy and our relations with other countries can receive only secondary consideration.

Tomii: In spite of difficulties raised by Argentina [such as the ban on coded communications], Japan is maintaining its neutrality [towards the Argentinian ban], and I personally have done my best to promote cordial relations between our countries. I would be very pleased if you would cooperate with me.

Ramirez: I shall do my best. [Here Tomii later noted that Ramirez was less than enthusiastic in this reply.]

Tomii: Argentina's foreign policy should be based on a world-wide point of view, taking into account the situation in Europe and east Asia, as well as in America. It should not be concerned only with events of the moment, but should take the past and the future into account as well. I would like to have Your Excellency's views on these comments, and, if there is any way Japan can help Argentina through her present difficulties, I will be only too glad to cooperate.

Ramirez: Even though I may agree with you in theory, we may nevertheless be forced to abandon that broader type of policy for, in order to maintain it, we must be strong, and at present we are embarrassed by our lack of various types of mechanized weapons. We have been trying to obtain them but the United States absolutely refused to ship us any. All the neighbouring countries are receiving arms from the United States and are constantly increasing their military preparations. We cannot guarantee that these nations do not harbour hostile intentions towards us, and even if Argentina maintains her neutrality she will need arms and war materials. I would therefore like to reveal to Your Excellency a method by which you can put into effect your desire to cooperate.[12]

Tomii then replied that he was willing to take up with the Argentine Foreign Minister any proposal Argentina might care to make, but Ramirez expressed a desire to 'deal directly'. It was then decided to have Colonel Enrique Gonzalez, Chief Secretary to Ramirez, submit a proposal to an attaché at the Japanese Embassy. Gonzalez held a meeting with the attaché the following day, during which he made the following statements:

The United States is now doing everything in its power to force Argentina to abandon its neutral position. It is supplying all the neighbouring countries with arms, and is surrounding us with a ring of steel. It will not grant our request for arms unless we break relations with the Axis, and it refuses to pay the slightest attention to the attitude of Great Britain, which is not in accord with the US policy. Even if Argentina should resolve to build up its defences in the face of this opposition, she would not succeed unless she received supplies from other countries. We would therefore be very pleased if Japan would supply us with urgently needed war materials. If Japan consents to supply us with munitions we will have our own ships carry cargoes of wheat and meat to Japan. These same ships will then take on cargoes of war materials in Japan. Argentina will make every effort to obtain safe conducts from all the countries concerned.

Argentina would like to obtain immediately 200 kilotons of ore, which is urgently needed for the production of arms. She would also like to import weapons such as anti-aircraft guns, precision instruments for planes, and strategic materials such as rubber.

If the Argentine government persists in maintaining its neutrality, the United States will revive long dormant questions of South America border adjustments, and this may ultimately lead our neighbours to take recourse to arms. In that event Argentina would like to request the armed aid of Japan.[13]

Tomii immediately reported this conversation to Tokyo in a secret message, admitting as he did so that he had not studied the proposal very deeply, highlighting however, the delicate military and political connotations of the proposal he added:

It is rather strange if this was a simple, sincere military proposal, since the difficulties involved in carrying it out would be tremendous. The fact that Argentina would like to have the transfer of war materials carried out publicly, leads me to suspect that her underlying selfish motive is to apply pressure on the United States in her negotiations to obtain arms from that country. As far as the shipment of ore and war materials is concerned, it might be possible to conceal the shipment of these urgently needed supplies for a while, but they are bound to be discovered sooner or later, and that will put Argentina in such a predicament that she will have to break relations with the Axis.

In so far as armed assistance in the case of hostilities in South America is concerned, it is almost out of the question geographically speaking. This was often discussed with the Naval Minister of the Castillo government,[14] but a deadlock was always reached when it came to the shipping problem. Furthermore, the German government once received a similar proposal.[15]

Since the fall of Castillo, Argentina's situation has become more acute, and unless she can compete with the various countries of North and South America, she will succumb to their pressure and break with the Axis. Hence we cannot flatly turn down a proposal of this sort, and by carrying on negotiations regarding this matter we may at least be able to postpone a break until such time as the general war situation takes a favourable turn for the Axis.[16]

US authorities throughout the war continued to place heavy pressures on Argentina to abandon its pro-Axis stance and to put a complete stop to Axis espionage activities which were then being carried out in that country. In October 1943, the US Treasury blocked the funds of the Banco de la Nacion Argentine and also those of the Banco de la Provincia de Buenos Aires, a total of 25,465,000 pesos (US$1.5 million). In August the following year the Treasury also blocked the Argentine gold reserves deposited with the US Federal Reserve Bank – a total of 2,550,000,000 pesos, (US$150,000,000) worth of gold. The funds were not released until after the end of the war.

ALLIED ACTIVITY

Also hot on the Axis wires was speculation as to where the Allies would next strike. Sicily was widely believed to be the likely target, mainly because of the various pieces of intelligence information which were then coming in from a wide variety of sources. The Allies were, of course, planning on doing just that, and were extremely interested in any secret communications concerning the subject. They were fortunate enough to receive several such reports, one in particular dated 8 June, from the Japanese Military Attaché in Rome to the Foreign Ministry in Tokyo, gave precise details of German strengths in Italy.

On 9 July, US and British airborne troops made a night landing on Sicily and the following day the main landings on Sicily took place. Throughout the many theatres of war, momentous events were unfolding. On 12 July, the greatest tank battle in history took place near Prokhorovka and the Russians went over to the counter-offensive. Three days later the Soviets launched offensives near Orel. On the same day the Japanese lost forty-five aircraft in air-combat over the Central Solomons. By 22 July, US troops had captured Palermo and three days later Mussolini resigned and was arrested. Marshal Badoglio took command of the Italian Army and formed a government. The following day martial law was declared throughout Italy and the Fascist Party was dissolved. Two days later Roosevelt broadcasted the Allies' terms for the surrender of Italy.

On 24 July, a staggering and unprecedented 20,000 people were killed during an RAF bombing raid on Hamburg. Ambassador Oshima later held a detailed conversation with German Field Marshal Erhard Milch, who admitted that the raids over Germany were having a terrible effect. Oshima coded transcripts of these conversations and forwarded them to Tokyo, so giving the Allies details of the successes of their raids and the general state of German morale. In one conversation Oshima quoted Milch as stating:

> ... to tell the truth, those air raids are certainly terrible. Look at what happened to the Ruhr; what terrible losses we sustained there in productive machinery. We are doing our very best to defend ourselves from the enemy planes. We are using plenty of anti-aircraft guns and trying to increase our fighter planes, but we have so much territory to protect that it isn't easy.... Therefore for the time being we are going to concentrate on the production of fighters and destroyer planes and give the production of bombers second place. We want to increase our defences primarily.[17]

Oshima left this meeting with a heavy heart, convinced that Germany was taking a far greater pounding than Milch was admitting. In an appendix to his coded message he added:

> From what Milch said, I judge that the German air arm is in considerable difficulty at present and has to expend great efforts merely for defence. In addition to this the Russian drive and the

Italian upset are causing them anxiety, therefore all they can do is go on the defence.[18]

INTERNAL PRESSURES

It was about this time that a series of events occurred which provided the American authorities with an enlightening illustration of the characteristics which seemed to be common among members of the Japanese diplomatic corps. It was an example of how tightly wound people like Suma and Morishima were, how their suspicions were not reserved only for members of the enemy nations, but that at times those suspicions could also be pointed at members of their own intelligence gathering cadres.

In July 1943, a representative of the Italian general staff informed the Japanese government, through the Japanese Legation in Rome, that an American intelligence agent had stolen the code books of the Japanese Legation in Lisbon. Tokyo promptly instructed Suma in Madrid to send a man to Lisbon to investigate. The investigator was not to advise the Lisbon Legation of his mission.

During the week of 4 July, Secretary Miura of the Madrid Legation arrived in Lisbon and made his investigation. As directed he kept the object of his mission strictly secret, not even telling the head of the legation, Minister Morishima. Miura was received at the legation with considerable suspicion and was treated with hostility and irritability by his Lisbon colleagues. He reported this hostility to Suma, saying that although he was being 'very nice' to the Lisbon staff, they were 'treating him ill'.[19] After returning to Madrid, Miura reported that he doubted whether the code books had been stolen, but he did express uneasiness over the fact that the Lisbon Legation had been forwarding to Tokyo a large volume of *Fuji* Intelligence reports – supposedly furnished by a former Portuguese Foreign Office employee. Miura however believed that these reports were probably not authentic, and suggested that the person supplying them may have been a double agent working for the Allies. The alleged purpose of this scheme was to make Lisbon transmit messages which could then be more easily decoded by US code-breakers. The Japanese, of course, did not realize that the US counter-intelligence units had no need to carry out such subterfuge as they had been reading the messages for years. On 9 August, after receiving Miura's report, Tokyo advised Morishima that the Allies might be supplying him with fake *Fuji* reports in order to make it easier for them to read Japanese codes, and that Morishima should make a prompt investigation of the activities of the person who supplied them to the legation. Morishima then began to suspect the real purpose of Miura's visit to Lisbon, and he made a hurried and special trip to Madrid to confront Suma and verify his suspicions. The next day, Suma sent the following report to Tokyo:

> Yesterday Mr Morishima came to Madrid. He had received your message about the *Fuji* reports and he pleaded with me to tell him whether or not Miura's visit to Lisbon some time ago had something to do with the matter. Now, sir, Mr Morishima is an honest patriotic man and one of my colleagues. I could not bear to keep this secret from him any longer. I am sorry not to have been able to comply with your request for secrecy, but that's how it is.[20]

Suma's disclosure greatly distressed Morishima and on 25 August, after considerable thought, Morishima sent the following communication to Tokyo:

> Some time ago Secretary Miura of our Legation at Madrid came over here to Lisbon. I learned afterwards that he had come on a secret mission to investigate all the ins and outs of my espionage net. I did not like this so I said to myself: 'I will go immediately to Spain and warn Minister Suma to see that nothing like this ever occurs again.' I go over to Madrid and, lo and behold, I find that my own Foreign Office asked them to send a man to investigate me, how did all this start? I am sure a message from Military Attaché Shimizu in Rome [who had supplied Tokyo with the story of the stolen code books] to you started it all. At that time I was doing everything within my power, in view of the seriousness of the situation, to see that no slip-up occurred, and of course, none of the code books got out. In my previous message I wired Hidaka [Japanese Minister to Italy] to inquire of the Italian government what it knew, and have never yet received any reply from Italian government sources. I know just how careful the Foreign Office is about its codes. I have followed instructions and if you have any more instructions I will follow them. That is the duty and most natural duty of an emissary, but if it is a fact that the code books have gotten outside my office, simple resignation or hara-kiri would not cure what has already been done.
>   You don't wire me anything; you have a member of another office come here and investigate me and my people, and then you learn about our set-up from them. Is this a civilized way to treat a man? It reminds me of the hideous punishment of bygone ages and those damnable GPU agents. This certainly will not give us who serve you in the field much faith in your own department. Take

me, for 23 or 24 years I have given my services, humble as they were, to the Foreign Office, and in all that time I have never heard of anything like this. I have never known another man to be treated as I have been treated. Now I know that codes are the very life of the Foreign Office, and now that suspicion has been cast upon me, I can never live it down. People will always be whispering behind my back. It was a sneaking dirty trick if you ask me. Would you please condescend to consider that I resign.

As for your message 105 [the instructions to investigate the persons who supplied the *Fuji* intelligence reports], I will answer it when I feel a little better.[21]

On the following day, although apparently not feeling much better, Morishima undertook to answer Tokyo's instructions. He stated:

I too always realized that if these *Fuji* reports were planted by the enemy they might even be used as a basis for deciphering our messages or to furnish us with misinformation at critical junctures. Considering the latter case, I have always endeavoured to examine them carefully for veracity, and, as for the former problem, I have always paraphrased them as much as possible. I know that we need a cipher machine. The main reason why I pleaded with you so hard to send me one was that I wanted to send you these intelligences with it. When you finally sent it, without waiting for any instructions, I sent them all through the machine, and if you will take the trouble to check in the Foreign Office, you will find that that is true.

The man who furnishes us with these intelligences is ———— [name deleted by US censors] ... His fifth-column activities for the Axis while he was in Rio became so conspicuous that the Brazilian government ... [almost expelled] him. His own government recalled him.

If you want to know more about these circumstances and his character you can learn it from Ambassador Ishii, Minister Mori and Section Chiefs Kudo and Inowe.[22]

Because of some irregularity or other in April of this year [the *Fuji* informant] was fired. It so happens that he and Secretary Komine had been chums since the old days in Rio, so I had Komine pal around with him for four months and find out all he could about the world situation. Then for the first time I had [the informant] approached with the idea of getting Portuguese code messages. Arrangements were made and since then he has been furnishing us with the *Fuji*'s. [This informant] hates the present Portuguese Foreign Office and the British and Americans extremely. His peculiar psychology will be described to you by the officials I have just mentioned.

As I have informed you, he gets these reports from typist friends of his, etc. You know how dangerous it would be for me to try to look behind the scenes and find out how he works it. It would be a very delicate matter to try to find out through just what channels he gets these Fuji's. I must keep on good terms with the Portuguese government, and if I make one mis-step a rupture of relations might result. I am sure you will agree with me that that is true.

After all it was the office of the Italian Chief of Staff that tipped you off, so I think it is the key for any investigation that is undertaken. If you know for sure that any codes have leaked out of my office I would appreciate it if you would let me know.[23]

Also on the 26th, a number of staff at the Lisbon Legation loyal to Morishima, sent a message of protest to the Japanese Foreign Office – although it has never been made clear which of Morishima's staff actually sent this message:

We all feel that, regrettable as it is, you have gone contrary to a long established tradition of the Foreign Office. In case this causes Mr Morishima to resign, in view of present circumstances, it will be a practical impossibility for any of us to continue our gruelling work here. We therefore ask that we be removed to some other office where we will not have anything to do with Mr Morishima's successor.[24]

In a message to Tokyo on the same day, Minister Suma in Madrid added his own contribution:

In view of the circumstances, it seems that Minister Morishima will choose the course of resigning. He himself wired you that this situation was without precedent. For my part, I am sick at heart after investigating him in this high-handed way. It is only natural that he should be indignant and utterly discouraged.

Now let me tell you, Mr Morishima has for many years worked himself to death, and if you would explain to him that the step you took was absolutely necessary from the point of view of the very serious matter of maintaining the secrecy of codes, it would be a glitteringly generous thing. I hope that you will listen to me and handle it as I suggest.[25]

On 27 August, the Japanese Foreign Office in Tokyo sent the following message to Suma:

The only reason why we ordered you to carry out this investigation is that the last thing in the world we want is to let the security of our code be jeopardized. We just wanted a cool, honest third party to do a good job of investigation for us. That you did and we thank you very much.

It is not that we had any suspicions of the Legation in Lisbon. As a result of the investigation some things were found out which will require the close attention of that Legation, but we found absolutely nothing at all to blame them for. You see the trouble was that the military attaché in Rome sent us some information and we simply had to act on it. Please communicate this in a suitable manner to Minister Morishima, and tell him to cut out worrying and rest easy.[26]

After this brief furore of intense diplomatic wrangling, the situation within the legations seems to have returned to normal. Suma continued to send his observations and intelligence reports, those he collected himself and reports from the *TO* net. At this time also, G2 became aware of another spy working for the Spanish Foreign Office, this was Chief of the Information and Press Division of the Foreign Office, the Marquis de Rialp. According to the secret reports which quoted Suma's own statement, Rialp called upon Suma on the evening of 26 August 1943 to tell him that he had just received a message from the Spanish Ambassador in Washington (Gardenas). The message contained 'a report from a most reliable strictly secret source concerning the items decided upon at the recent Quebec Conference.' Rialp stated that the report was of the utmost importance and that he knew the Japanese would be especially interested in it. He went on to warn Suma however: 'Never let anyone know that I told you this.'[27] Rialp then gave Suma the substance of the secret document which Suma duly forwarded to the Japanese Foreign Office with the admonition to be 'extremely careful how you handle this message because we must consider Rialp's position, the seriousness of the matter, and what is yet to come.'[28]

On the war front, at this time the Allies were making large advances – advances which were causing Japanese diplomats around the world to fear that the governments to which they were accredited would soon move from neutral or pro-Axis leanings, towards a more pro-Allied stance. On 12 August there was a large scale German evacuation of Sicily. Two days later Rome was declared an open city and on 17 August the Americans entered Messina and all resistance in Sicily ceased. RAF bombers were destroying secret German rocket sites at Peenemunde, and on 22 August the Germans evacuated Kharkov. On 3 September the Allies landed in Italy opposite Messina. Four days later Hitler and Reichsmarschall Hermann Goering ordered a complete evacuation of the Ukraine, and the following day Badoglio and General Eisenhower announced the surrender of Italy.

As these events were occurring, Foreign Minister Shigemitsu, in Tokyo, fearing that his legations in Spain and Lisbon would soon be called upon to close, sent the following message to Suma and Morishima:

Make arrangements now so that regardless of difficulties, you can continue to communicate with us in the event of an emergency. If you use a secret transmitter, your contact should be with [Oshima] Berlin. If you use agents or mail, deal with Vichy or Berne. For the present you must of course be careful not to give the impression that we are afraid the government to which you are accredited is moving towards a break with the Axis.[29]

TANGIER

At this time, too, the Japanese Foreign Office considered closing down its Tangier station. The Tangier apartment – as US Authorities well knew – had very little to do with diplomacy but was purely an espionage base for the staff stationed there. However, Tokyo, fearing that the Allies might suddenly take over the administration of the International Zone in which the office was situated, thought that it might be prudent – for the sake of code security more than anything else – to close the station down. Suma quickly reported to Tokyo that he had talked with the agent in Tangier, Obayashi, and that Obayashi had informed him that there was no indication of any abrupt change in the conditions there. Suma went on to say that communication by aircraft between Tangier and Lisbon was still possible and that, even if the worst were to happen, the Spanish Air Force had guaranteed to supply a plane to evacuate the Japanese agents at the Tangier office. Suma added:

The agency in Tangier has become doubly important since Italy's surrender and since the Straits of Gibraltar have become the gateway to both the Pacific and the Indian Oceans. It is also a suitable spot from which to observe closely the activities of the administration in Algiers. If we were now to move the agency to some place such as Algeciras [Spain], it would be extremely difficult to replace the intelligence network which has been built up in Tangier with a good deal of trouble over a long period.[30]

Suma concluded with the statement that he had instructed Obayashi to remain in Tangier until further notice and asked for confirmation and approval of his decision. Suma also informed Tokyo that he had replaced his old secret transmitter (installed in June 1943) with a new semi-portable transmitter which at that time was being tested out. Suma stated that he expected soon to use the transmitter to contact the Japanese legations in Paris and Vichy. He also said that in case Spain broke diplomatic relations with Japan, he would take the transmitter with him to Paris. The United States and Britain had been pressing the Spanish government to suppress the activities of espionage agents in Spanish Morocco and Tangier – the Allies were primarily concerned about the actions of German agents in these areas, but the results of this pressure were also brought to bear on the Japanese agents, who were working at times with the German agents through information exchanges. By mid-November the Spanish had successfully pressed a demand for the recall of at least one German spy. A message on 17 November to Tangier from the German Foreign Office disclosed:

> In accordance with the Spanish desire, Lieutenant-Colonel Reche, head of German Intelligence in Spanish Morocco and Tangier will be recalled. Berlin hopes that this action will re-establish tranquillity for some time to come. An officer who is entirely new to the region is being considered as successor to Reche, but before any decision is reached the matter will be discussed further with Spanish officials. In the meantime Vice-Consul Krueger in Tangier, who is head of German Intelligence there, will exercise a kind of general supervision without the knowledge of the Spanish Legation, since he is one of those who knows local conditions best.[31]

Under great strain, the Japanese spy Obayashi in Tangier sent a message to Tokyo stating that Allied pressures had become a serious problem, but that the time had not yet come for the withdrawal of the 'last Japanese agency in Africa'.[32] He emphasized that his espionage work in Tangier had become more important than ever.

At around this time also, Suma – obviously feeling the pinch of a notoriously tight-fisted Japanese Foreign Office – sent a coded message on 6 October stating that because of the precipitous rise in the cost of living in Spain, his staff were 'eking out an impoverished existence', and that the entire Japanese colony in Madrid was 'in a sad plight'.[33] Accordingly, the Minister requested Tokyo for a substantial increase in funds, pointing out that neutral observers in Spain quite naturally drew comparisons between Japanese and Anglo-Saxon diplomats and that, '... the impression is current that we Japanese are cheapskates and not worth having anything to do with'.[34]

MORE ALLIED PROGRESS

For the following few months, Suma and Morishima continued with both their diplomatic work and also with their clandestine espionage activities. Information from the *TO* agents in the US was apparently diminishing, but the messages from Tangier continued to be regular and of vital importance, keeping the Axis supplied with much needed details of Allied troop and shipping movements through the Straits of Gibraltar. By mid-December, the Russians had opened the winter offensive and were advancing on a wide front. On Christmas Day the Allies landed on New Britain and the following day the Royal Navy sank the much vaunted German battleship *Scharnhorst*. January was a busy month militarily. The Soviets advanced into Poland and the Ukraine, General Eisenhower was appointed Supreme Commander of the Allied Expeditionary Force, the 5th Army occupied Anzio and Nettuno, and US troops made a successful invasion of Kwajalein Atoll and other islands in the Marshall group. By 8 February, the top secret decision to invade Europe at Normandy had been made and plans for Operation Overlord began in earnest.

Security surrounding Operation Overlord was, of course, extremely tight. Axis powers, suspecting that the invasion was imminent, had instructed its agents to obtain – at whatever cost – precise details of the landings. Literally thousands of Allied personnel knew many of these details and the chances of a leak were exceedingly high. On 17 April 1944, in an effort to counter the security risk, Winston Churchill took the unprecedented step of ordering the withdrawal of most diplomatic privileges. He instructed that all diplomats then living in England could no longer send radio messages in code, they could no longer use the previously sacrosanct diplomatic pouch, and no diplomats or any of their families could leave the country until at least the end of June. This effectively blocked any kind of subversive communication from pro-Axis embassies and consulates such as those of Spain and Portugal.

In Spain, Suma continued to battle with a progressively more antagonistic Spanish government as Franco – reading the tides of war with some accuracy – moved away from pro-Axis to pro-Allied sentiments. This change in sentiment was also the result of intensive British and US pressure, restricting the vital flow of petroleum, and indeed the temporary suspension of all US oil imports and other vital commodities into the country. On 28 January 1944, the US State Department announced that the loading of Spanish tankers with petroleum products for Spain had been suspended. The Department stated that the steps had been taken pending reconsideration of trade and general relations between Spain and the United States in light of the trends of Spanish policy. The announcement added:

> The Spanish government has shown a certain reluctance to satisfy requests deemed both reasonable and important by the State Department, and concerning which representations have continuously been addressed to the Spanish government for some time past. Certain Italian warships and merchant ships continue to be interned in Spanish ports.[35] Spain continues to permit the export of certain vital war materials such as wolfram. Axis agents are very active both in continental Spain and in Spanish-African territory as well as Tangier. Some portion of the Blue Division[36] appears to be still involved in war against one of our allies (Russia), and reports have been received indicating the conclusion of a financial arrangement between the Spanish government and Germany, designed to make available to Germany substantial peseta credits which Germany unquestionably expects to apply to augmenting espionage and sabotage in Spanish territory and to intensifying opposition to us in the Iberian Peninsula.[37]

This decision was not an easy one for the Allies to make, but it came at a crucial time when they were about to embark on colossal military operations, and the activities of Spain in allowing espionage to continue on such a vast scale could have meant at least the partial failure of those operations and a large loss of Allied lives. The effects of the oil cancellation on Spain were immediate. The limited supplies which the Allies had previously allowed to be imported into the country were not on such a scale that reserve stocks could have been built up, and the Germans at this time did not have sufficient supplies themselves to send tankers into Spain in an effort to alleviate the shortages. Shortly after the US embargo, Madrid radio announced a statement quoting the Spanish Commissariat for Fuel giving details of immediate fuel restrictions, these restrictions also extended to the use of cars by foreign diplomats.

By now Suma was incensed about the lack of petrol and the ramifications for Japanese/Spanish relations and the obvious problems this caused to his intelligence net. On 1 February, Suma reported to Tokyo:

In view of the circumstances, I took it upon myself to go and tell the German Ambassador that Germany should supply Spain with gasoline for public and military use. I pointed out to him that such a move would raise the prestige of the Axis and have a fine effect on Spain by saving her from her present crisis. Ambassador Dieckhoff [The German Ambassador to Spain] replied 'That is a very fine idea. I promise you that right now I am going to ask Berlin to do it'.[38]

The following day, Suma spoke to one of his informants, the Marquis de Rialp, Chief of the Press and Information Section of the Spanish Foreign Office who told him:

In two all-night secret sessions, the Spanish Cabinet has decided to withdraw the volunteer units of the Blue Division, to turn over to the Allies Italian merchant vessels in Spanish harbours, to abrogate the commercial agreement between Spain and Germany and to exercise a stricter surveillance over the activities of Axis spies. [Even allowing the United States to cooperate in this endeavour].[39]

Thus the Spanish Cabinet had decided to yield to four of America's six demands. The only point to which the Cabinet refused to yield was for the granting of coastal defence installations. No decision had then been reached about the sixth demand, that of turning over to the US all Italian warships in the Balearics. On 4 February Suma reported that he had spoken to his old friend and colleague, the former Spanish Foreign Minister, Serrano Suner, who stated:

It was discovered that the United States and Britain, adopting measures similar to those used against Argentina, had been plotting a *coup d'état*, making use of the public unrest caused by suspension of gasoline shipments. Concessions had to be made although they were kept at a minimum; as it was, we were only barely able to weather the storm ... Spain is alive to the fact that further Anglo-American pressure may be applied as the war progresses.[40]

In this, Suner was expressing the obvious. The Allies were stating publicly that they wished nothing more than to maintain Spain's neutrality – yet, as we have seen, there was enormous pressure to drop exports to Germany and to evict all Axis spies from Spanish territories. Such political and economic manoeuvres did little to bring the Spanish public over to the side of the Allies, and throughout the country there was a general feeling that the Americans and the English were placing unnecessary pressure on Spain and its people. According to Suma, reports were coming in claiming that among the people there was, 'a spreading wave of indignation at the presumptuous and offensively pugnacious manner of the Anglo-Americans – particularly the English.'[41] Suma claimed the resentment was originally developed within the ranks of the Franco government and the people were rallying behind their government. The English and Americans had not expected such unanimous indignation and were taken aback by it. Suma continued:

Of course it would be wrong for me to say that the struggle is already over, in fact it is just beginning. The Anglo-Americans will demand that no more wolfram be supplied to Germany and will probably ask for all of the mercury which Spain produces. The enemy is also considering a plan to deprive Spain's textile industry of American exports of cotton, and thereby also instigate labour disorders. The final means of economic pressure would be to cut off Argentina's grain shipments to Spain, a measure which would be very serious in view of the fact that there has been a terrible drought in Spain in recent weeks. The enemy's ultimate goal – as in Argentina – is undoubtedly to force a break in relations with Germany. Whether the enemy succeeds in the case of Spain will depend in good part on the future development of the overall military situation.

The Allied intensified check on Spanish uses of gasoline and raw materials is a subterfuge to enable them to extend their network of agents into the smallest villages. We must also realize that German agencies in Spain – the embassy, consulates, units of the Nazi party and our intelligence organization – will all be placed under especially strict scrutiny and that their operations will be made more difficult in every way.[42]

The following day, Suma had one of his periodic meetings with the Marquis de Rialp, who stated:

Almost all the members of the Blue Division who remained on the Eastern front have been killed in the sector near Leningrad. Thus the Anglo-Americans have no further cause for complaint about our military aid to Germany. The Allies are screaming about all the wolfram we have contracted to send to Germany, but Spain has not budged an inch. As you know, the Anglo-Americans are ferreting out Axis espionage activities in Spain, and are composing lists of Axis spies which they will lay under Spain's nose if necessary. We Spaniards are trying, by granting a minimum of concessions, to obtain a modification of the Anglo-American methods. Of course there are still difficulties, but in general things are going along nicely; unless something unforeseen happens, we may be able to import gasoline as usual by March.[43]

To understand more fully the implications of the gasoline restrictions, and the part those restrictions played on Japanese espionage nets, we have to look at conditions within Spain at this time. Ravaged by the Spanish Civil War, the Spanish economy was in tatters, much of its gold reserves, a vast fortune worth tens of billions of dollars, had been moved to Russia during the war and Stalin had not only refused to release it, but had also charged the Spanish government exorbitant fees for its transportation and security. With Franco's anti-Communist government in power, the release of the gold seemed unlikely. The details of this gold transfer are interesting not only for their curiosity value, but also, as demonstrated, its theft played a large part in Spanish foreign policy during this crucial period. Had Spain still retained the gold she could easily have purchased sufficient quantities of fuel from other neutral countries by paying well over market value – despite formal US policies. The fact that she did not have the gold eventually forced her to conform to US policy, a factor which did much to influence Axis espionage activities in Spain.

No Spanish government could at this time find the means to provide the food and raw materials to repair the ravages of the war or to reach towards a pre-war standard of living. Even before the material and social wreckage of the Spanish Civil War, when cotton, coal, machinery, fuel and chemicals could be imported and easily paid for by the relatively small volume of exports to markets closed to Spain during the Second World War, Spain had not been self supportive. The wearing out of irreplaceable transport and the lack of fuel as well as coal all severely restricted the growth of the economy. Even after the end of the war, foreign correspondents were reporting that the countryside was filled with starving peasants.

THE POLITICS AND ECONOMICS OF JAPANESE ESPIONAGE

Shortly after the imposition of fuel restrictions in Spain, the Argentine government released details of (primarily cosmetic) government actions allegedly to smash all spy rings in that country. At his weekly press conference on 6 February 1944, Colonel Gonzalez, the Minister and Secretary to the President, announced that Argentine counter-intelligence operatives had discovered the existence of three Axis spy nets, two German nets and one Japanese. He said that the Argentine Federal Police, with the aid of army officers, had discovered one spy ring operating under the control of the German Embassy, and another under 'a representative of Hitler', a German industrialist named Harnisch, who had been living in Argentina for twenty-five years. He was alleged to have had an Argentine wife and Argentine-born children, and that the rivalry between the two German rings had led the police to the discovery of the Japanese secret organization which worked out of the Japanese Embassy and in close collaboration with the Germans. Gonzalez defended himself against pro-Axis critics by claiming that Japanese espionage activities in the Argentine were prolific, and that his government had not merely bowed to Allied pressure. He also said that the Japanese espionage activities were far clumsier than any of the German operations. Gonzalez stated that several arrests had been made. Among those arrested were the German Military Attaché, General Friedrich Wolf, and the Japanese Naval Attaché, Rear-Admiral Katsumi Yukoshia. Both men were later released and little, if any, real action was subsequently taken against these spy rings, although one of the German agents, Herbert Jurmann, took his interrogation sufficiently seriously, he committed suicide by jumping from a window at the Buenos Aires Central Police Station.

Information published by the Argentine authorities during the following weeks was imprecise and sketchy. It was in fact less elaborate than the contents of a forty-page memorandum sent by the United States government in January 1943 to the Consultative Committee for Political Hemisphere Defence at Montevideo. This memorandum gave the names of thirty Axis agents and the texts of several intercepted messages sent by Axis spies regarding movements of ships and details of precautions taken by the United Nations against the ravages of German submarines. When the government of President Ramires broke off diplomatic relations with the Axis governments in January 1944, the reason given was that the Axis powers had committed acts of aggression against other American countries from Argentine territory, with the connivance of the German and Japanese governments, and because Argentina was being used as a centre for South American espionage. The problem was further compounded when British authorities in Trinidad arrested Osmar Alberto Helmuth, a young Argentine citizen who had just been appointed Argentine Auxiliary Consul to Barcelona. Helmuth was being detained for spying. The Argentine government stated that they had dismissed Helmuth from his post and had ordered a full investigation. On 24 March, a brief supplementary report was issued by the Argentine government stating that a new anti-espionage department, the 'Federal Co-ordination' was to be created. At this time too, police referred for the first time to the clandestine operations during which precious metals and other strategic products, including diamonds, were being shipped in secret aboard Spanish ships to Germany. The authorities also admitted that they had seized an aircraft, two yachts and a launch, all of which had been used for espionage activities.

At this time, too, the Allies were continuing to bring enormous pressure on the Franco regime to have all Axis spies removed from Tangier. Air services had also been curtailed and on 17 January, Suma held a meeting with the Spanish Foreign Minister and took the occasion to complain about the inconveniences of not being able to pass freely between Tangier and Spain. He asked Jordana if there might be some way around the difficulty. Jordana replied: 'Spain has to put up with the situation because she is entirely dependent on Great Britain and the United States for oil. Japan is already enjoying treatment not accorded to others, since a Japanese military observer has been allowed to stay on in Tangier.'[44]

On 27 January, the day after Argentina broke relations with the Axis (after considerable political and economic pressure from the US), Japanese Foreign Minister Shigemitsu informed Suma that he had plans for preserving the flow of intelligence from Buenos Aires. Shigemitsu's suggestion, which he said had originated from Japanese Ambassador Tomii in Argentina, was to make a deal with the Buenos Aires correspondent of the Spanish weekly publication *Economista*. Suma was instructed to ascertain whether the *Economista* home office in Madrid would be agreeable to such an arrangement. Two days later, Suma advised Tokyo that a member of his staff had held discussions with the editor of *Economista* who had 'no objections in principle' to the Japanese proposal. Shigemitsu then instructed Suma to complete the necessary arrangements. Shigemitsu stated: '... that Tokyo would be satisfied – at least for the time being – with the correspondent's standard material on finance, economics, labour and social problems.'[45] He also stated that payment was to be made directly to the correspondent when a regular channel of communications had been established between Tokyo and Ambassador Tomii in Buenos Aires. Until that time, Suma was to make payments – the amount of such payments was left to Suma's discretion. But getting payment to the agents in the field continued to be difficult. Even as early as 1942, after most of the South American republics had broken diplomatic relations with Germany Italy and Japan, Axis espionage agents began to finance their operations with currencies obtained on the black market. In Argentina many of these currencies were obtained through a black market currency agent named Lestoille. For example, six days after Argentina broke off diplomatic relations with Germany, the German Foreign Office sent the following message to their embassy in Buenos Aires: '150,000 pesos are available at ... [name deleted by US censors]. Please arrange to have them picked up there and then acknowledge receipt by a telegram in clear.'[46]

Allied bombing of Germany was now at its height and the German cities were sustaining enormous damage. At around 3 a.m., on the night of 29 January, a particularly heavy bombing raid took place during which a demolition bomb, weighing almost two tons, landed just 2 yards from the Japanese Embassy causing irreparable damage. A great many other bombs, including incendiaries landed in the immediate vicinity and fires broke out on the second floor of the embassy. Ninety per cent of the furniture and fittings were destroyed. Ambassador Oshima was forced to resort to using the cellar of the building as his office and residential quarters.[47] However the following night another heavy Allied bombing raid took place and the embassy was again extensively damaged, Oshima soon afterwards moved his headquarters to Boitzenburg, leaving a small group of diplomats in Berlin to keep in touch with the German government.

THE IMPORTANCE OF NEWSPAPERS

It is perhaps also worthy of noting that much of the vital intelligence information being beamed back to Japan by the various diplomats and espionage agents was only what was ordinarily available from newspapers, magazines and technical journals. The Germans on several occasions requested their agents in the field to obtain 'factory journals' and the Japanese, too, put a great deal of faith in such materials. Newspapers like *The Times* and *Time* magazine were greatly prized by Axis intelligence services, and both Japan and Germany knew that these publications in particular could be relied upon to report the facts, without embellishment – accurately and without favour. Indeed, most British newspapers, and to a lesser extent American newspapers, contained only the barest of propaganda, and the propaganda published was almost always truthful or at least based upon truth. On 27 January, Foreign Minister Shigemitsu sent the following message to Minister Morishima in Lisbon:

> The enemy technical magazines which you send us, containing information on aviation and other subjects, have been put to a great variety of uses. I know that you have experienced great difficulties in getting hold of this material, and I want you to know that it is regarded in all quarters here as intelligence of enormous value. Please continue to collect and send to us everything you can get on this sort of thing.[48]

Morishima's Legation in Lisbon had a large section of personnel devoted to gathering intelligence from such sources. In April 1943, Morishima had advised Tokyo that English and American newspapers and magazines constituted their principal source of information about the Americas. He stated that *Time* and *Life* magazines ordinarily arrived by clipper, within a week after publication, and that the *New York Times* was scarce and usually two weeks to a month late. He added that technical and specialized magazines were extremely difficult to get. Early in 1943, Tokyo had instructed Morishima to obtain:

> ... in addition to other publications which we have already asked you for, the following American journals: *American Economic Review, American Heart Journal, Chemical Abstract, Federal Reserve Bulletin, Harvard Business Review, Iron Age, Journal of Applied Physics, Journal of the American Medical Association, Monthly Labour Review, Physical Review, Review of Economic Statistics, Survey of Current Business* and *World Petroleum*.[49]

The Americans were, of course, quite aware of the value of such publications to the Axis powers. There were substantial pressures brought to bear on newspaper editors and journalists not to divulge information which may have been of assistance to the enemy. But America was and is a democracy, and the widespread censorship experienced by journalists in Axis countries, under fascist and dictatorial rules, could not be imposed to any large degree in the United States. As we have seen, the Americans were naturally extremely careful and sensitive about the radio intercept intelligence which was providing a wealth of information concerning the Axis powers. Following the Battle of Midway, in June 1942, the *Chicago Tribune* published a headline 'Navy had the Word of Jap Plans to Strike at Sea'. This was followed by a detailed report, written by journalist Stanley Johnston, explaining that Admiral Nimitz had known in advance the Japanese Order of Battle and diversionary tactics. How Johnston came by such knowledge remains uncertain but, despite strict security precautions for the handling of such material, he almost certainly read one of the de-crypted messages which had been left lying around on the ship, the USS *Barnett* to which he had been assigned as war correspondent.

COOPERATION WITH THE FASCISTS

The Japanese at times also worked closely with the Fascist Italian Military Intelligence Bureau, exchanging information and possibly sharing assignments. On 28 January 1944, Major General Shimizu, Japan's Military Attaché in northern Italy, had an interview with a man known only as Dr Foschini who was at the time organizing the SID, the Military Intelligence Bureau of the Italian National Defence Ministry. (Another secret US report identified Dr Foschini as 'a member of, and perhaps the head of the new Fascist Republican Military Intelligence Service').[50] From Shimizu's report of that meeting it appears that Foschini had by that time assembled a staff of several hundred men, including about forty-five officers. The SID had been set up into four main divisions: a general administrative division (Zeta), an espionage section (Delta), a radio intercept section (Iota), and a code-breaking section (Beta). However the principal intelligence sources were espionage and cryptogram interception.

On 28 February, Shimizu reported that the Germans had been keeping a close watch on Foschini because of the activities of his agency, and that he had been dismissed, presumably because of the excessive size of his intelligence organization as compared with the small Italian Army. Shimizu noted Foschini's departure with some regret, since an agreement had been reached to place intelligence at the disposal of the Japanese when the radio intercept system had become established.

However, by early March, the SID had been reorganized and a new head, Colonel Candeloro De Leo – formerly in charge of the Italian Intelligence Service at Palermo – had been appointed. Shimizu visited De Leo on 6 March and later submitted a report to Tokyo on the new intelligence organization. The report also noted that the system of gathering intelligence by means of large-scale radio interception – the policy of the former bureau chief – had been temporarily suspended, and that special emphasis was being placed on counter-intelligence. The report also stated that the total personnel of the department had been reduced to eighty men. Despite this report, by 23 March, when Shimizu forwarded another secret message to Tokyo, it seems that the interception of Allied radio messages had continued. The location of this secret agency was reported to have been at Volta Mantovana, about 12 miles south of Lake Garda. Counter espionage agencies under the control of SID were set up in eight other Italian centres, including Rome, Turin, Genoa, Florence and Milan. All were under the control of a Lieutenant-Colonel or Major.[51]

GERMAN INTELLIGENCE ORGANIZATION

Meanwhile, in Portugal and Spain, both Suma and Morishima must have been extremely concerned to learn, in early February, that the German Foreign Office had sent a circular to all their diplomatic posts in neutral countries stating that a decision was soon to be made as to whether the German Intelligence Organization should be extensively cut in all neutral countries. Shortly afterwards a number of incisive steps were carried out to curb politically dangerous clandestine activities in Spain. Berlin issued orders that sabotage of Allied vessels in Spanish ports was forbidden. The German Ambassador to Spain ordered German intelligence agents in Madrid who were not directly subordinate to the German Embassy to move their offices out of the Chancery, and advised all such agents that the embassy would no longer request diplomatic immunity for them. The Ambassador told them that Spanish authorities had hinted that diplomatic immunity for such secret agents could no longer be guaranteed. Diplomatic immunity was crucial to such undercover work. Without it, espionage activities would have been severely curtailed, if not stopped altogether. Shortly afterwards, Axis agents began gathering information on British and American secret agents working in Spain and Portugal. They started to investigate the total number of diplomatic officials at Allied embassies and legations. They compiled a list of diplomatic agents who were not career men, a list of diplomatic personnel who had at any time been involved in any kind of intelligence gathering, especially intelligence against neutral countries, and a list of representatives who were protected by diplomatic passports but who were not bona-fide members of the diplomatic mission to which they were attached, for example American petroleum attachés. The diplomatic pressure also continued in Tangier. On 18 March, Suma reported to Tokyo a conversation he had had with German Ambassador Dieckhoff regarding the withdrawal of German agents from Tangier. Suma quoted Dieckhoff as saying:

> In order to lessen Anglo-American pressure on Spain, Germany has decided voluntarily to recall some of her agents from Tangier. In all, 12 persons, including 2 Vice-Consuls are to be withdrawn. The first of them left two weeks ago. If the question of closing down the German Consulate at Tangier were to be broached, it would inevitably re-open a discussion about the legality of Spain's occupation of Tangier. Consequently the two sides have tacitly agreed that the above-mentioned withdrawal of intelligence agents will close the matter for the present.[52]

On 17 March, Lieutenant-Colonel Hasebe, one of the Japanese espionage agents based in Tangier, advised Madrid:

> As the war in the Pacific grows more active, intelligence on the movements of ships to the Indian Ocean by way of the Mediterranean has become increasingly important. I am responsible for the observation of ship movements through the straits of Gibraltar, but it is difficult for me to discover whether incoming ships remain in the Mediterranean or sail on to the Indian Ocean. Therefore I recommend that Imperial Headquarters formally request the German High Command to make available its reports on ship movements in the Red Sea area.[53]

In fact, on at least one known occasion prior to this message, the Germans had turned over to the Japanese, intelligence on movements of warships east of Alexandria.

On 28 March, the US State Department made a formal request through their Ambassador in Madrid (Hayes) to urge the Spanish Foreign Office to ask the Japanese spies in Spanish Morocco and Tangier to abandon their posts – the request was met with only stony diplomacy.

Spain, of course, was procrastinating over the matter of the Italian warships, and Jordana candidly admitted as much to Suma. He also conspiratorially added: 'In spite of recent developments concerning the activities of Axis spies in Tangier, it does not seem that there is going to be anything to cause you Japanese any trouble.'[54]

Despite these diplomatic pressures, Japanese agents throughout their various areas of operations continued to forward their reports, including the details of an Allied build-up for the expected second front. In Berlin, Oshima and his staff were working under terrible conditions; as the bombing of the city continued rations were short, money was difficult to obtain and liaison with the German authorities was diminishing. On 12 March, Oshima forwarded to Tokyo the following report:

> Although emergency repairs have been made to our business office, the greater part of the office and also the official residence [which includes the living quarters] are in such a bad shape that we shall not be able to use them much longer. In the present conditions of those buildings, difficulties arise which hinder the prosecution of our work and adversely affect the health of our staff. Furthermore, a large number of typists employed in our office have lost their homes and will not be able to continue their work unless we provide living quarters for them within the embassy.
>
> Because the bombing of Berlin has intensified, all other foreign diplomatic establishments have taken refuge in the country and plan to make no more than two visits a fortnight to Berlin. My staff, however, is distributed between Berlin and Boitzenburg and keeps on working day and night through the bombings.[55]

Even under such difficult circumstances, the intelligence reports still flowed frequently through Berlin. One such report stated: 'At present there are probably not more than 20 divisions of American troops in England. Since the beginning of the year troops have been arriving at the rate of one division a week.'[56]

A few days later, there came another report from espionage agents within Britain:

> [Number missing through poor radio transmission] ... divisions from the United States, including one tank division arrived on the west and southwest coasts of England at the end of February. Another US infantry division of 17,800 men arrived in England in the latter part of February. According to aerial reconnaissance of the Woolwich-Thames area, practice landings are being carried out with the battleship *King George V* and a large number of auxiliary landing boats. Since February a large number of landing craft from the Mediterranean has been noticed. In February two American bomber squadrons were transferred from Tunis to England.[57]

JAPANESE AGENT DEFECTS

US Intelligence operatives were given an enormous boost, in late April 1944, when an important Japanese diplomat/espionage agent, based in Stockholm, defected to the Allies and openly offered his assistance to the Allies in their war against Germany.

The agent, a man named Sakimura, had been based at the Berlin Embassy, under Oshima. In the Autumn of 1943 he had been transferred to Stockholm on a temporary basis, but despite pressure from Oshima and others at the Berlin Embassy, he has steadfastly refused to return to Berlin, claiming that his work in Stockholm was not completed. Decoded transcriptions of the secret Japanese diplomatic radio traffic disclosed that his superiors first became concerned about Sakimura in December 1943. The embassy in Berlin recalled with considerable uneasiness that he 'at one time had communistic views' and an investigation was started in an effort to discover whether he was in contact with Communists in Stockholm.

Before leaving for Stockholm, Sakimura had been working on a study of the German iron and steel industry, under the auspices of the Japanese Iron and Steel Control Corporation. According to the Berlin representatives of that association, his behaviour at that time had not been at all suspicious, nor had he stolen any confidential documents.

In September 1943, Sakimura went to Stockholm on his own initiative and at his own expense. Some time afterwards he was taken ill and went to hospital. On 4 December 1943 he suddenly disappeared from the hospital.

By 17 January, private detectives assigned by Ambassador Oshima to watch Sakimura's movements had discovered that he was on intimate terms with the 20-year-old Jewish wife of a Swedish merchant, of Jewish extraction, and had taken lodgings with her family in a house just outside Stockholm. However, no evidence of communistic activities on Sakimura's part could be found – his only associations were with the families of the Swedish merchant and his wife, none of whom were Communists. Sakimura's only other activity was, 'going in and out of the municipal library'. During the course of the investigation, one Japanese official in Berlin attributed Sakimura's irregular conduct, in the past at least, to the influence of his life in Germany. The official stated:

> While in Germany he noticed the presence of certain types of privileges not found in Japan; high German officials were not subjected to the same regulations regarding food and clothing as the ordinary German, and were able to live in a far different style.[58]

In fact, Sakimura had become aware of the Final Solution for the Jewish problem – probably through his contact with the Jewish family – and had pledged himself to work for the destruction of the Third Reich.

Sakimura's defection was an event which very much angered Suma in Madrid. In a message to his colleagues in Stockholm he remarked that Sakimura had been an able man, that in his capacity as a representative of the Iron and Steel Control Association he had made extensive trips all over Germany studying economic questions, and that the Allies could therefore make excellent use of him. Suma concluded:

> Unless we settle the matter promptly and effectively before Sakimura reaches enemy territory, I am afraid that a serious situation may develop. Under these circumstances it seems to me that there is no other course open to us but – setting aside all lukewarm or humane methods – to take drastic steps by availing ourselves of the assistance of some organization such as the Gestapo, and eliminating him.[59]

ALLIED PRESSURE ON SPAIN

Finally, in late April, an agreement was made between the Allies and Spain for the removal of a ban on oil shipments. On 2 May 1944, the US State Department announced the terms of the agreement which included the stipulation that Spain would close the German Consulate and, 'other Axis agencies in Tangier'. Wolfram exports were to be cut once more, all Spanish units withdrawn from the Eastern Front and the Italian ships interned in Spanish harbours were to be released. The following day, 3 May, Suma spoke confidentially to Hans Dieckhoff the German Ambassador in Madrid, and reported to Tokyo that Dieckhoff was, 'annoyed at Spain's very poor performance on the question of the Tangier consulate'.[60] According to Suma, Dieckhoff said that he had kept his government minutely informed of the progress of the negotiations, but had not then received any hint of possible German counter measures. Suma added his own thoughts to the message: 'Although there is likely to be considerable German reaction over the Tangier question, in view of the general situation the matter will probably end by being dropped.'[61]

The following day Suma advised Tokyo:

> In a confidential dispatch, Foreign Minister Jordana today earnestly requested that Lieutenant-Colonel Hasebe be instructed to withdraw to Madrid without delay, since his continued residence in Tangier is not in accord with diplomatic practice in

Spain, which requires Embassy and Legation service attachés to be stationed permanently in Madrid. I have sent a written reply to Jordana pointing out that in several recent conversations he has declared that in all probability Hasebe's status would not be affected, that I have so informed Tokyo, and that this sudden request for his withdrawal is most surprising. I concluded by stating that I would like to see Jordana and discuss the matter with him in person.[62]

On 7 May, Suma reported that he had received a, 'diplomatically worded but strong note' stating that Jordana would be very glad to receive him on 8 May, and to hear him say that Hasebe had been instructed to return to Madrid. Suma went on to say that Germany, considering it unwise to stir up trouble with Spain before the opening of the second front, was withdrawing its agents from Tangier, and that, if Japan insisted on making an issue of Hasebe's recall, Japan would find herself standing alone.

Suma added:

> It would be wise, before the Spanish authorities force us to retreat, to arrange to have suitable Spaniards take over Hasebe's intelligence organization, and then, at the appropriate moment, recall him to the legation in Madrid.[63]

In this endeavour, Suma was emulating German moves for the continuation of espionage activities in Tangier. As early as 3 March 1944, Germany, anticipating that German agents would eventually be ordered to withdraw from Tangier and Spanish Morocco, made arrangements for a substitute network of Spanish secret agents to take over intelligence operations in those areas. On 8 May, Hasebe reported from Tangier that the Spanish Consulate-General had formally notified him that the Spanish government wished to have the Japanese agency in Tangier closed and removed to Madrid. Hasebe replied that negotiations on the subject were being carried on in Madrid, and that his actions would depend on whatever orders he received from his government.[64]

That same day, Suma held his meeting with Jordana – a meeting of polite diplomatic manoeuvring and equal determination.

> *Suma:* The request for Lieutenant Colonel Hasebe's recall is hard to explain merely as a matter of protocol; isn't there some other reason for it?
> *Jordana:* The request is connected with the abolition of the

German Consulate-General in Tangier, provided for in the recent agreement between Spain and the Anglo-Americans.

Suma: If that is the case, it is impossible to tell to what limits Anglo-American presumption may go and we Japanese cannot let the matter pass unchallenged. I myself have always done my utmost to explain Spain's position to my country, in spite of such instances ... as [Spain's] refusal to agree to raising our mutual legations to embassy status – instances which have been more difficult to understand in view of the fact that Japan recognized the Franco regime from the very beginning. Unless I know Spain's future plans in relation to England and the United States, I shall have the greatest difficulty in explaining recent developments to my government.

Jordana: England and the United States contend that Spain has exceeded the limits of neutrality in her protection of Japanese interests, ... [and] that we break off diplomatic relations. The agreement which we have just been compelled to conclude with England and the United States represents the maximum modification of their demands to which they would agree, and I ask you to appreciate the great efforts which Spain has made to obtain such a relatively mild settlement. Hasebe's recall from Tangier will assist Spain in its diplomatic handling of the matter, and I beg you to use your good offices to have the recall promptly effected.

Suma: Might I suggest – purely on my own responsibility – moving Hasebe to Tetuan. [*Sic*].

Jordana: Germany has made the same suggestion with respect to her agents, but for the present at least a camouflage of that sort is not possible. From the Axis point of view, it is much more desirable that Tangier remain in Spanish hands than that it should come under the control of England and the United States.

Suma: May I ask whether this agreement with England and the United States specifically guarantees that the concessions included are the limit to which Spain will go?

Jordana: The Anglo-Americans want to lease air bases in Fernando Po and the Balearics, citing the Azores agreement [leased from Portugal] as a precedent. However we have refused this request on the ground that Spain's position is entirely different from that of Portugal and Turkey who both have alliances with Great Britain.

Suma: The status of Attaché Hasebe is a matter which concerns the [Japanese] General Staff, and therefore I must await instructions from Tokyo before giving you a final answer.[65]

In fact, a later German report discloses that, in accordance with instructions from the German Foreign Office (and despite Jordana's statement that such a camouflage would not be possible) twelve German agents in Tangier, including the Chief of

German intelligence in the region, were transferred to Tetouan. The members of the German Consulates in Tangier and Tetouan, as well as German agents in Spanish Morocco and Madrid, all believed that this measure would eventually lead to renewed pressure from both Great Britain and the United States, and that within a short space of time the Tetouan Consulate would be forced to close and that all Germans would be expelled from Spanish Morocco.

Finally, bowing under the immense diplomatic pressure, Suma relented, advising Tokyo:

> When Spain's recent agreement with Britain and the United States was concluded, Foreign Minister Jordana made firm representations about the withdrawal of Lieutenant-Colonel Hasebe. Since you in the Foreign Office have decided that if circumstances rendered his withdrawal inevitable, it should be carried out spontaneously ... I have accordingly issued orders for Hasebe's return.[66]

Since February, Axis agents had been attempting to gather evidence of English and American espionage activities in Spain, Portugal, Spanish Morocco and Tangier, and in June Berlin advised the German Military Attaché in Madrid that:

> As a means of exerting counterpressure, Germany has demanded the expulsion of 20 Anglo-American agents from Tangier and Morocco. Spanish Foreign Minister Jordana received the demand favourably. The list of agents will be expanded and more proof will be given.[67]

Confirming that, even at this late stage in the war, the Japanese were still sending secret agents into America, at the end of April, Suma asked Japanese Foreign Minister Shigemitsu if he had any special instructions for a Spanish secret agent who was shortly to sail for America. In his reply, dated 13 May, Shigemitsu said that: ... as detailed and concrete intelligence as possible was wanted with regard to:

> 1. Naval matters – location of the US fleet, progress of the construction of battleships of the Montana class, 45,000 ton class aircraft carriers and heavy cruisers of the Alaska class.
> 2. Shipping – the movement of ships from American ports to the Pacific and Indian areas.
> 3. Army matters – the Order of Battle of the American Army, including the US Marines, the assembling of troops especially on the west coast of America and in the Alaskan and Aleutian areas.[68]

On 6 June came D Day, and the entire focus of the war changed overnight as the Allies landed vast amounts of troops and stores on the French coast between Cherbourg and Le Havre. On 7 June the Allies reached the beautiful old town of Bayeux. Three days later the Allied beachhead expanded and General Montgomery established his HQ in Normandy. By 12 June all Normandy beachheads were linked and the front extended for more than 50 miles.

FINANCIAL PROBLEMS

At this time also, the British were making moves to dry up the flow of money used to pay Axis espionage agents. On 7 June a Lisbon-based member of the Sicherheitsdienst (Nazi Party Secret Intelligence Organization) reported that the British had requested *Banco Espirito Santo* in Lisbon (and possibly other banks such as the *Banco Pinto Sottomayor*) to return to the German Reichsbank all official German deposits and to grant no more credit to representatives of the *Abwehr* – (the Armed Forces Secret Intelligence Organization which oversaw espionage activities). The agent stated that it was possible that *Banco Pinto Sottomayor* which controlled SD (the much feared SS Security Service) credits might be prevented from making payments to SD personnel, a step which, according to the Lisbon agents, '... would finish us, as neither the legation nor the *Abwehr* has a large monetary reserve.'[69]

The Japanese, too, were having problems with financing their espionage activities, especially during 1943/44 when they encountered enormous difficulties getting hold of neutral currencies. Towards mid-1944, however, Suma and other intelligence chiefs had made considerable progress towards solving their economic problems.

In mid-1943, Japan's needs for Swiss francs were running at a level of at least 40 million francs per annum. These francs were easily negotiable and therefore perfect for payments into various countries where espionage agents were operating. Payments within Germany and Italy presented no problems, as the Germans were willing to provide unregistered marks in exchange for yen credits in the Far East, and the Italians were also supplying lire on the same basis. Elsewhere, however, the Japanese were unable to buy local currencies with yen, and had to provide some generally acceptable currency, usually Swiss francs. In addition to their own needs, the Japanese had to supply Swiss francs – presumably in relatively small amounts – for the Thai and Manchukuoan missions in Europe. Because of the successes of American and British warships in preventing the movements of war supplies from Europe to Japan, Japan's earlier need for francs had been greatly diminished as there were very few products for which payments had to be made. However, by 1944, in order to meet their mounting diplomatic and espionage needs, the Japanese almost certainly required somewhere in the region of 20 million Swiss francs a year. Until the spring of 1943 the Germans had supplied the Japanese with sufficient neutral European currencies to keep them going, but by that time the Germans themselves were running short. Accordingly, they politely but firmly told the Japanese that no more Swiss francs would be forthcoming unless the Japanese would agree to provide gold in exchange, and they suggested that the Japanese could, at their own risk, ship gold to Europe on German submarines.

When the ramifications of these financial difficulties were realized, the Japanese adopted a number of emergency measures. They ordered all Japanese representatives in Europe to curtail their activities in the interests of economy. Somewhat grudgingly they shipped a certain amount of gold to Europe. By March of 1944, at least 4 tons had arrived and 2 more tons were en route. The total of six tons would net about 30 million Swiss francs, In addition, the Japanese did manage to sell several shipments of pearls in Europe, supplying Morishima in Lisbon with a sum in US dollars as a result. Morishima then sold these dollars on the black market, exchanging them for Portuguese escudos. From the sale of these pearls, the Japanese netted somewhere in the region of 2 million Swiss francs.

At the beginning of 1944, the Japanese hit upon one more expedient, which, from their point of view, would have been a most satisfactory method of solving their financial problems. The US and British governments had for years been paying out substantial amounts of money through the Swiss and the Red Cross for the relief of American and British nationals in the Far East – principally in China. For some time both the Swiss and the Red Cross had obtained the Chinese currency required for those payments by selling Swiss francs in Shanghai where the Japanese still sanctioned an open money market. Outside China, the Swiss often used Far Eastern currencies owned by Swiss nationals who were reimbursed by American and British payments in Switzerland.

However, on 1 January 1944, the Japanese issued regulations providing that all relief payments in the Far East would have to be made with funds provided by the Yokohama Specie Bank, and that such funds would have to be paid for with Swiss francs at the official rate of exchange. The new arrangement had three immediate effects. It diverted into Japanese hands the Swiss francs normally sold on the open market in Shanghai, it greatly increased the total number of Swiss francs required for payments in China (the Swiss had been able to buy Chinese currency on the Shanghai market at 1/15th to 1/20th of the official rate), and it ensured that all relief payments outside China would provide the Japanese with Swiss francs.

In compliance with these regulations, the Swiss deposited 7,150,000 Swiss francs in the Yokohama Specie Bank, for which they received Chinese currency at no better than the official rate. However, Tokyo, fearing that the Swiss would take reprisals restricting the use of Japanese franc balances in Switzerland, proposed a compromise agreement under which the rate of exchange for future relief transactions be at double the official price. Even at this more favourable rate, the Japanese created for themselves a very handy source of Swiss francs. At twice the official exchange rate, the cost of American relief in occupied China alone was around 10.5 million Swiss francs per year. Thus much of this American money was finally used to pay for Japanese espionage activities directed against America and its allies.[70]

At the end of June, Japanese Foreign Minister Shigemitsu reminded all his representatives in European capitals that: '... recent developments in Europe have made it very difficult for us to carry on intelligence activities,' and directed them, 'to re-examine present methods and consider new channels of intelligence – keeping in mind the possibility that certain neutrals may break relations with us.'[71] In a reply of 11 July, Ambassador Oshima in Berlin stated:

> It is quite possible that such neutrals as Turkey and Portugal will enter the war or, under pressure, will at least curtail the activities of Axis agents. Accordingly, Japan should arrange to transfer at least part of her intelligence organizations in those nations to other countries. For example, some of the agents in Portugal could be transferred to Spain, and some of these in Sweden should be moved. Competent Japanese personnel will always be needed, and steps should be taken so that people experienced in this kind of work do not end up by being interned.
>
> As to the desirability of Switzerland being an intelligence centre, she will probably remain neutral, but is not as strategically located for intelligence purposes today as she was during the last

war when Germany and France were the chief belligerents. Moreover, if communication between Switzerland and the Iberian peninsula were cut off, Switzerland would be of questionable value as a base for gathering intelligence.

Heretofore the Embassy in Berlin has not been particularly concerned with collecting enemy intelligence, and Germany is not an entirely satisfactory base for such activity. However, part of the espionage organization could be based in Germany, where it might be possible to develop contacts with the Germans and arrange to use materials which they collect.[72]

PROBLEMS WITH *TO* AGENTS

However, by July, the Japanese were becoming more and more uneasy about a possible exposé of their dealings with Spanish espionage agents. For more than two years, an unnamed informer (actually the head of the *TO* net) had been selling information to Suma in Madrid. This agent had first acquired Suma as a customer through Serrano Suner, when Suner had been Spanish Foreign Minister. The exact degree of intelligence and its value to the Japanese gleaned through the *TO* net has never been discovered, but US authorities were convinced that it was never very great. In January 1944, one of the *TO* agents – a Spanish national – was charged in Canada with espionage and forced to leave the country. Shortly afterwards the British asked Spanish Foreign Minister Jordana to make a complete investigation of the matter and Jordana promised, '... a most rigid inquiry'. Yet it must be remembered that Jordana was fully conversant with the operations of the *TO* net. Not long afterwards an informant began supplying Suma with some alarming stories about the development of the investigation, and subsequent messages between Suma and his superior, Foreign Minister Shigemitsu in Tokyo, revealed some interesting facts, including that, as of 5 July Suma had been told that the investigation had uncovered the name of the head of the *TO* net in Spain, and that the matter had been referred to a Spanish military tribunal. Suma was also informed that US Secretary of State Cordell Hull had sent Jordana a personal letter proposing that Spanish representation of Japanese interests be supervised by a US appointed committee, and that restraint be exercised over the *TO* head (i.e. military detention), until the incident had been settled. According to Suma this information sent the *TO* head into immediate hiding.

By 8 July, Suma had arranged with the Germans to have the

TO head spirited across the border at San Sebastian. The intelligence chief was to live quietly in Paris for a while at Japan's expense. He was provided with the equivalent of around US$500 per month for this purpose. Suma was extremely concerned that as a result of the affair, Anglo-American pressure might cause Spain to break off diplomatic relations with Japan, and that Portugal would automatically follow the Spanish example. If that had occurred, Suma would have lost the valuable vantage point for espionage which the Iberian Peninsula afforded.

On 11 July, Japanese Foreign Minister Shigemitsu told Suma:

> ... that we shall absolutely not accept any responsibility for this affair'. He added that it was important to keep Spanish-Japanese relations from, 'getting out of hand', and that if representation of Japanese interests in the United States were handed over to another country, the Americans might impose 'onerous stipulations'. Shigemitsu said that if Spain made representations to Suma about the matter, he was to stall by saying that he would have to get instructions from Tokyo, 'taking every precaution not to make matters worse.

By 11th also, Suma was further upset by an event concerning another *TO* agent. The agent had recently returned to Madrid for a rest. He told Suma that he had been about to go back to the United States to continue his spying activities, but the US Consul at Bilbao had prevented him from sailing. According to the agent, the matter was then taken up with the US Ambassador who, after making an investigation, had expressed regret over the Consul's action and had become so suspiciously cordial that the agent was left wondering whether to return or not. It could have been a trap designed to lure the agent back to the United States where he could have been tried for espionage.

Suma suggested to Tokyo that he might try to persuade the agent to, '... return by a safer route, since the loss of such an experienced and able individual at the present time would be too bad.' Tokyo however decided that the Japanese were already in deep enough trouble through the use of such agents, and ordered Suma to refrain from interfering.[73]

SITUATION WORSENS FOR AXIS POWERS

But by now, the war was progressing with great rapidity. By early July 1944, US forces had annihilated the Japanese garrison on Siapan and leading Japanese Admirals Nagumo and Yano had been killed. By 9 July the 2nd Army had taken Gretteville-sur-Oden, and in Finland the Russians had crossed the Vuoksi. By 18 July, US Forces had entered St Lô and the Japanese had retreated from Imphal Kohima. Two days later came the unsuccessful bomb plot against Hitler's life. Also, at this time, came the fall of the Tojo cabinet, which was replaced with a firmer and more objective group of men. In the reshuffle, Foreign Minister Mamoru Shigemitsu took over the vastly influential Greater East Asian Ministry (GEA), in addition to his position as Foreign Minister. On 24 July, Shigemitsu sent out a GEA circular to his foreign representatives exhorting them to greater efforts. The distinctly Nelsonian message, which was given wide circulation, is particularly noteworthy because it was sent out almost immediately after the Cabinet shift and contained several unusually objective admissions:

> The overall war situation is becoming serious. The enemy have already broken through our inner South Seas Defence Zone, so that from now on transportation between north and south is going to be increasingly difficult. In addition, the enemy will try to destroy our production and resources by air raids.
>
> In Greater East Asia we must expect a deterioration of peace and order, a weakening of cooperation, an increase in the tendency to revolt, and a decline in the supply of munitions and other materials.
>
> Japan is facing an unprecedented national crisis and it is essential that the union of Asiatic peoples and their cooperation in the production of materials continue. We are expecting all of you to do your utmost as one body to meet the life and death demands of the nation.[74]

As the situation became increasingly more difficult, particularly for Germany, the German secret police and intelligence organization RHSA (Reichs Sicherheitshauptamt, the Reich Security Head Office) began to take steps to ensure that in the case of a break in diplomatic relations with Spain (or Portugal and Turkey), a number of 'stay-behind agents' would continue the work. If relations were not broken with Japan, then these agents would work in conjunction with Japanese agents. On 2 August, Japanese Ambassador Kurihara in Ankara sent the following communication to Ambassador Oshima in Berlin:

> The Germans have asked us to collect Near Eastern and Turkish intelligence for them after the German Embassy is closed. At your discretion therefore, please pass on to the German authorities the intelligence which we send to you.[75]

By now, the British had presented to the Spanish authorities a list of more than 600 Germans they wanted to have expelled from the country. While most of these were only commercial representatives, at least three of four dozen were espionage agents.

At this time also, Spanish Foreign Minister Jordana was replaced by a new Foreign Minister, José Felix Lequerica, who had been serving as the Spanish Ambassador to Vichy. Lequerica had been an intermediary between France and Germany and had been instrumental in arranging the armistice of 1940. He was later honoured at Vichy with a double ceremony, receiving the Grand Cross of the French Legion of Honour from Marshal Pétain, and the Grand Cross German Eagle.

On 11 August, the Marquis de Rialp, Head of the Press and Information Bureau of the Spanish Foreign Office (and one of Suma's informants), issued a statement:

It was decided to appoint Lequerica because he obtained the consent of the Germans to make Paris an open city and acted as intermediary for the Franco-German armistice. He is also on good terms with both Britain and America. A person of such experience will be in a good position, whatever develops, to play the part of mediator for European peace, a role which Spain has earnestly desired for a long time.

Lequerica is an excellent person to maintain the policy of strict neutrality. However, his leanings may well be towards Great Britain since he comes from a wealthy family in Bilbao – a decidedly pro-British area, and he had been to England a number of times prior to the Spanish Civil War.[76]

The following report from the Madrid representative of the RSHA outlined the Axis feelings towards Lequerica:

Unlike Jordana, Lequerica is a civilian; accordingly, he has less understanding of the needs of military intelligence, but is also less aware of its extent. On the question of expulsion of [Axis] agents, he is more skilful and courteous than his predecessor, but he is bound by the agreement of 2 May [with England and America], and insists on the departure of 50 agents. Of great advantage to us is the fact that General Martinez Campos [Chief of the Intelligence Section of the Spanish General Staff] is friendly with Lequerica, so that certain influence can be expected through him. The new Foreign Minister is intelligent and skilful and possesses literary talent, but he is vacillating and somewhat weak when faced with a firm attitude.[77]

On 14 August, Suma held his first official interview with Lequerica. It was cordial and polite, and no mention was made of the presence of Japanese secret agents on Spanish soil. Likewise, the German Ambassador Dieckhoff's interview, conducted at almost the same time, did not broach the subject of intelligence gathering in Spain or by Spanish nationals in other countries.

Shortly afterwards, the Marquis de Rialp was appointed to represent Spain at the inauguration of Cuba's new President, Grau San Martin, on 10 October. Rialp applied to American Ambassador Hayes for a visa to visit the US for about a month after the Cuban celebrations. On 29 August, Suma advised Tokyo of Rialp's proposed tour and went on to say:

In view of the fortunate fact that the Spanish Ambassador, Minister and Councillor in Washington, and the Consul General in New York are all friends of Rialp, he has asked me privately to let him know without hesitation if he could be of any assistance to Japan. Rialp has displayed a friendliness towards Japan that is beyond calculation; accordingly, if you have any instructions as to matters of particular importance, please let me know by September 3 at the latest.[78]

Rialp's information, however, had never been very important – nor had it been very accurate. Shigemitsu's reply came promptly: 'It is unlikely that we would derive much advantage even if we should ask Rialp to do anything specific for us. Therefore just ask him to let us have his impression of trends in America.'[79]

Over the following weeks, the diplomatic and political pressure steadily mounted on the Axis powers to decrease their intelligence services in Spain. On 22 September, the Spanish Bureau for the Maintenance of Peace and Order in Madrid arrested seven German residents for refusing to comply with an order to leave the country. In a confidential interview with General Franco, the US Ambassador later stated that Franco had said that he neither liked not trusted the Japanese, and that he would be ready to break off diplomatic relations at a suitable time. Suma was extremely worried as the anti-Axis trend mounted throughout the country and, on 23 September, he complained to Lequerica that the tone of the Spanish press had recently changed and that statements had appeared openly criticizing Japan's intentions. Lequerica replied:

Quite frankly I fully understand Japan's feelings and will take appropriate measures. Please do not worry about that. I am sure you can understand that, under the present circumstances, it is extraordinarily difficult to maintain neutrality and to avoid breaking off diplomatic relations.[80]

NOTES

1. SRS 1020, 9 July 1943.
2. SRS 1020, *ibid.*
3. SRS 1017, 5 July 1943.
4. SRS 1023, 12 July 1943.
5. SRS 1023, *ibid.*
6. SRS 1030, 19 July, 1943.
7. SRS 1031, 20 July 1943.
8. On 5 July 1943, Foreign Minister Jordana told Suma that 'Spain has finally obtained an understanding with the Germans who have confidentially agreed to let the aviation company Iberia be converted into a concern financed totally by Spain.' According to an earlier report from Suma, the company had been 49 per cent German owned.
9. SRS 1028, 17 July 1943.
10. SRS 1028, *ibid.*
11. SRS 1033, 22 July 1943.
12. SRS 1033, *ibid.*
13. SRS 1033, *ibid.*
14. Dr Ramon Castillo, advocated through his Foreign Minister Dr Ruiz Guinazu, a tough pro-Nazi policy. Castillo was overthrown by military junta in June 1943.
15. A secret German message of July 1942 disclosed that the then Buenos Aires Chief of Police and later (for 3 days) Foreign Minister in the Rawson Cabinet, had submitted to German Chargé d'Affaires Meynen a proposal that, because of the growing military might of Argentina's neighbouring nations, Germany supply Argentina with military equipment – to be delivered by German blockade-runners or taken away by Argentine ships from Spanish ports. Thereafter, according to Meynen, he was approached on the same subject by the Chief of the Spanish Commercial Mission in Buenos Aires and also by the Argentine Minister to Denmark who was home on vacation at the time.
16. SRS 1033, *ibid.*
17. SRS 1064, 22 August 1943.
18. SRS 1064, *ibid.*
19. SRS 1075, 2 September 1943.
20. SRS 1075, *ibid.*
21. SRS 1075, *ibid.*
22. Ishii was a former Ambassador to Brazil, Kudo and Inowe were on his staff, nothing is known about Minister Mori, although there were at least three prominent Moris employed in the Japanese diplomatic corps. None of these men however was of ministerial rank.
23. SRS 1075, *ibid.*
24. SRS 1075, *ibid.*
25. SRS 1075, *ibid.*
26. SRS 1075, *ibid.*
27. SRS 1082, 9 September 1943.
28. SRS 1082, *ibid.*
29. SRS 1089, 16 September 1943.
30. SRS 1101, 28 September 1943.

31. SRS 1135, 1 December 1943.
32. SRS 1135, *ibid*.
33. SRS 1115, 12 October 1943.
34. SRS 1115, *ibid*.
35. This shipping technically belonged to Marshal Badoglio's pro-Allied government, which was officially recognized by Spain.
36. Spanish nationals fighting on the side of Germany on the Eastern Front. By this time however, their withdrawal was only an academic point, as a large percentage of these volunteers had been killed.
37. *The Times*, 29 January 1944.
38. SRS 1202, 5 February 1944.
39. SRS 1205, 8 February 1944.
40. SRS 1205, *ibid*.
41. SRS 1205, *ibid*.
42. SRS 1205, *ibid*.
43. SRS 1205, *ibid*.
44. SRS 1189, 23 January 1944.
45. SRS 1212, 15 February 1944.
46. SRS 1214, 17 February 1944.
47. SRS 1199, 2 February 1944.
48. SRS 1203, 6 February 1944.
49. SRS 1203, *ibid*.
50. SRS 1385, 9 July 1944.
51. SRS 1385, *ibid*.
52. SRS 1249, 23 March 1944.
53. SRS 1274, 17 April 1944.
54. SRS 1251, 25 March, 1944.
55. SRS 1251, *ibid*.
56. SRS 1251, *ibid*.
57. SRS 1251, *ibid*.
58. SRS 1288, 1 May 1944.
59. SRS 1300, 12 May 1944.
60. SRS 1303, 15 May 1944.
61. SRS 1303, *ibid*.
62. SRS 1296, 8 May 1944.
63. SRS 1303, 15 May 1944.
64. SRS 1303, *ibid*.
65. SRS 1304, 16 May 1944.
66. SRS 1313, 25 May 1944.
67. SRS 1356, 7 July 1944.
68. SRS 1305, 17 May 1944.
69. SRS 1336, 17 June 1944.
70. SRS 1346, 27 June 1944.
71. SRS 1368, 19 July 1944.
72. SRS 1368, *ibid*.
73. SRS 1370, 21 July 1944.
74. SRS 1383, 3 August 1944.
75. SRS 1388, 8 August 1944.
76. SRS 1403, 23 August 1944.
77. SRS 1403, *ibid*.
78. SRS 1414, 3 September 1944.
79. SRS 1416, 5 September 1944.
80. SRS 1438, 27 September 1944.

6   The Beginning of the End

By 30 September 1944 the Lisbon branch of the German
RSHA Military Section had advised Berlin that, according to the
heads of the Portuguese police, Anglo-American pressure on
Portugal for the rupture of Portuguese-Japanese relations was
mounting, and Portuguese Premier Salazar was expected to make
a decision on the matter within the week. It was also reported to
the Germans that such moves against the Japanese in Portugal
would help to influence Spanish policy in the same direction. At
this time, preparations were under way to move a large
percentage of the intelligence department of Morishima's
Legation to Spain, although Suma was resisting this move,
claiming that such an action would further jeopardize the already
extremely fragile Spanish-Japanese relations. But time was
running out. The Japanese Military Attaché in Lisbon stated:
'Although we can always devise lots of policies of delay, such as
those which have formed Japan's basic policy vis à vis Portugal, I
do not think they will be very effective against American and
English pressure.'[1]

During the last week of September, the Spanish Cabinet held a
series of meetings during which the problem of Axis relations was
discussed in detail. At Foreign Minister Lequerica's insistence, it
was decided to prohibit all newspaper articles abusive to Japan,
and notification to this effect was sent to the Press Bureau of the
Ministry for Spanish Home Affairs. When the discussion came
around to the question of diplomatic relations, the War Minister
insisted that while Spain had at first been a non-belligerent
associated with the Axis, she was now strongly neutral, and that
such neutrality did not permit breaking off with one side only. He
claimed that, if relations were to be broken, then they should be
broken with all belligerents. After heated debate, Cabinet
decided that suitable restrictions should be placed on the
activities of Axis diplomats – primarily espionage activities.

INCREASING FINANCIAL PROBLEMS

At this time too, Suma and Morishima again became concerned over banking restrictions and the flow of money for espionage purposes. In September 1944, the Yokohama Specie Bank representative in Germany complained that: '... in deference to England and America,' Swiss banks were refusing to make remittance of Axis funds to Spain and Portugal. The representative noted that in order to avoid the restrictions, it had become necessary to set up 'straw men' (false accounts) in whose names the remittances could be made. Early in October 1944, Tokyo again became concerned over a Domei (newsagency) dispatch from Zurich, stating that the Swiss banks were further limiting the services they would perform for Axis clients. Tokyo asked the legation in Berne for more details.

On 10 October Kojiro Kitamura, the Berlin representative of the Yokohama Specie Bank, who was then in Switzerland, replied that late in September the Swiss Banking Association had sent the following secret notice to banks throughout Switzerland:

> The opening of any new account for a foreigner living or visiting Switzerland, while not prohibited, should be permitted only after a most careful study of the particular circumstances involved. As for the existing account of a foreigner living outside Switzerland, the balance must not exceed the highest balance in the previous year.[2]

The restrictions were actually being imposed to help prevent the vast river of gold and currencies which was flowing from Germany at this time. Government officials, SS officers, diplomats, and even private citizens, anticipating that the end of the war was close, were sending enormous sums out of the country – funds which had usually been stolen during the course of the war, often from concentration camp victims. Kojiro Kitamura stated that Swiss banks were not opening any new accounts for Axis clients, and commented that the banks were becoming 'more weak-kneed than ever'.[3] He stated that they had succumbed to pressure brought by England and the United States to prevent the escape of money from Germany. He commented, however, that the Germans already had a good deal of money tucked away in various types of currencies and gold, much of it under Swiss names. Yet these restrictions were to prove a fierce barrier to the continued espionage activities of the Japanese.

The following day Kitamura reported that he had discussed the matter with Paul Hechler, the Assistant General Manager of the

Bank of International Settlements. The president of the bank was an American, Thomas H. McKittrick. Kitamura was himself a director of the bank.

According to Kitamura, Hechler stated: 'The establishment of new accounts ... is altogether impossible. The restrictions on existing accounts ... applies whether or not a diplomatic official is concerned and whether or not the owner of the account resides in Switzerland ...'[4] Kitamura later stated:

> Although the measures were primarily intended to strangle Germany, they would also seriously effect the Japanese, and that I think that we, like Hechler, must anticipate the worst. As a temporary measure it would be wise for us to place Yokohama Specie Bank funds – as far as possible – in the National Bank, and to withdraw our personal deposits in 100 franc notes and keep them ourselves. Just now the deposits of the [Japanese] ministers and other diplomatic officials are receiving special treatment and I think they are safe, but there is no reliable guarantee for the future.
>
> As for the possibility that the accounts of Japanese [citizens] or of our bank will be frozen, the National Bank and the Banque Federale have both assured me that at present there is absolutely no danger.[5]

The principal Japanese accounts in Switzerland were with the National Bank and the Banque Federale. At this time there was still room for expansion in these bank accounts – up to the stipulated previous year's high. An indication of deposits may be gained from Kitamura's later report which stated that the previous year's high in the Banque Federale had been more than 10 million francs.

Five days later, on 16 October, Kitamura sent a further message to Tokyo indicating that he had attempted to withdraw 2 million Swiss francs from the Banque Federale in Berne, apparently pursuant to instructions from Tokyo. However the bank had expressed a wish to limit cash withdrawals by the Japanese Legation to just 100,000 francs, and asked the reason for so large a withdrawal. Kitamura recommended that the matter not be pressed, since to do so might have 'stimulated the Swiss to strengthen the restrictive measures against foreigners'.[6]

AGENTS' DIFFICULTIES

Even at this late stage in the war. Axis agents were still being smuggled into the US – not only new agents, but agents who had spent several years in the field, had returned to Spain or Germany for a rest, and were now being returned to duties. As we have seen, at least one *TO* agent was certainly allowed by Suma to return to Madrid for a brief period, but as the war progressed, it was becoming increasingly more difficult to get such agents back into operation because of Allied domination of the Atlantic.

In the Spring of 1944, a German vessel, referred to in secret German communications as the *Jolle*, ran the blockade from Europe to South America, (where many of the agents destined for North America were landed). In late June it reached a point on the Argentine coast near Mar del Plata, some 200 miles south of Buenos Aires, where at least two agents, and possibly more, complete with radio equipment and other supplies, were put ashore. Whether the *Jolle* was a surface craft or the code name for a submarine was not clear to G2 at this time. However, within a few months more evidence came to light about this and other similar clandestine operations.

Late in June 1944, one of the agents who had been landed from the *Jolle* delivered to a leader of an Axis espionage organization in Argentina, a secret ink device and chemical products, then valued at around 75,000 Reichmarks. The chemicals were to be sold in order to finance espionage operations. By now, the American counter-intelligence operations had discovered that the *Jolle* was, in fact, a French fishing smack named the *Santa Barbara*. On 16th or 17th of September 1944 it returned to Vigo, Spain, where Axis mail and propaganda films were delivered to members of the German Legation. There were eight or nine Axis agents on board, all but one of them, and the vessel itself were interned by the Spanish authorities (an event which would have been unheard of twelve months previously). Several members of the crew managed to evade internment and succeeded in escaping to Madrid where they went into hiding. Another voyage to deposit even more agents in South America was planned, this time aboard the *Prinz Adalbert*. However, British intelligence agents later discovered that the voyage had been abandoned.[7]

BURGEONING DIPLOMATIC PRESSURE

Further diplomatic pressure was brought to bear on Suma when the Japanese in the Philippines unexpectedly seized some valuable Spanish property. The property concerned the sugar plant and refinery in Tarlac belonging to Spanish-owned Compania General de Tabacos de Filipinas. After a cool meeting between Suma and Lequerica, the Japanese Foreign Minister in Tokyo ordered Ambassador Murata in Manila to sort the problem out. In a message of 27 November, Murata stated:

> The Tarlac plant has some of the finest equipment on Luzon and controls extensive sugar plantations. However production at the plant has recently fallen off despite our direction and encouragement, and this has adversely affected our alcohol programme on Luzon, which is already at a critical state because of enemy air raids and the difficulty in importing sugar from Negros. The army tried to lease the plant and plantation, but the company stated that, in view of its neutral position, it could not grant a lease. Consequently the army ... decided to requisition and administer the factory and plantation.[8]

The plant was of vital importance to the Japanese, one of its principal activities had been the production of ethyl alcohol, primarily for the use of Japanese military and Philippines puppet government vehicles. Because of US domination of the Pacific, very few supplies were now reaching the Philippines and petrol was almost non-existent. Many cars and trucks were being powered by charcoal gas and pine nut oil.

On 1 December, the substance of Murata's report was sent to Suma with the instructions that Suma tell the Spanish that the Japanese intended to relinquish control of the plant as soon as the necessity for it ceased. In light of the impending break in diplomatic relations, Suma was also instructed to discuss the terms of a suitable compensation package.[9]

AGENTS TRANSFER TO SWEDEN AND SWITZERLAND

By December 1944 many of the Japanese espionage agents based in Portugal had been moved, three were transferred to Stockholm to continue intelligence work and, because Suma refused to have them in Spain, five had gone temporarily to Berlin. As a result of Japanese policy to build up intelligence services in Sweden and Switzerland, the number of secret agents in those two countries had, by 1 December, increased by eleven and six respectively. On 11 November, Japanese Minister Kase in Berne had reported that Geneva was becoming an important centre for collecting intelligence on America, England and France, and he recommended that the Japanese open an office there. He suggested the possibility of reopening the Consulate-General – closed since 1941 – or alternatively establishing a Red Cross or newspaper office (as espionage fronts). Kase was careful to point out that the reopening of a Consulate-General might be opposed by the Swiss, who, '... had been deferring to the Anglo-Americans.'[10]

On 6 December, however, Kase advised Tokyo that the Swiss had agreed to the re-opening of the Consulate-General because they were anxious to facilitate Japanese cooperation with the Red Cross. Yet the Swiss were still worried about the increase in Japanese personnel and wished the Geneva staff to be limited to two men, both of whom were to be selected from among the Japanese already in Switzerland. Kase informed Tokyo and asked for two men to be appointed. One of the leading Japanese intelligence agents in Switzerland at this time was Lieutenant-General Okamoto. Okamoto was head of a 'liaison mission' decided upon at a conference of government and military leaders in Tokyo in October 1942, and sent to Europe early in 1943. The activities of the mission were never entirely clear, but Okamoto – after a stay in Berlin – spent several months inspecting and reporting at length on conditions in various European countries. He took up residence in Berne in November 1943, and had begun to set up his office as Military Attaché by January 1944, after which he was instrumental in sending a stream of intelligence to Tokyo. In December that year Okamoto was suddenly taken ill, apparently suffering from a stroke, and he asked Tokyo to have him relieved of his duties.[11]

Japan's relationship with Sweden and Switzerland during the war was a curious one. Japan certainly made many secret deals – especially with Sweden – to buy badly needed war materials, and the espionage activities set up by the Japanese in both those countries was studiously ignored by the relevant authorities. The secret purchases from Sweden involved ball bearings and large quantities of piano wire. These items were sent from Sweden to Germany, Italy and occupied France, where they were taken to Japan either by blockade runners or by German submarine. These purchases were completed despite a promise made in August 1943 by the Swedish Foreign Minister to the US Ambassador in Stockholm, that no further licences would be granted for Swedish exports to Japan, and that those licences already issued would be revoked. Yet on 25 November, 1943, 15 tons of piano wire was shipped to Japan, the first part of a 70 ton order. The Japanese Military Attaché based in Stockholm at the time reported to Tokyo: 'We have received an export order for the rest and we expect to ship it early in January'. Shortly afterwards, the Japanese Military Attaché in Berlin advised

Tokyo that he expected to purchase 120 tons of piano wire within days, and that a large portion of the wire would be delivered within the month. The piano wire was being used by the Japanese in the construction of aircraft and also in the manufacture of ball bearings.

In August 1944 the Japanese Foreign Ministry transferred from Morishima's Legation in Lisbon to the Legation in Stockholm the task of collecting published intelligence, newspapers, journals, magazines, etc. Tokyo also recommended at this time that the services of Swedish correspondents be recruited for the purpose of intelligence gathering. Two added agents were soon afterwards transferred to Stockholm. The Swedes knew that both agents were Japanese spies, yet they made no protest to the Japanese government.

Late in 1944, the Allies became aware that Sweden and Switzerland were both passively assisting the Japanese in further building their espionage nets. On 8 October the Japanese Foreign Office authorized the setting up of a diplomatic post in Zurich. At the same time Tokyo authorized the Japanese Military Attaché in Berne to add a further five agents to his staff, and recommended that a Red Cross representative be moved to Geneva in order to collect intelligence and to observe the general situation.

By now, of course, the various Allied offensives against Germany and Japan were progressing with speed and efficiency. On 20 October the United States had invaded the Philippines at Leyte, using the largest fleet ever gathered in the Pacific, and within weeks the Japanese forces, under General Tomoyuki Yamashita, began falling back to northern Luzon. By 10 November, the Russians were across the Danube and US Forces were bombing Iwo Jima. On 12 November, RAF Lancasters sank the pride of the German fleet, the *Tirpitz* and four days later American forces captured Kalemyo, severely restricting Japanese military and espionage communications. By 24 November, the Allies were across the Saar and the French had taken control of Strasbourg. On the same day US B-29 bombers, flying from bases in the Marianas, delivered a bombing raid directly on Tokyo. On 8 December, USAF aircraft began a seventy-two day bombardment of Iwo Jima and the following day the Red Army almost encircled Budapest. Eight days later the Battle of the Bulge – Germany's last great stand – commenced. Shortly afterwards, Turkey officially broke diplomatic relations with Japan, and espionage activities from that country were severely restricted. On 4 January, Japanese Ambassador Kurihara in Ankara reported to Tokyo that Turkish Foreign Minister Saka had that morning given him an explanation of Turkey's break. According to Kurihara, Saka stated: 'On 28 December I received a memorandum from the British and American Ambassadors demanding that we break off diplomatic and commercial relations with Japan. In the position in which you know Turkey to be, we were forced to consent.'[12]

The following day Kurihara dispatched a supplementary report on the same interview he had had with Saka, stating:

> Saka urged us to understand that the relations between the two countries have, so to speak, assumed the form of a temporary suspension, in view of the increasing complications of internal relations. Considering Turkey's situation, I feel that this is a frank statement of her awkward position.
>
> Needless to say, however, I feel that the recent events in Turkey have been brought on by my own unwise negligence, and I am utterly abject.[13]

Kurihara also reported that 'on the basis of reciprocity', the Turks were willing to give his staff freedom of movement and the privilege of sending messages in code until their departure from the country. The departure was scheduled for 10 January, but Kurihara managed to obtain firstly a week's postponement, and then a postponement of several months.

By now, plans were advancing for the reassignment of Japanese spies acting as news correspondents in Europe. As we have noted, the spies were to be sent to both Sweden and Switzerland. As of 1 December 1944 there were fifteen agents acting as correspondents based in Berlin, some of whom had previously been working in Portugal and Turkey.

On 4 January, Japanese Foreign Minister Shigemitsu told Minister Kase in Berne to proceed with the plan to increase the number of spies in these countries, but to proceed with the utmost caution. Kase had advised Shigemitsu on 1 December that he was trying to obtain entry visas for a number of 'correspondents' attached to *Domei*, *Asahi*, *Nichinichi* and *Yomiuri* newspapers and news agencies. In a 2 December radio-telephone conversation with Tokyo – monitored by US listening posts – a Japanese spy in Berlin stated that he had recently accepted a position with *Yomiuri*, and that he and another *Yomiuri* correspondent in Germany were to be transferred almost immediately to Switzerland.

In reply to the information supplied by Minister Kase, Japanese Foreign Minister Shigemitsu stated:

We should not give the impression that our 'correspondents' are making a mass exodus to Switzerland, since that would displease the Germans and the Swiss and provide material for enemy propaganda. However since Switzerland may become an important base for our intelligence activities, I think it would be advisable, if possible, to have one or two of our European 'correspondents' go there.[14]

'M' AND 'I' INTELLIGENCE REPORTS

The Portuguese office was still functioning at this time as a central gathering depot for espionage work, despite the enormous Allied pressure being brought to bear on the Portuguese government to have the Japanese Legation closed and its few remaining diplomats and agents expelled. One of the types of intelligence being channelled through Minister Morishima at Lisbon was called 'M' Intelligence, and was allegedly based upon information supplied by an informant in Lisbon who claimed to be operating at least two separate espionage nets working principally for the Japanese. The 'M' reports were certainly diversified and covered a large area, including the Soviet Union, although, according to specialists at G2, many of these reports were inaccurate, often '... fantastically so'.[15]

Another coded Japanese intelligence source termed 'I' Intelligence, was still flowing through the beleaguered Japanese Legation at Ankara. On 13 January 1945, Minister Kurihara in Ankara forwarded a message to both Foreign Minister Shigemitsu in Tokyo and to Suma in Madrid. The message stated:

I believe it is important for us in our prosecution of the war to be fully informed of political developments between Britain, the United States and the Soviet Union, as seen from this part of the world – and particularly as evaluated by Turkish government circles. Accordingly I have introduced the person connected with 'I' intelligence to Spanish Minister Rojas here, and have arranged that in the future intelligence shall be communicated through him to the Spanish Foreign Office in Madrid which will pass it on to Minister Suma.[16]

Three days later Kurihara told Suma: 'We have been able to bring this about chiefly because the Turkish government – bearing relations with the Soviet government in mind – is anxious to maintain an unofficial link with Japan and Germany through Spain.'[17]

Kurihara also advised Suma that the necessary funds for the

operation were to be provided jointly by Germany and Japan, and that the reports received by Suma – which Kurihara said would arrive two or three times each month – should be forwarded without delay not only to the Foreign Office in Tokyo, but also to Ambassador Oshima in Berlin.

On the 19 January, Kurihara reported to Tokyo that according to word received from the Spanish government (through Minister Rojas), the Spaniards had agreed to pass the reports on to Suma, providing they were not concerned with military matters.

The accuracy of the 'I' reports is difficult to assess. While some of the reports were certainly factual and informative, many of them consisted of little more than speculative comments on political activities, especially in the international sphere. They frequently displayed a hostile attitude towards Russia, and reiterated the theme that serious disagreements existed between Russia and England and England and the United States which could have had far-reaching effects on Turkey's international position. In one specific case, the 'I' reports gave the Japanese misleading information – either deliberately, as misinformation, or simply through ignorance. On the other hand, US intelligence analysts stated that the 'I' reports seemed to reflect the views of the Turkish government, in so far as could be ascertained from other diplomatic and intelligence sources.

It was clear, however, that Kurihara himself had considerable confidence in the 'I' agent. In his 16 January message to Suma, Kurihara stated that the 'I' agent was:

> ... thoroughly conversant with all intelligence obtained by Turkish government agencies and that examination of his reports shows that he has given us not only general estimates formed in government quarters, but also intelligence relating to the secret relations between Anglo-Americans and the Soviets, and that he had done it promptly and accurately.[18]

The Japanese radio traffic coming out of Ankara indicated that 'I' was an unnamed employee of the Turkish Secret Police. Before the Turco-German break in diplomatic relations he had been one of the key secret agents attached to the German Embassy in Ankara – actually the head of German espionage in Turkey. When the Turco-German break occurred, Kurihara, at the request of the Germans, took over various German intelligence activities, including the 'I' arrangement, and the Germans transferred to the Japanese Embassy about 80,000 Turkish pounds (US$64,000) for, 'allowances for contact men'. Since that time, Kurihara had used Japanese diplomatic channels to keep in touch with the Germans, and had sent messages to, and received replies from, SS Oberführer Schellenberg, the head of the military and political intelligence sections of the RSHA, and other intelligence chiefs in Germany. On 4 January, 1945, in anticipation of a Turco-Japanese break in diplomatic relations, Kurihara paid over to 'I' the entire balance (15,000 Turkish pounds) remaining from the original fund the Germans had left for 'contact men'. 'I', it seems had a great hunger for money. Despite the large payment from Kurihara, one of the first messages received from 'I' after the Turco/Japanese break, was transmitted to Oberführer Schellenberg in Berlin on 5 January which read: 'I shall continue to observe developments as convenient. The financial situation is precarious. Please replenish my account with the Societe de Banque Suisse Geneva. Account number ND 90030.'[19]

THE FAR EAST

At this time too, Minister Morishima in Lisbon was urging his government to consider a withdrawal of Japanese troops from Portuguese Timor. Ever since the original invasion of Timor, the question of the occupation had been a political and diplomatic nightmare for Morishima, and on several occasions the Portuguese government had threatened a break in diplomatic relations unless Japanese troops were withdrawn and the occupation ended. Despite Morishima's continued pleadings to the Japanese Foreign Office, there seemed to be no softening in Japanese attitude towards the question. The Japanese Foreign Minister on several occasions stated that under no circumstances would troops be withdrawn, but that the Japanese would do everything else possible to avoid a break in diplomatic relations.

On 24 January, facing a rising wave of Portuguese opposition, and citing the importance of continued intelligence gathering, Morishima tried once more, stating that while he realized that the Timor problem was then in abeyance, both he and his Military Attaché believed that the time had come for a withdrawal of Japanese troops. He stated:

> If Japanese troops remain on Timor, America might conceivably use that fact as a pretext for demanding that Portugal turn over Macao for use as a base. Moreover Portugal – in order to improve her 'moral position' may even raise the question of Macao herself. Lisbon is a valuable centre for obtaining intelligence, particularly about the enemy's movements of troops in the Far East, and a

rupture in relations between Japan and Portugal should therefore be avoided. By giving in on Timor, Japan might even be able to improve their present intelligence set-up.[20]

The Japanese Foreign Office considered Morishima's request with care before replying on 18 February that, if the need should arise, they would consider the possibility of allowing Portuguese troops to be dispatched to Borneo, but that Japan would not commit herself to the withdrawal of its own troops.[21]

In Madrid, Suma too was fighting for his diplomatic life. As General MacArthur's troops pushed the Japanese in the Philippines higher into the dense interior of Luzon, and as the Puppet Philippines government, under President Laurel, was forced to abandon Manila, the Spanish promised to immediately recognize the legitimacy of President Osmena's government – the government which was to be installed under temporary American military control after the capture of the Philippines. This move was considered in Japan to be a serious rift in Japanese-Spanish relations, and in Madrid, Suma was urging that the Japanese not be incautious in the event of a Spanish recognition of Osmena's government. He asked them, '... not to be hasty', and urged them to, '... tolerate the intolerable' and, '... overlook the matter entirely'.

Suma stated with infinite diplomacy:

> In any case, if America and Britain are successful in getting Spain to recognize the Osmena government, their next step will certainly be to demand emphatically that Spain relinquish her diplomatic representation of our interests. It may therefore be necessary to consider in advance the problem of the future protection of our interests.[22]

As the Allies advanced on Berlin, the Japanese diplomats in that city were taking whatever precautions were necessary. On 2 February, the Japanese Military Attaché advised Tokyo that he had begun, on his own authority, to make certain prearranged security measures, including the burning of some of the top-secret cryptographic materials in anticipation of the possible fall of Berlin. At the same time, Ambassador Oshima advised that on 1 February, all Japanese nationals (mainly officials and their families formerly stationed in France and Italy), living in Brueckenberg, 100 miles west of Breslau, had been evacuated to Neuruppin, 53 miles northwest of Berlin, where, in October 1944, Oshima had rented a castle.[23] As the Allied bombardments of major cities such as Berlin and Hamburg continued, so conditions and facilities diminished. By 7 February, the Germans were arranging to move part of their short-wave broadcasting facilities from Koenigswusterhausen, 15 miles southwest of Berlin, and had informed Ambassador Oshima that Japanese-sponsored propaganda broadcasts, which had previously been sent out over those facilities, and which were sometimes used for delivering secret messages to agents in the field, would have to be discontinued. On the 9th, a member of Oshima's staff was advised that the move was to be to somewhere in southern Germany, and that there was very little hope of resuming the Japanese broadcasts in view of the restrictions on the use of electric power and retrenchments in installations.

By now too, the Japanese were expecting any day that the Swiss would freeze their special funds, thus effectively neutralizing any further espionage activities. Increases in the amounts of monies paid by the Allies to Japan for the welfare of Allied captives, had supplied Japan with even more reserves of the vital Swiss francs – most of which were deposited in a special account at the Banque Nationale Suisse in Zurich. In anticipation of a general freezing of their assets, the Japanese took several precautionary steps at the beginning of February 1945. Sometime between 8 and 17 February, 2 million Swiss francs were remitted to Stockholm, by this time one of the major centres for Japanese espionage. On 16 February, a secret courier left Zurich for Berlin carrying with him half-a-million Swiss francs. On 17 February, an unsuccessful attempt was made to send one million francs by wire to Portugal. However, on that same day, the Japanese Military Attaché in Berne reported that because of intense American and British pressure, Switzerland would no longer handle Japanese remittances to either Spain or Portugal.

Also on the 17th, Kojiro Kitamura, the Yokohama Specie Bank representative then in Switzerland, withdrew 2 million francs from the relief payments account with the Banque Nationale, and placed the money in the bank's custody under his own name. A 17 February report from Japanese Minister Kase stated that the amount withdrawn by Kitamura had been added to a previously withdrawn amount of 3 million Swiss francs of 'emergency capital'. On the same day, Kitamura advised that: '... as counter-measures against the freezing of deposits,' he intended on the following day to withdraw from the Banque Nationale a balance of 1.5 million francs of diplomatic establishment money, and a, 'considerable amount of the deposits for Army and Navy Attachés and other individuals of the diplomatic establishment.'

That the Japanese would not submit to a restriction on the use of their funds in Switzerland without retaliation, was suggested in a 17 February report from Kitamura to the Japanese Foreign Office in Tokyo which stated:

> In view of the origin of the Japanese funds [US relief payments], and the fact that as of today they are entirely free exchange, if the Anglo-Americans persist in these demands [on Switzerland], it will be possible for Japan to threaten Switzerland and England and America with discontinuance of relief for English and American prisoners in East Asia. [Most of which was not arriving anyway.] I hope that we may make this protest at once through the countries representing our interests. Aside from this, it will also be possible to consider freezing deposits of the Swiss in Japan, refusing to allow remittances, etc.[24]

The problem was further complicated by an earlier request from the Swiss authorities concerning the health and welfare of all Swiss nationals in the Far East, especially those nationals in Borneo. On 14 February, in reply to several queries from Minister Kase and his Military Attaché, Japanese Foreign Minister Shigemitsu replied:

> The reason we have no news about the Swiss nationals is because they are all in the [Japanese] Navy area and there is no [communication] with Navy headquarters in cases of this sort. We have made frequent requests of them but have, annoyingly enough, received no answers at all.[25]

Shigemitsu went on to say, however, that word had finally been received from Borneo and that all the Swiss nationals there were in good health except for two who had died of illness and two others who had been executed in December 1943, '... on the charge of leading an attempted armed revolt against the Japanese Army.'[26] Shigemitsu added that this news would doubtless have: 'an unpleasant effect on the Swiss at a time when there was increasing enemy pressure on Switzerland,' and told Kase not to pass the news on to Swiss authorities 'for the time being'.

In Berlin, Ambassador Oshima was still able to obtain money for general running and espionage expenses, but only just. Allied bombing on 3 February had seriously damaged the National Bank, and two days later the Berlin Branch of the Yokohama Specie bank reported that, 'the business of all banks appears to be almost at a standstill.' On 19 February, Kojiro Kitamura, reporting from Switzerland added:

We do not yet know what emergency measures banks in Germany have taken, but at present there seems to be no particular change (in the conduct of their business). The Reichsbank was heavily damaged by the recent air attacks, but I understand that by using the basement it has been able to reopen for business.

At all the banks recently, great throngs have been making withdrawals, not for the purpose of buying necessities, but apparently in preparation for evacuation. The Reichsbank has announced its decision to issue new paper money without watermark in order to speed up its printing.[27]

By now, Ambassador Oshima was becoming extremely concerned about the increasing difficulty in gathering intelligence information on England and America from Germany. On 13 February he pointed out the danger to Foreign Minister Shigemitsu, and again recommended that as many as possible of his espionage agents be transferred to the neutral countries of Portugal, Spain, Sweden and Switzerland. Oshima warned, however, that any transfers to Sweden and Switzerland would have to be carried out as inconspicuously as possible because of the large number of Japanese officials who had already entered those countries.

On 17 February, Shigemitsu issued instructions that Consul Kuroda in Hamburg,[28] be sent to Sweden, and that four other agents on Oshima's staff be sent to Switzerland. Two of the transfers ordered by Shigemitsu immediately hit snags. On the 21st, Oshima protested that one of the men was invaluable to his work in Germany, and on the 22nd, for some unexplained reason, Shigemitsu postponed Kuroda's move.

Shigemitsu also requested information on the difficulties of travelling from Germany to Portugal and Spain. Two days later Oshima replied that air connections between Berlin and Lisbon were irregular, but that there were still five or six flights a month, so that it would be possible for Japanese agents in Germany to reach posts on the Iberian Peninsula. In fact, at this time the US Military Attaché in Madrid had reported that according to, 'a fairly reliable source', Lufthansa service between Germany and the Iberian Peninsula had been cut to two round trips a month because of the German aviation fuel shortage.

Shortly afterwards, German intelligence authorities shared with Oshima the difficulties they were experiencing in placing their agents into Spain, a difficulty previously unheard of. The RSHA warned Oshima that all espionage agents dispatched to Madrid should be given 'very strict instructions'. Quoting a warning given by the Madrid branch of the RSHA, the Germans continued:

> In some cases recently, Spanish police – and therefore presumably enemy services – were fully informed even before [an agent's] arrival, because mistakes were made in preparation for the journey from Germany. It cannot be sufficiently emphasized that the situation has changed here [in Madrid]. Spanish friends are no longer as willing as before to cloak errors of form with a mantle of love – nor in the main are they in a position to do so. The assistance they give is also conditioned to a very great extent by the degree in their confidence in the ingenuity and intelligence of their German partner on not getting them involved by stupid behaviour.[29]

Meanwhile, in Berne, Minister Kase was laying plans for stepping up his intelligence operations. On 21 February, he submitted to Tokyo an expense budget for the year which was more than twice that for 1944, explaining as he did so that the increase was necessary to offset the diminishing activities of other Japanese intelligence-gathering offices in Europe. Kase explained: 'It is actually possible to send newspaper correspondents of this country, with whom we have contacts, to England, France, Italy and the Balkans, in order to find out about the activities of the enemy and of the Russians.'[30]

AFGHANISTAN

Attitudes towards Japanese intelligence activities were also changing in Afghanistan. In July 1944, the Japanese Legation in Kabul ran into serious difficulties with their espionage activities. At that time the Chief of Political Affairs of the Afghan Foreign Ministry (who had himself supplied the Japanese with intelligence on India) advised the Japanese Chargé that the British and Americans had apparently obtained proof of the Japanese Legation's espionage activities, and he warned the Chargé to show due respect in future for Afghanistan's neutrality. In October that year, Japanese Minister Shichida, based in Kabul, reported to Tokyo that it was becoming increasingly more difficult to gather intelligence since the Afghans had, '... begun to exercise a more rigid surveillance of our activities'.[31] Nevertheless, Shichida still managed to forward to Tokyo a number of espionage reports, most of which concerned Soviet and Iranian affairs, which had been supplied by agents who attributed their information to contacts within the Afghan Foreign Ministry. In February 1945, Shichida proposed to the Foreign Office in Tokyo a detailed budget for espionage activities during the forthcoming fiscal year (starting April 1), which was substantially the same as the estimate which he had submitted for 1944/45. The new budget contemplated espionage activities in India, Iran, Russia, Sinkiang and in Afghanistan itself. However, Shichida's operations quickly received another major set-back. On 8 February, the Afghan Political Affairs Department again seriously upbraided Shichida for the espionage activities of one of Shichida's staff. The Afghan official from the Political Affairs Department stated that news of the agent's activities could probably be prevented from 'leaking out', so that he would not make a formal protest over the issue. However, he suggested that it might be a good idea to send the agent back to Japan. Shichida was told that a 'certain refugee' from Uzbek in Turkestan had confessed to the Afghan secret police that, among other things, the Japanese espionage agent in question had used him as an intermediary for sending spies into India, and had tried to find out the contents of reports sent in by the Afghan Military Mission in India and by the Afghan Ambassador in Moscow.

In advising Tokyo of the affair, Shichida noted that the Afghan government had, '... become more cautious and vigilant than ever', and that it had become, 'increasingly difficult to keep in touch with our spies ... and to obtain information from India.' He recommended that the blown agent be recalled in order to avoid adding to the 'many circumstances which might serve as a pretext for breaking relations.'

On 17 February, Foreign Minister Shigemitsu in Tokyo directed Shichida to have the disgraced agent leave Kabul as soon as possible, adding that, '... in spite of your clever handling of matters, I regret to say that as the war develops the attitude of all the petty little neutral countries towards us grows more hostile.'[32] On 19 February, the Afghan Political Affairs Chief expressed to Shichida his satisfaction that the agent was being recalled to Tokyo, and asked the Minister in the future to keep a close check on the activities of his staff members to, '... see to it that they are as circumspect as possible in their conduct.'[33] Shichida concluded from this that the Afghan authorities would not expose any facts about their subversive activities unless it again became an embarrassment to them.

DETERIORATING SPANISH/JAPANESE RELATIONS

In Madrid, Suma was facing another test of his diplomatic skills. News of the atrocities which had been carried out in Manila – primarily by members of the Japanese Navy against Filipinos and Spanish nationals – had been released in the Spanish press. As the American forces had stormed the besieged city, the Japanese had turned on the civilians, particularly in the old Spanish citadel of Intramuros, and thousands had been brutally butchered. This atrocity caused an outbreak of anti-Japanese feeling when details were released in the Spanish press. Indeed, press coverage of the events was fully sanctioned by the Spanish government as a calculated way of deliberately deteriorating Spanish-Japanese diplomatic relations. Shortly afterwards, the Spanish government took the unprecedented step of deciding to stop representing Japanese interests in the United States and elsewhere in protest over the atrocities.

On 23 March, after talking with Spanish Foreign Minister Lequerica earlier in the day, Suma suggested to Tokyo that, 'by consenting at once to a certain amount of indemnity, we can save face for the Spanish government and prevent the situation from becoming any worse.'[34] Suma added that it might then be possible 'to carry on conversations looking towards a resumption of the protection of our interests.'[35]

In a report of 25 March, Suma's Military Attaché stated that although Spanish General Staff members were waiting for an official report from Japan on the atrocities, they did not consider that a critical diplomatic situation was then imminent. The attaché concluded that while the public was being stirred up by the press campaign, '... final steps are not likely to be taken soon.'[36]

On 25 March, Japanese Foreign Minister Shigemitsu cautioned Suma: '... in view of the deterioration of Japanese-Spanish relations', to be particularly careful not to allow Japan's intelligence-gathering activities to be used against her. Two days previously, on 23 March, the head of the Political Affairs Bureau of the German Foreign Office had said to Ambassador Oshima in Berlin:

> The Spanish press campaign against Japan is part of Franco's flirtation with the United States, and Franco doubtless intends to decide on what further measures to take towards Japan after he has observed the American reaction to the propaganda. I think it

now impossible that Franco will break off relations with Japan, but I do not think he will do anything like entering the war against her.[37]

A few days prior to this, an agent of the Madrid branch of the RSHA Military Section had advised Berlin that, with the arrival of US Ambassador Armour in Spain, there were increasing signs from various quarters that Allied pressure, '... is now beginning on a larger scale'. The agent went on to state:

Serious Spanish measures [against the Axis] must be expected in the first three weeks of April. The pressure will probably not be restricted any longer to individual questions such as the expulsion of agents, etc., but will be directed against [Axis] influence in all sectors with the objective of a break in relations. The present incident with Japan [the Manila atrocities] is fundamental in this connection, concessions with regard to Spanish attitude towards Japan will be of little interest to the Spanish public, and therefore easy to obtain ... My personal impression is that an elastic defence – similar to that which has been successfully conducted in the last eight months – will now be most appropriate in all sectors for maintaining the [Axis] position here as far as possible.[38]

On 24 March, Suma proposed that he submit to the Spanish authorities, as a communication from the Japanese government, a statement to the effect that although the reports of the atrocities were 'baseless propaganda', if there were indeed any Spanish nationals who had been harmed during the violent fighting between Japanese and American forces in Manila, '... that fact is very greatly regretted in view of the friendly relations between Japan and Spain.'[39] Suma went on to state that if any of those sufferers was in need of financial relief, the Japanese government was prepared to offer appropriate compensation and: '... it is of course desirable that with this in view, Japanese-Spanish relations should be restored to their previous status and that Spanish representation of Japanese interests be continued.'[40]

On 28 March Japanese Foreign Minister Shigemitsu replied that he considered Suma's suggestion to be a good one, but that in order to avoid having third countries making similar claims, it would be better for Suma merely to, 'discuss the matter informally with Spanish Foreign Minister Lequerica'. Shigemitsu told Suma to bear in mind that if many of the estimated 2,000 Spaniards in Manila were to make claims of any size, Japan's budgetary and exchange difficulties would be extremely complicated, so that grants would have to be small and restricted to persons actually in need. But it seemed that diplomacy had already begun to work its calming magic. Soon afterwards, Suma's Military Attaché, quoting, 'a man close to Franco' stated that Franco had modified his original intention to break relations with Japan or 'even to declare war,' and that the 'problem can be solved by a Japanese reply providing full material and psychological compensation enabling Spain to save diplomatic face.'[41]

On 28 March Foreign Minister Shigemitsu hedged his bet over Spanish-Japanese relations by instructing Ambassador Oshima in Berlin to seek German help in overcoming the crisis. The German authorities immediately complied and instructed Chargé von Bibra in Madrid to intervene with the Spanish government. Suma later reported that von Bibra, after consulting with him on 2 April, saw Foreign Minister Lequerica the next day and told him that '... the German government earnestly hoped for an amicable settlement of the Philippines affair.' According to what von Bibra later told Suma, Lequerica replied that he too hoped '... the affair would not impair relations between Japan and Spain,' and promised that he would continue his, 'endeavours to find a solution.'[42]

On 4 April, the US Secretary of State brought the big guns to bear in an effort to curb Axis espionage emanating from Spain. He advised his representatives in London, Madrid and Stockholm that he was ready to authorize an immediate diplomatic approach in Madrid in an effort to have the Spanish funds of German and Japanese assets frozen. But rumours of this impending financial crisis had been circulating through Axis circles for a while. On 12 March, the pay office of the Madrid Branch of the RSHA Military Section advised Berlin that according to, 'an increasingly persistent rumour', German (and Japanese) bank credits were shortly to be blocked in Spain, and that the German Overseas Bank (the Banco Alleman Transatlantico – the Madrid Branch of the Deutsche Ueberseeische Bank of Berlin), was recommending that its German clients withdraw their money.

In a message of 23 March, the German Embassy in Madrid instructed their Consulate in Santa Isabela (in Fernando Po), to withdraw official funds from the local banks because of the impending freeze. The embassy added that the information should be passed onto German nationals on a confidential basis, in order that 'harmful political effects do not occur.'

On 5 April an official of the Madrid Branch of the RSHA reported that '... three months salary reserve for every member of the local organization had been deposited with responsible group leaders. The next day the branch advised Berlin that

300,000 pesetas had been, '... deposited for the most part with Spanish secret police for security reasons.' Also on the 6th, Chargé von Bibra sent a very urgent report to Berlin stating: 'Signs are visible to me which do not make it appear that the repeated reports of Spanish plans to introduce measures placing limitations on the right of disposal over [Axis] assets, will turn out to be true.' Von Bibra stated that his source of information was Senor Carceller, the Spanish Minister for Industry and Commerce.[43]

AGENTS IN FINLAND

Meanwhile, Major-General Onodera, the Japanese Military Attaché in Stockholm, was pressing ahead with plans to establish a comprehensive espionage net to gather information about Russia, using Finns and Estonians, and also through an ambitious project utilizing anti-Soviet activities in Finland. In a 25 March report the Stockholm branch of the RSHA passed on to Berlin information said to have been obtained two days previously by Onodera from a Finnish colonel:

A Finnish resistance movement has been founded on cycles [*sic*] of the Finnish Army. It is to be headed by the present Chief of the Finnish Army General Staff [as of 26 February, 1945, this post was occupied by Lieutenant-General Aksel F. Airo], and will comprise 40 guerrilla battalions. In each local militia district there is one battalion and four specialist battalions. These illegal formations are abundantly equipped with light and medium weapons.[44]

In a separate message, sent the same day, the RSHA Stockholm branch advised: 'Major-General Onodera was engaged in a programme of trying to gather intelligence on Russia through Finns and Estonians.'[45]

One agent, presumably working with the Finnish militia and reporting through Onodera, had developed a spy network which included highly trained radio-equipped agents in Finland. The agent was attempting to extend his spy ring's activities to the Leningrad area and also into 'inner Russia'. The RSHA was hoping to arrange through Onodera for radio communication between the Finnish spy net and the RSHA in Berlin, via the Japanese. Two days later, Berlin answered the second report stating that while it was, in principle, ready to give all possible support and assistance to the Finnish network, more detailed information on the project, especially whether or not there would be collaboration with Sweden, was needed before a decision could be reached.

GERMAN COLLAPSE

By this time the war in Europe was reaching its bloody climax – conditions in Germany were eloquently described by Japanese Consul Kuroda, who sent a detailed report on what he had witnessed to Tokyo. Kuroda stated:

> As a result of the intense air attacks and machine-gunning, refugees are pouring into the streets and fields. The food situation is deteriorating and there is a serious lack of the necessities of life. The people are indeed in dire distress. Since the collapse of the Western Front, the war can hardly be called war, but is rather, I regret to say, a vast and one-sided display of destruction and bloodshed by the enemy. Accustomed to wishful thinking, and neither attempting nor wanting to face facts, the German people now find themselves up against the worst. In their bewilderment, they are filling the air with their murmurings.
>
> Enemy columns are now approaching Bremen, and since Bremen and Hamburg are linked by a super-highway, it may be assumed that the enemy will reach Hamburg a few days after completing the occupation of Bremen.
>
> Only a few days stand between ourselves and our fate.[46]

By now, certain diplomats and espionage agents were making plans to escape the coming Allied fury of war. Since early September 1944 – three months after the Allied landings at Normandy – the Japanese Navy Ministry in Berlin had been contemplating a shift of key personnel from Germany to neutral countries in the event of a German collapse. However, one such move involving a naval captain to Sweden, in March 1945, almost immediately ran into seemingly insurmountable difficulties. Early that month, Vice-Admiral Abe, Japan's representative on the Tripartite Commission in Berlin and Japan's ranking naval officer in Europe, recommended that Captain Ogi, of the Berlin office, be appointed Naval Attaché in Sweden (the existing Naval Attaché was merely to remain as an 'adviser'). Admiral Abe pointed out to his superiors in Tokyo that: '... the position occupied by Sweden will be extremely important in the future from the stand-point of intelligence ...'[47] Tokyo duly made the appointment on 1 April and twelve days later Ogi left for Copenhagen to await a Swedish visa.

The following day, however, 14 April, Japanese Minister

Okamoto in Sweden reported that the Swedes had turned down the request for Ogi's visa, because they had: '... decided not to permit any further increase in our staff.' (The Swedes by now were, of course, well aware that the Japanese were filling the embassies, legations and consulates of neutral countries with espionage agents and spy nets). On the 16th, Minister Okamoto, fearing diplomatic upheavals, recommended to Tokyo that the matter should not be pushed since it was important not to provide the Allies with a pretext for forcing Sweden to break relations with Japan. Okamoto observed that the affair was part of an overall secret plan of escape from Germany to Sweden for ten or more Japanese officials, and that Ogi's appointment to Stockholm was an integral part of this plan. Okamoto's Military Attaché, Major-General Onodera, was allegedly in on the escape plan and, according to rumours, this group (Abe, Onodera, etc.), were going to attempt future peace contacts in Sweden. However fantastic this may have seemed, almost immediately, Minister Okamoto in Stockholm received a message from the Japanese Foreign Minister Togo (who by now had replaced Shigemitsu during another cabinet reshuffle), instructing him to take up the Ogi matter with the Swedish authorities '... in view of Sweden's extreme importance in the international situation.'[48] In accordance with that order, on the 17th, Okamoto went to see the Swedish Vice-Minister of Foreign Affairs. According to Okamoto's later report, the Vice-Minister explained that the Americans had been persistently requesting a reduction in the number of Japanese diplomats in Stockholm, and that Sweden had had to agree not to allow any increase. However, Okamoto managed to extract a promise from the Swedish Vice-Minister that the decision in Ogi's case would be reconsidered. He later assured Tokyo that he was going to do, '... his very utmost to bring about a solution by hook or by crook.'[49] In a message of the 17th to the Japanese Embassy Berlin, Okamoto described another part of his conversation with the Swedish Vice Minister, stating:

> I sounded out the Vice-Minister as to whether there was any way for the Japanese in Germany to take refuge in Sweden. He revealed that visas would not be provided for them, but that since there was no way to deport Japanese who might come by plane, small boat, etc., it was planned [merely] to intern them.[50]

Despite this information, the Japanese Foreign Ministry continued to make strong representations to Sweden in efforts to have the Japanese admitted. By 5 May, Okamoto had advised

Tokyo that on the 3rd of that month, the Swedish Foreign Ministry still refused to accept either Ogi or Admiral Abe and the ten other Japanese diplomatic staff. However, soon afterwards, (5 May) the entire group of twelve men arrived at Malmo – a Swedish port opposite Copenhagen – aboard a German Navy minesweeper. The men were detained but not interned, as were eight Japanese Navy officers – all of whom were believed to have been involved in various forms of espionage work – and who had arrived the day before at Ystad, in southern Sweden.[51] Abe was later allowed to communicate with Tokyo and stated, 'In view of the fact that this country's treatment has been generous ... until I advise you, please consider that my authority and duties of Chief Naval Officer in Europe remain the same for the present.'[52] In fact, Vice Admiral Abe and Military Attaché Onodera were later involved in covert moves to establish unofficial peace negotiations between Japan and the Allies. They used as their intermediary a man named Eric Erickson, a former Swedish oil businessman who had completed some espionage work for the Allies, obtaining valuable details of German oil production.

THE NOOSE TIGHTENS

At 10 p.m. on 21 April, Japanese Councillor Kawahara in Berlin filed an urgent message to Tokyo:

> This morning the Under Secretary of Foreign Affairs [von Steengracht] and the head of the Political section [Henke] left Berlin. Although the German High Command and Foreign Minister von Ribbentrop are still here, I think they also will leave sometime today or tomorrow. The battle line is very near and shells have already begun to fall within the city, so I have decided to destroy all my cryptographic materials.[53]

By 24 April, the world in Berlin was grinding to a halt and Japanese diplomats were already beginning to disassociate themselves from the Nazis – especially so because of the news of atrocities which was now sweeping the world as the dreadful death camps were one by one liberated. On 24 April, in the light of persistent rumours that Hitler and many of his top staff would attempt to escape Berlin and fly directly to Tokyo, via the North Pole and Bering Straits, aboard a specially modified JU 290 aircraft, Japanese Minister Kase, in Berne, forwarded an urgent message to the Japanese Foreign Office in Tokyo:

In view of the fact that as the collapse of Germany draws near, the enemy has begun a ferocious atrocity campaign against Nazi racial policy and the like, any impression that Japan is following a policy of identity with the Nazis to the bitter end should be avoided so far as possible. From that point of view, even this sort of rumour may give one cause for anxiety on behalf of the [Japanese] Empire.[54]

On 27 April, Japanese Minister Kase in Berne forwarded to Tokyo an account of a conversation which had recently taken place between Kojiro Kitamura, the Yokohama Specie Bank representative then in Switzerland and three officials of the Banque Nationale Suisse, the president of the bank (Ernst Weber), the vice president, and the bank's general manager. According to the account written by Kitamura, the Swiss officials observed that Germany was, 'standing on the edge of a miserable end such as has not been seen in all history'. The bank officials reiterated the stand which Switzerland had made over the possibility of freezing Japanese funds and urged Kitamura do his best to make known to Tokyo how the Swiss felt about the future prospects of Japan, should Japan consider emulating Germany and fighting to the bitter end.

Weber said:

It is plain that Japan will not be able to fight the whole world after Nazi Germany goes down. If Japan exhausts herself to the point of meeting such an end as Germany's, her recovery will be almost impossible and her very existence as a nation and people will be endangered. Taking a long-term point of view, Japan should plan towards bringing about peace.[55]

Kase later stated:

According to a person who is well informed about US affairs, the impression of experts is that the new President[56] is anxious at this important moment not to impair his position by taking a false step, but the Secretary of State [Cordell Hull], since he must sooner or later retire from office, wants to have the honour and glory of finishing the war with Japan while he is in office. The person in question, therefore, wonders whether it would not be good policy on Japan's part to take this opportunity of approaching the Americans.[57]

By now, Ambassador Oshima had completely abandoned the devastated Berlin and moved his embassy staff to Badgastein. On 27 April, he reported to Tokyo:

When we left Berlin, it was our intention to accompany the

German government for, as I had indicated to you, I had assumed that the German government had intended to retire to southern Germany ... however as might have been expected from the character of the Führer, he decided to show his people the way, and would not tolerate the idea of leaving Berlin. As a result, the other top leaders have also remained in Berlin, and it now appears likely that they will avail themselves of this opportunity to die the death of heroes at the front. It is quite probable that they have already made provision for the continuation of the Nazi regime in the event that they are killed when Berlin falls. However I must confess that at the present time it is difficult to foresee the future course of events throughout Germany.[58]

Oshima's future at this time, and also that of his staff and agents was certainly under a menacing cloud. His report to Tokyo went on to state that he had not decided what to do himself, but that it seemed to him the only feasible plan appeared to be to 'escape to Russian-occupied territory.' He added that he was, '... carefully studying the possible treatment we might receive after being taken into custody by the enemy.'[59]

On 27 April, Great Britain and the United States refused the proposed armistice delivered by Count Bernadotte from Himmler. The following day in Italy, Mussolini and his mistress Clara Petacci were captured near the Swiss border and executed by partisans. On 30 April, Hitler married Eva Braun and committed suicide with her. Shortly afterwards, the Russians overran the Reichstag buildings. The end of the European war had arrived, but Japanese endeavours, especially espionage endeavours, were to continue, where possible, unabated.

ESPIONAGE AGAINST RUSSIA

At this time came the first news of another Japanese espionage mission against their old enemy, the Russians. In August 1944, the Japanese fishing vessel *Kosei Maru* (about 30 gross registered tons), with a crew of eleven men, had been seized by the Russians some distance northeast of the mouth of the Tumen River, on the Korean Siberian border southeast of Vladivostok. The Japanese had immediately demanded the release of the vessel and crew, insisting that she was a simple fishing craft and had not violated Russian territorial waters. In February 1945, however, Japanese Foreign Minister Shigemitsu secretly advised Japanese Ambassador Sato in Moscow that the *Kosei Maru* had actually been operating under a navy charter at the time, and had been engaged in searching for 'Russian floating mines'. After the seizure, the Russians had discovered secret data and unusual sea charts (indicating defence installations, etc.) on board the vessel, which clearly indicated that the *Kosei Maru* was not a simple fishing smack, but a fully fledged spy boat. What happened immediately after the boat's seizure is not clear, the skipper either committed suicide, or was killed 'offering resistance'. The mate, a man named Maeda, after receiving a 'severe interrogation', had been forced to confess both the vessel's connection with the Japanese navy and the nature of its crew's espionage activities.

On 25 April, Ambassador Sato in Moscow advised the Japanese Foreign Office that a Soviet Foreign Commissariat official had handed a note to a member of Sato's staff which stated that a Russian court sitting in camera had sentenced Maeda to ten years forced labour for having, '... deliberately violated Soviet waters for the purpose of collecting spy intelligences.' The Soviets had also decreed that the *Kosei Maru* should be confiscated. According to Sato, the Soviet official brushed aside the objections of the Japanese that Maeda had not received a fair trial, and stated unequivocally that the matter was closed, and that there 'was no room for appeal'.[60]

Indeed, the Soviets were beginning to intensify their methods of countering Japanese espionage and also of finding out more of Japanese espionage methods and secret codes.

Early in May 1945, Japanese Ambassador Sato in Moscow advised Tokyo that the Russians had informed a member of his staff that on 2 May a Japanese agent and diplomatic courier named Kanezaki, while travelling over the Trans-Siberian en route to Moscow, had, '... died as a result of strangulation when he swallowed vomit brought on by an extreme state of alcoholic intoxication.' Sato was also advised that Kanezaki's companion, a courier named Shibayama, had become very upset over Kanezaki's death and so had engaged, 'in such scandalous behaviour as throwing empty saké bottles at the persons in charge of the train and attempting to commit suicide.' Shibayama was therefore, 'seized, bound and put to bed'. Sato asked Tokyo to send him detailed information as to the contents of the sealed diplomatic pouches which the two couriers had been carrying, stating that he wanted to check to see if they had been, 'lost or opened'.

On 6 May Japanese Foreign Minister Togo replied that the couriers had been carrying two official pouches which had contained, among other things, top-secret cryptographic material for Sato's use, and also, 'four secret documents on code instructions for the Japanese Military Attaché in Moscow.'

On 7 May Sato reported that when several members of his staff had boarded the train at Yaroslavl on the 4th, Shibayama had told them, 'in fragmentary outpourings,' that, '... the whole affair was planned by the Russians; the passengers were all Soviet spies, the Russians had regarded the couriers as quite drunk, the Japanese wine had been poisoned and the cigarettes also.'[61] Sato noted however that tests made after the party's arrival in Moscow on 5 May (by the Russians themselves) had revealed no trace of poison in either the saké or cigarettes, and that in the opinion of a member of his staff, Shibayama was, 'not a very admirable man,' and had been, 'suffering from traumatic delusions.'[62]

Also on 7 May, Sato advised Tokyo that investigation of the two pouches carried by the couriers had revealed that they contained seven bundles of diplomatic communications, of which just three did not appear to have been tampered with. There was also evidence that the remaining four bundles – containing three of the four secret documents on code instructions for the Military Attaché – had, in fact, been opened, since, among other things, the outer seal of each bundle appeared to have been pasted up again, the inner seals of three bundles 'appeared to have been replaced by brand new ones', and the pasted opening of the fourth bundle was covered with a small strip of white (Russian made) paper. It was never proved that either of the couriers had been deliberately poisoned, but it seems likely that the operation had been carefully mounted by Soviet counter-intelligence in an effort to discover the Japanese codes. Sato himself did not conform to this theory. On 9 and 10 May he communicated long reports to Tokyo on the subject. His personal conclusions were that Kanezaki had probably died of natural causes, since there was no evidence of poison and that the Soviets would not have attempted such a clumsy method of obtaining information about the Japanese codes and ciphers. However, Sato admitted that it seemed extremely likely that the Soviets now knew the codes. He advised Tokyo: 'In any event, the only safe course is to act as if the pouches had been opened and their contents read.'[63]

Tokyo apparently agreed with Sato on this point, for a few days later Minister Togo instructed Sato to burn all the cryptographic material sent to him in the two pouches. The affair ended with the caution not to let the Soviets realize their suspicions. The Japanese closed the incident by simply sending the Russians a formal statement of regret for the trouble the two couriers had caused, and requesting that Kanezaki's body and personal effects, together with a copy of the autopsy report, should be turned over to the Japanese.

NOTES

1. SRS 1449, 8 October 1944.
2. SRS 1462, 21 October 1944.
3. SRS 1462, *ibid.*
4. SRS 1462, *ibid.*
5. SRS 1462, *ibid.*
6. SRS 1462, *ibid.*
7. SRS 1467, 26 October 1944.
8. SRS 1512, 10 December 1944.
9. SRS 1512, *ibid.*
10. SRS 1535, 2 January 1945.
11. SRS 1537, 4 January 1945.
12. SRS 1543, 10 January 1945.
13. SRS 1543, *ibid.*
14. SRS 1545, 12 January 1945.
15. SRS 1553, 20 January, 1945.
16. SRS 1559, 26 January 1945.
17. SRS 1559, *ibid.*
18. SRS 1559, *ibid.*
19. SRS 1559, *ibid.*
20. SRS 1566, 2 February 1945.
21. SRS 1589, 25 February 1945.
22. SRS 1569, 5 February 1945.
23. SRS 1570, 6 February 1945.
24. SRS 1584, 20 February, 1945.
25. SRS 1588, 24 February 1945.
26. SRS 1588, *ibid.*
27. SRS 1586, 22 February 1945.
28. Also a highly experienced espionage controller and agent.
29. SRS 1602, 10 March 1945.
30. SRS 1594, 2 March 1945.
31. SRS 1603, 11 March 1945.
32. SRS 1603, *ibid.*
33. SRS 1603, *ibid.*
34. SRS 1620, 28 March 1945.
35. SRS 1620, *ibid.*
36. SRS 1620, *ibid.*
37. SRS 1620, *ibid.*
38. SRS 1624, 1 April 1945.
39. SRS 1627, 4 April 1945.
40. SRS 1627, *ibid.*
41. SRS 1627, *ibid.*
42. SRS 1634, 11 April 1945.
43. SRS 1638, 15 April 1945.
44. SRS 1647, 24 April 1945.
45. SRS 1647, *ibid.*
46. SRS 1639, 16 April 1945.
47. SRS 1644, 21 April 1945.
48. SRS 1644, *ibid.*
49. SRS 1644, *ibid.*

50. SRS 1644, *ibid.*
51. SRS 1660, 7 May 1945.
52. SRS 1664, 11 May, 1945.
53. SRS 1646, 23 April 1945.
54. SRS 1645, 22 April 1945.
55. SRS 1654, 1 May 1945.
56. Harry S. Truman. President Roosevelt had died on 12 April.
57. SRS 1658, 5 May 1945.
58. SRS 1655, 2 May 1945.
59. SRS 1655, *ibid.*
60. SRS 1657, 4 May 1945.
61. SRS 1664, 11 May, 1945.
62. SRS 1664, *ibid.*
63. SRS 1669, 16 May 1945.

7   The Final Stand

Japan was now standing alone against the Allied might. Germany and Italy had fallen and the Allies could concentrate on defeating the final enemy

On 2 May, 1945, Japanese Foreign Minister Togo advised all his diplomats in neutral countries that Japan would recognize the fact of Germany's surrender only when a formal announcement was made. He also took the opportunity to reiterate several of Japan's policies now that they stood alone.

> At a recent Cabinet meeting, we decided on measures to be taken in case Germany surrendered. Our basic policy is designed to control unrest caused by Germany's surrender and to renew the determination of our 100,000,000 people to fight to the end.[1]

In the turmoil of Northern Italy at this time, the Japanese Ambassador to Italy, Shinrokuro Hidaka, was attempting to flee with his staff and his agents before the US authorities could catch up with them. It was believed within Japanese diplomatic circles that Hidaka had been arrested because he had been in possession of a pistol, but this report proved erroneous. On 3 May, Japanese Minister Kase in Berne stated that the previous day he had received a message from Hidaka to the effect that Hidaka had requested permission for a party of twenty-eight Japanese (his staff and agents) to enter Switzerland at Muenster, on the Swiss border, about 100 miles northeast of Milan. However Hidaka had been refused entry by the Swiss frontier authorities.

Kase advised Tokyo that, '... although considerable difficulty is to be anticipated, he was taking the matter up with the Swiss government and military authorities.'[2]

The fall of Germany had also caused even greater fears by the Swiss concerning their continued practice of allowing Japanese diplomats to use large amounts of Swiss francs for what – even the Swiss realized – were largely espionage purposes. The 17 February Swiss decree freezing German assets was not, as the Japanese had feared, applied to their holdings in Switzerland.

However, the Swiss, in compliance with the Allied requests, were continuing to restrict the limits of Japanese remittances from Switzerland to other countries in Europe. Further, as the Japanese fortunes of war waned, and Swiss protests against the treatment of their nationals in the Far East mounted, Japanese representatives in Switzerland became ever more fearful of tighter restrictions on Japanese funds.

Accordingly, the Japanese in Switzerland now began to transform their funds by converting them into cash, gold and government notes. They were also considering plans to make down-payments on long-range purchases from Swiss manufacturers. In addition to this, the Japanese were still threatening that if further restrictions were imposed, they would retaliate by discontinuing relief for Allied internees and prisoners in the Far East. The Japanese were also trying to find ways to remit sizeable amounts of money from Switzerland into Sweden and Russia.

The plan for the transfers to Sweden, approved by Tokyo on 1 May, was to sell an amount of gold worth 5 million Swiss francs to the Swedish branch of the Riksbank in Switzerland, and to obtain the equivalent in Swedish kroner in Stockholm. On 4 May however, the Yokohama Specie Bank representative in Stockholm advised that the Swedes were unwilling to buy the gold in Switzerland, although they had no objection to exchanging kroner for Swiss francs. The Stockholm representative concluded that such a plan would bring no advantage since, '... we will have the same difficulties in paying over to the Swedes the Swiss francs received in return for the gold.'

However the plans to get funds into Russia were progressing more favourably. On 17 April Kojiro Kitamura, the Yokohama Specie Bank representative in Switzerland, advised Tokyo that the Banque Nationale Suisse had been unwilling to remit funds to Russia in view of the poor state of relations between the two countries, but that the bank appeared, 'more or less willing to act as intermediary, changing the Swiss currency into American dollars and ordering payment into the USSR State Bank account in the Federal Reserve Bank of New York.'[3] Kitamura asked for authority to, '... sound out the inclinations of the Americans through the Banque Nationale.'[4] Tokyo immediately favoured this proposal, but was holding up further action until it could be determined whether the Russians would supply roubles at the 'diplomatic rate'. (12 roubles to the dollar instead of the official exchange rate of 3.5 roubles to the dollar.)

On 7 May Spain officially broke off diplomatic relations with Germany, and the German Embassy and consulates were ordered to destroy immediately all their secret files and codes. The following day Berne authorities publicly announced that they had lodged with Japan a strong protest demanding better treatment of Swiss subjects and that, '... steps to meet this situation have already been undertaken and others are under consideration.' The note of protest first demanded, '... immediate and effective improvement in the condition of Swiss nationals in Japan and the areas occupied by Japanese forces.'[5] In particular, the note requested a satisfactory explanation of, and reparations for, the killing by the Japanese Army of twelve Swiss subjects in Manila (during the widespread atrocities which took place as US forces attacked the city), and for the execution of a Swiss priest in the Gilbert Islands in 1942. The Swiss also demanded that the Japanese police should no longer persecute and arrest Swiss nationals without cause, and they expressed 'grave alarm' over the 'third degree tactics' which had been employed against a Swiss subject named Treichler.

Treichler had been the manager of the Yokohama branch of the Zurich firm of Siber Hegner. He was arrested on 6 December, 1944 and charged with espionage. On 17 June Yoshiro Ando, a new and friendly Chief of the Political Affairs Bureau of the Japanese Foreign Office, informed the Swiss Minister in Tokyo (Gorge), that the case of Treichler – who by now had been sentenced to six years imprisonment for the violation of Japan's National Security Law, would be brought directly to the Supreme Court of Appeal, and if found innocent, the Japanese were ready to assist Treichler to secretly leave the country.

One of the steps made by the Swiss in efforts to force Japanese compliance to their demands was to postpone consideration of Japan's request that the Swiss take over from Spain the representation of Japanese interests in the United States and several other countries, namely Canada, Cuba, Panama, Colombia, Venezuela, Salvador, Ecuador, and, of course, Spain itself. Another was to debar from Switzerland the twenty-nine Japanese diplomatic officials – including Ambassador Hidaka, then trying to gain access into Switzerland from Italy – and to consider the eviction of Ambassador Mitani (formerly accredited to the Vichy regime), and, '... other diplomats who have fled here from Germany.'[6]

On 25 May Foreign Minister Togo informed Minister Kase in Berne that the, 'quarters concerned' (presumably the Japanese Army and Navy who were responsible for the atrocities), had agreed that a certain amount of consolation money should be paid to the families of the those killed. Kase was instructed to point out to the Swiss that a, 'fair investigation' of the Swiss charges was difficult at that time, but that Japan was offering the money, 'as a means of pacifying Swiss public opinion and improving Japanese-Swiss relations.'[7] Togo added: 'It goes without saying that in case it should be difficult to satisfy the wishes of the Swiss, you have full discretion as to details of amount and method of payment.'[8]

Japanese funds lodged in just one account of the Banque Nationale at this time amounted to over 50 million Swiss francs – almost all of which had come from US relief payments – a vast sum if it were to be used principally for purposes of espionage, propaganda and subversion, and a fund which, used propitiously, could have wreaked inestimable damage to the Allies. After receiving the message from the Japanese Foreign Office, Kase approached Max Petitpierre, Head of the Swiss Political Department, and was told that a total of 1 million francs would be acceptable compensation for the families of those killed. Kase contacted Tokyo and urged them to accept the figure, pointing out that if they did not appease the Swiss government, they might lose the entire 50 million if it were frozen indefinitely, and all espionage activities would have to be suspended. The terms were immediately accepted.

Meanwhile, in Portugal, Minister Morishima – who had still not appeased the Portuguese government over the Timor question, was making valiant attempts to revive his flagging espionage network in America. On 21 July, as peace manoeuvres were under way in Switzerland, he sent a message to the Japanese Foreign Office:

> We have been trying to arrange for communication with America, and lately, as a result of secret negotiation with ——— [name deleted by US censors], formerly head of a spy organization attached to the OKW and since then concerned in similar work on behalf of the German authorities, we have been trying at his suggestion to revive the spy network which he had established.[9]

According to G2 counter-intelligence experts, the man to whom Morishima was referring was undoubtedly a successful former German agent based in Portugal. He had arrived in Lisbon late in 1940 and according to the US military attachés in Portugal, had been given a diplomatic card by the Portuguese government. He was the controller for several agents in the US, including a former US naval officer who had acted as a spy for the Germans and was now about to be recruited for Japanese espionage. The remainder of Morishima's message gave further details of this naval spy:

> Fortunately radio communication between America and Lisbon is possible, and a number of messages have arrived without hindrance. The parties in America – although it is not clear whether they agree with our proposals – have been told that as soon as their relationship with us is cleared up, we think there will be no difficulty. It has also been arranged that we should receive radio apparatus and codes.
>
> [The controlling agent] has been in contact with us for quite some time past, and is known to the [Lisbon] Legation. His opposite number in America is a former American naval officer with German affiliations. His rank is about that of lieutenant-commander; he took part in the war, was discharged on account of illness, has since been serving as head of an office connected with the Navy Department, is at present living in New York, and appears to have a relative in Berlin who is engaged in trade. He has already furnished fairly reliable information, and has in particular, it seems, played a useful part as a radio contact for German agents in America. Moreover, in a reply to an enquiry from here, he has said that it would be possible to create a contact point on the Pacific Coast.
>
> Hitherto, I have felt that although there was no particular difficulty in obtaining somebody on the spot to do the work, it could be extremely difficult to arrange satisfactory means of communication. Radio bases are fortunately available, and, looking at the matter from the point of view of espionage, I should like – since the suggestion has come originally from us, and in view of the personalities of those concerned – to give the scheme a trial in close cooperation with the service attachés.
>
> The necessary monthly expenditure would be about 200 contos [at official rate approximately US$15,000], an amount which I regret to say I cannot defray out of the funds in hand. If you agree that the scheme should be put into operation, please let me have a remittance by telegraph of 1,200 contos [approximately US$90,000] for six months.
>
> I should be grateful for an early decision, since the matter involves the persons I have mentioned as well as the Legation. The service [Navy and Army] attachés agree [with the foregoing].[10]

But, as tensions mounted, as the Japanese continued to ignore Allied demands for an unconditional surrender, the Japanese were also forced to turn anxious eyes towards Russia. The Soviets believed that now was the most opportune moment to strike at Japan. For many years the Soviets had been restlessly seeking Japanese territories and valuable fishing rights. With the war in Europe concluded, they could now begin to move troops and war equipment east towards Vladivostok. Realizing this, the Japanese began to increase their espionage activities in Soviet Russia. At this time they did not seem to have established a sophisticated network of espionage agents, and relied generally on the observations of couriers and diplomats. For example, Ambassador Sato in Moscow advised Tokyo, in June 1945, that his couriers – all of whom were trained in elementary espionage – had observed 171 troop trains carrying an estimated total of 120,000 troops and various items of military equipment. Two further messages in July reported that two couriers had, during the period 29 June to 6 July, observed a further 202 eastbound military trains while travelling west over the Trans-Siberian from Chita to Moscow. Evidently the Soviets were bringing massive forces into line for a possible invasion. Other courier/agents reported that they had counted these trains carefully. Eighty-eight of them were unidentified, but of the remainder, the couriers counted 2,932 cars carrying troops (a total of 117,280 troops at the normal rate of 40 men to a car), 2,920 motor vehicles, 144 heavy tanks, 126 pursuit planes, 84 anti-tank guns, 81 cannon and 91 anti-aircraft guns. The couriers stated that the artillery units '... had the appearance of being front line units,' and that several of the vehicles were, 'considerably damaged,' suggesting that they had been transferred directly from the Western Front.[11] Such alarming reports now began to flood into Tokyo.

THE POTSDAM ULTIMATUM

After the fall of Berlin, Allied heads of government met in Berlin for the Potsdam Conference, at which a complete and unconditional surrender was demanded from Japan. The Potsdam Declaration was issued on 26 July.

On 30 July, the Japanese flatly rejected the Potsdam ultimatum, stating that it was, '... unworthy of consideration, absurd and presumptuous.' The end was now close. In a carefully worded message to Tokyo, Ambassador Sato in Moscow eloquently stated:

> In the final analysis, we will have to determine our own attitude to the Three Power (Potsdam) Proclamation and then, equipped with some concrete proposal for ending the war, seek the good offices of the Russians... As you say, the days are numbered when we can bring the war to an end before the enemy lands on our mainland, and this causes me to feel very deeply the pressure of time. Much

as I regret to say it, this is the natural conclusion we must reach, now that we have lost mastery of the air and command of the sea. Only two months ago I remember the War Minister stated before a special meeting of the *Diet* [Japanese Parliament] that if the enemy should attempt to invade the mainland, he would be utterly destroyed first on the sea and then on the land at the water's edge. This was evidently a miscalculation, since the past month has clearly demonstrated that there is no longer any ground for statements of this kind. Since we are about to contend with an enemy who has accumulated a great deal of experience in landing operations, and since we have only such meagre material with which to defend ourselves, we cannot avoid the conclusion that in the final analysis is it only a question of time until we will have to surrender after having again made innumerable sacrifices ... I cannot cease hoping that the government and the Military will not neglect this crucial hour and, assuming full responsibility, will arrive at some concrete plan for ending the war.... I therefore implore you to report this to the Throne with all the energy at your command, and I will be truly grateful for your trouble. Furthermore, I also request you to permit my message to be read by the leaders of the Supreme Council for the Direction of the War. In this way I earnestly hope to help stimulate our Empire to reach a final determination.[12]

But it was already far too late, for by now of course the Americans were preparing to drop atomic bombs on some of Japan's key cities and there was no longer any requirement for Japanese espionage. After the destruction of Hiroshima on 6 August the Soviets finally declared war on Japan. The date was 8 August. The following day a second US bomber flew to Kokura – another of Japan's heavy industrial cities – with the intention of dropping the next atom bomb. When the aircrew arrived over the city they found it covered with dense cloud, and under instructions proceeded to Nagasaki which was, of course, obliterated. On 10 August the Japanese broadcast their terms for surrender:

The Japanese government are ready to accept the terms enumerated in the Joint declaration which was issued at Potsdam on July 26, 1945 by the heads of the governments of the United States, Great Britain and China, and later subscribed by the Soviet government, with the understanding that the said declaration does not compromise any demand which prejudices the Prerogatives of His Majesty as a sovereign ruler.[13]

The end had finally arrived. It was an end which had been brought about more by the incredibly dense firebombing of

Tokyo and other major cities rather than, as is popularly believed, the destruction caused by the two atom bombs.

On 12 August, at 4.04 p.m. Tokyo time the radio station at Hsinking, a station often used by the Japanese Embassy for espionage and propaganda broadcasts, sent the following message: 'With this we are shutting down. Keep up the good fight.'[14]

The feelings of the Japanese diplomatic staff at this time could probably be summed up in a moving plain text message Ambassador Sato in Moscow sent to his family in Fukushima:

> We may yield once to force, but what can conquer the strength of spirit? So long as that remains our people is not destroyed. The future may be dark, but let us bind up our wounds, keep back our tears, and face with good cheer the task which comes next: to devote ourselves body and soul to the restoration of our nation.[15]

DESTRUCTION OF RECORDS

At 9.59 p.m. Swiss time on 14 August, Minister Kase in Berne reported to Tokyo that all his files of coded messages, secret documents and accounts – many of which detailed payments to espionage agents through the various diplomatic posts such as Suma's in Madrid and Morishima's in Lisbon, had been destroyed. Kase stated however that, '... for the present' the legation was retaining its cryptographic materials.

At 11.20 p.m. Swiss time on the 15th, Kase advised Tokyo that he had that evening received from the Swiss Foreign Ministry, a note from the American government. The note, as transmitted by Kase, ordered the Japanese government to, 'immediately instruct its diplomatic and consular offices in neutral countries to surrender custody of all property and archives to representatives of Allied powers'.

Fifty minutes later Kase sent word to Tokyo that most of the secret financial records of the former embassy in France had been destroyed during the day, but that the records of the former embassy in Germany were being retained pending receipt of instructions from Tokyo.[16]

At 6.30 p.m. Swiss time on the 16th, the Japanese Foreign Ministry sent to Minister Kase in Berne its reply to the American demand that the Japanese surrender to Allied representatives custody of all diplomatic and consular property and archives in neutral countries. The reply, which Kase was instructed to deliver to the Swiss Foreign Ministry read: 'Inasmuch as this demand is not covered by any of the stipulations of the Potsdam declaration which we have accepted, the Japanese government cannot agree to this demand of the United States government communicated to the Swiss government.'[17] The Japanese Foreign Office also advised Kase that Japan's missions in Sweden, Portugal, Ireland and Afghanistan were being informed of the American request and of the Japanese reply. The Japanese Legation in Spain did not exist at this time. Spain had severed relations with Japan in April 1945. However former Minister Yakichiro Suma and many of his staff – including his intelligence agents – remained in Madrid after the closure of his legation. He managed to maintain some communication with the Japanese Foreign Office through the Swiss Legation in Madrid.

In Stockholm, Japanese Minister Okamoto was adamant that he was not going to hand over to the Allies any of his top secret intelligence files. In a conversation with the Under Secretary of the Swedish Foreign Ministry on the 18th, Okamoto stated that he had no intention of handing over these sensitive files, and that the Americans could not, '... do what they wanted without legal basis'.[18] In concluding his report to Tokyo, Okamoto commented, 'I imagine there will be more demands on this subject from the British and Americans at the time of concluding the armistice agreement or at some other time.'[19]

On the 14 August Switzerland finally froze all Japanese funds then in Swiss accounts. Three days later Sweden did the same. Sensing what was about to happen, Kojiro Kitamura, the Yokohama Specie Bank representative in Switzerland, withdrew 5 million Swiss francs (approximately US$1.125 million) from a safe deposit box of the Banque Nationale Suisse, and sealed the money in a suitcase. He then arranged to have the bag turned over to a friendly Swiss citizen on the faculty of the University of Basle, who, 'as soon as the situation settles down,' was to transfer the money to the legation safe in Berne. Because of the fund freezing order of the Swiss however, Kitamura's attempts made the same day to withdraw other funds from the Banque Nationale and the Banque Federale were unsuccessful.

In Sweden, the Japanese Naval Attaché had managed to convert into cash his total funds of almost 500,000 kroners (approximately US$115,000). On the 17th, Minister Okamoto in Stockholm was arranging to place in the safekeeping of individual members of his staff, one-fifth of the money in the custody of the legation. He indicated to Tokyo his doubt that the remaining four-fifths could be successfully hidden from the Allies. The amount given by Morishima was 1.5 million yen (approximately US$345,000) –

although the money was almost certainly in kroners, which at that time was equal in value to the yen.

It was not clear just what measures the Japanese in Portugal may have been taking to protect their funds, but on the 14th, Tokyo directed Minister Morishima to, 'instruct the Yokohama Specie Bank representative to withdraw deposits in such a way as to avoid irritating the Portuguese.'[20]

What exactly became of the money is not clear. Morishima must have been able to withdraw most or all of it, and to find somewhere where the American authorities could not lay hands on it, for, on 17 August Morishima took issue with the decision of the Japanese Foreign Ministry to reject the American demand for the surrender of all Japanese diplomatic and consular property in neutral countries. Morishima expressed the view that Japan's best course would be 'to either give in to the American demands, or to state that we would like to discuss the question again, after the Supreme Allied Commander arrives in Japan.'[21] Morishima pointed out in support of his position that compliance with the demand would not materially effect his legation since only small sums of money and various furnishings would be found by the Allies, and that rejection of the demand might cause the United States to effect the termination of Japanese diplomatic functions in neutral countries. Morishima was clearly successful in secreting a large amount of his funds for, by the following October, in the face of mounting Portuguese pressure for compensation over murdered Portuguese civilians on Timor, Morishima was able to offer the Portuguese government an immediate payment of 910 contos (about US$68,000) from his available funds.

On 19 August, however, the Japanese Foreign Minister replied that although Japan must carry out promptly the legitimate demands of the Allied powers, '... it is absolutely necessary ... to oppose their unreasonable demands by giving detailed explanations and, by making our position clear, to solicit their reconsideration.'[22]

Meanwhile, Japan's legations in Europe were proceeding with the destruction of their files and accounts. On the 19th, Minister Kase in Berne reported that in compliance with an order from Tokyo he had completed the destruction of his legation's financial archives – previously carried out in part, with the exception of '... records of recent advance payments to Japanese nationals.' Kase also stated that he had destroyed all other financial files in the custody of his legation, namely those of the former Japanese establishments in France, Germany, Belgium, Bulgaria and Austria, and of the Consulate-General in Geneva. (Many of these documents had allegedly contained detailed financial reports concerning the payments made to espionage agents. Had these details fallen into Allied hands, they would have provided a Pandora's Box of information concerning who had spied against the Allies during the war, names of contacts in Allied countries, methods of payment and methods of communications, etc).

On 18 August the Japanese Naval Ministry sent a message to the Japanese Naval Attaché in Stockholm, which was headed 'To all those within the Naval Service'. The message ordered the destruction of all cryptographic materials, 'except those currently in use or to be used in the future,' and all other secret documents classified as 'military most secret or above,' and documents which, 'might prove disadvantageous to Japan's foreign relations if they were to fall in enemy hands.'[23] The Japanese Naval Ministry added that materials then in use should be burned as soon as there was no longer need for them, but that, '... those which it is believed we will have need for in the future, we shall be able to keep in the publications office (presumably of cryptographic materials), in such a way that they do not fall into enemy hands.'[24] The message ended with the order: 'This dispatch is to be burned after it has been received and understood.'

On 25 August, the Yokohama Specie Bank, on instructions from the Japanese Foreign Office, advised its representatives in Switzerland, Sweden and Portugal that, 'in view of the present conditions,' it had been decided that the representatives of the Minister of Finance and of the Yokohama Specie Bank in those three countries should collaborate in collecting economic intelligence.

Representatives of the bank were instructed to emphasize intelligence concerning developments in finance, industry, imports and exports, labour and psychological trends in Great Britain, the United States, Russia and various other European countries. The bank added that the Japanese Foreign Office was particularly interested in the monetary and economic situation in Germany, and any information regarding the economic policies of Japan. Information so gathered was to be transmitted via the *Domei* newsagency.[25] However, Domei overseas broadcasts were shortly afterwards suspended on the orders of General MacArthur.

At this time, information from the diplomatic posts in Berne, Portugal and Sweden was, strangely, still being transmitted in code. On 6 September, the Japanese Foreign Minister sent a message to Minister Kase in Berne, with instructions that it was to be passed on to Sweden and Portugal:

> Since we have received no orders whatever from the Allied Supreme Commander regarding code communication, it will be our policy for the time being to continue to use the remaining cipher machines and code books. We are making preparations so that we can dispose of the cipher machines and code books at any time.
>
> Depending upon the situation at your place, take whatever steps are necessary in accordance with the above. In the event that code communications are suspended, I shall report that fact to you.[26]

By November, when it was almost certain that most of the incriminating evidence was long destroyed – the Japanese Foreign Ministry sent a plain text message to its Minister in Stockholm. The message was also addressed to the Japanese diplomatic posts in Ireland, Portugal and Afghanistan.

> You will without delay turn over to the Allied authorities all the designated property and documents – in their present condition – of Japanese diplomatic and consular offices in the country to which you are accredited. Thereafter, official relations with the government to which you are accredited will cease.
>
> It will be necessary to submit a report to the Allied authorities [presumably in Tokyo] stating that these instructions have been carried out. Therefore will you please send a wire to that effect immediately ...
>
> The recent Allied order [delivered by General MacArthur on 25 October] specifies that officials and personnel will be returned to Japan. Please report as soon as the time for departure is decided.[27]

And so the end finally came. All throughout the war, Japanese espionage activities were largely channelled through the Foreign Office in Tokyo, or, possibly to a lesser extent, through the Army and Navy Ministries. Now all that was over. For four years, vast amounts of secret and not so secret intelligence had been channelled back through these offices. It ended eventually with a simple, blunt and evocative message, broadcast on 2 November 1945 from the Japanese Foreign Office. 'With this wire as the last, we are discontinuing radio communication for a while because of [Allied] radio control.'[28]

FAILURE OF JAPANESE AGENTS IN THE US

It is perhaps ironic that despite the extensive work carried out by

Suma, Morishima, and many of the other Japanese diplomats who acted as spy-masters that not one of their secret agents in the US ever discovered any reference to the atom bomb, the Manhattan Project as it was known. More than 2.5 billion dollars was poured into the project, thousands of people were involved, filing clerks, engineers, secretaries, technicians, designers and scientists. In many instances not even these men knew what they were building, each stage in the bomb's construction was kept carefully segmented, not even Harry S. Truman knew of the project until after he took office on the death of Roosevelt. Yet despite this intense secrecy, there were leads of which any competent intelligence agent should have been aware. Tests were being prepared in Mexico, soldiers knew they would have to face some kind of exhaustive ordeal which involved a secret weapon. The Germans were certainly aware that the Americans and British were collaborating on the manufacture of an atom bomb, and were themselves involved in the race to complete the first one. Intelligence operatives were informed that a project must be underway somewhere – somehow, yet none, (with the exception of Soviet spies Allan Nunn May, Klaus Fuchs, and the husband and wife team Ethel and Julius Rosenberg who were later executed in Sing Sing prison, succeeded in penetrating the remarkable cover of secrecy and misinformation which enshrouded the project.

In this respect and in many others, the agents which Japan managed to infiltrate into the US and other countries were certainly failures. Thanks to the *Magic* Summaries and to the careful structure of British and American counter-intelligence, these operatives were rendered virtually obsolete even before they landed in the countries in which they were to operate. For many of them, the *Magic* Summaries almost certainly saved their lives. For captured espionage agents of foreign countries there was very little chance of survival. Almost every agent ever landed into the United States or Britain was caught and, in most cases, executed. (Other than those who were turned into double agents.) Probably the only agent the British failed to catch was codenamed 'The Druid'. Dropped by parachute near the South Wales city of Swansea, he sent valuable information back to Germany for several years. All other German agents were ill-prepared, poorly trained and easily caught.

AXIS AGENTS IN AUSTRALIA

In Australia, the activities of Axis espionage agents – also often through neutral operatives – received a fair amount of publicity during the war, and the Americans naturally shared much of their intelligence with their Australian allies. As far back as 1936, the Spanish Consul in Australia, Pedro de Ygual, was known to have had pro-Axis sympathies, although the Australian government of the day still endorsed his claim for official diplomatic recognition. The Commonwealth of Australia Investigation Branch, in a top secret 1943 report, stated that Ygual was a close associate of Mexican Consul Carlos Zalapa, a suspected spy, adding that (de Ygual) '... is not a suitable person for appointment to any of His Majesty's Dominions. Another cablegram from the Australian Department of External Affairs enciphered to the British External Affairs Officer in London stated:

10th February, 1943.

SECRET.

Señor Pedro de Ygual made no secret when in Australia that he was a Franco supporter. Letter to this department expressed pro-Franco sympathies. Sun newspaper issued poster on his departure: 'Consul leaves to help Franco'. Considerable press comment aroused by his placing documents in the care of the Italian Consul Commander Vitali, who was subsequently found to be actually engaged in espionage on behalf of the Italian government. De Ygual was close associate of Mexican Consul Carlos Zalapa, who is suspect in some circles of having pro-Axis views. Ramon Mas, former Spanish Consul, was confidentially interviewed and he stated that de Ygual is definitely pro-Axis, but when pressed could not give specific incidents. Information obtained from Australian Legation Washington shows that he was associated in America in 1941 with Ulrich von Der Osten, alias Julio Lopez Lido, a ringleader of German Espionage Agents.[29]

An indication that the US and Australian Intelligence organizations were working closely together can be seen from the following cablegram from the Australian Legation in Washington to the Department of External Affairs in Canberra, dated 24 January 1942.

Most Secret for Chief of Naval Staff from Naval Attaché.

United States Army Intelligence state that they have reliable information that the Axis are taking steps to place in Australia agents of Spanish nationality equipped with short-wave wireless sets. These agents would be on the staffs of Spanish Consulates. It is expected that these agents will attempt to pass through the United States and a close watch is being kept for them here.[30]

The contents of this cable were quickly security-upgraded from 'Secret' to 'Most Secret' and a closer investigation was made of all Spanish diplomatic staff. But details of most Axis espionage systems operating within Australia did not surface until well after the end of the war.

For example, in September 1945, the former Premier of Queensland William Forgan Smith made a statement to the press detailing his government's activities in curbing the activities of Japanese spy rings which had operated within that state. Forgan Smith said:

> It was obvious that the Japanese were going to tremendous pains to secure metals and agricultural products from Queensland, and it was equally obvious that they did not want our metals to make manicure sets. They wanted them to make guns and planes, and they were working in all sorts of underground ways to get them from us, they were thorough, but just not thorough enough.'[31]

Smith revealed that before he left for an official visit to London in 1937 he had formed very definite ideas about the activities of Japanese espionage agents and Japanese subversive commercial infiltration into Queensland. However, he claimed that special disclosures made to him by British counter-intelligence in Singapore had shown him the extent of this infiltration. Cables which he sent from Singapore were responsible for deeper probes, which resulted in a dramatic exposé of Japanese designs. When Smith returned from England, he made further disclosures to State Parliament. He explained that he had in his possession a number of revealing papers, statutory declarations, copies of letters and documents which dealt with the proposal to form a large Japanese company in Queensland. Outwardly the company seemed genuine enough, with Australian shareholders and directors, but it was in fact to be a dummy company to cover for Japanese financiers (straw men). Smith said that on the surface the company intended to engage in the business of mining iron ore, lead, wolfram, copper, tin and, 'all other metals'. He added:

> This company actually applied for leases in Queensland and in consideration of efforts to obtain the leases and do other works, certain persons as a beginning, were to get £20,000. In the

correspondence which I have it is fully disclosed that it was merely a dummy company.[32]

Smith added that, in addition to the establishing of such an industry, the company would also be involved in espionage, and especially in the surveying of coastal regions and defences. 'These interests had been given vital information concerning the depths of water and the geography of the northern reefs. They also had maps on which were indicated suitable landing places for seaplanes and airplanes.'[33] Smith stated that he had placed all this information at the disposal of the Australian Defense Department.

For many years prior to the war, the Japanese had been sending 'experts' to Queensland to map out mining fields. Official files showed that they had been particularly interested in the rich fields at Mount Isa and in the Cloncurry areas. The Japanese had formulated a plan by which they hoped to send raw metals to Normington and thence to Japan. They were also especially interested in Iron Island, a rich deposit in Broad Sound, approximately 100 miles from Rockhampton. Before they were arrested by Australian authorities, several Japanese had actually been in possession of the island. They had an established camp, a sophisticated method of radio communications and an excellent library, which gave the authorities a clue to Japanese special interests in Australia. There were textbooks on mining fields, statistics of mine outputs, stock-exchange reports and financial journals dealing with mining and pastoral companies. There were books on Australian travel, railway guides, and dozens of maps, including a complete set of charts of the Great Barrier Reef. Other maps had markings along flat coastal plains which could have been used for the landing of Japanese aircraft. The Japanese agents had a comprehensive portfolio of photographs dealing with Queensland scenes and industry. They were also keenly interested in Queensland sheep and cattle, they had the pedigrees of many of the prize animals from the stud farms to which they belonged. There were reports of industrial disputes, the morale of the people, and lists of exports.

According to previously secret reports recently released by the Australian Archives, the Commonwealth Investigation Service was fully aware of many more Japanese espionage activities throughout Australia. The documents reveal that intelligence was being bought by Japanese fishermen for just token payments. Head of the Brisbane Investigation Branch, Inspector Robert Wake reported to Canberra:

Undoubtedly there is a strong liaison between a few British inhabitants along the coast, certain of our local fishermen and the Japanese. Mostly there is distinct hostility, but there is some evidence of the exchange of goods and information and the cheapness at which some of these items cam be obtained in fair quantities from Japanese craft is a strong temptation, e.g. silk shirts are 2/6d whisky 2/9d a bottle and so on. There is also some evidence that near Cape Upstart and the Burdekin River and at other places along the coast, this trade was carried out on an organized scale and not limited to the local exchange with fishermen.'[34]

Inspector Wake gave details of many Japanese espionage operations and operatives, including an agent named Umeda who had completed an assignment to the Portland Roads area to ascertain the extent of iron ore deposits but had, 'gathered information far beyond that necessary for his purpose.'[35] The Japanese had agents on the Darling Downs, a rich agricultural centre, where they were particularly interested not only in pastoral produce, but also in the large flocks of locusts which sometimes swarm the region, believing these would be excellent subjects for chemical warfare experiments. They were interested in Toowoomba, Queensland's largest inland city, its industries and military capabilities, they had agents check the feasibility of landing operations on Fraser Island – the world's largest sand island – and only a few hours from Brisbane. They gathered information about the movement of cattle in Northwestern Queensland, with a view to using those statistics to plan for Japanese troop movements after an invasion. They gleaned information concerning the anchorages in the Sir Edward Pellew group of islands in the Gulf of Carpentaria, which would have been an ideal location for landing troops and equipment from Indonesia.[36]

In August 1940, the Special Branch presented a detailed report concerning the methods used by the Japanese, which stated that Chinese men who had been seconded into the Japanese espionage service, could be easily recognizable because they had a secret symbol tattooed in their right armpits. The report also gave details of several occidental people who were collaborating with the Japanese, including two Australian men living at Port McArthur on the western side of the Gulf of Carpentaria who had allegedly prepared secret plans of the harbour and had handed them over to the Japanese.

The extent of Japanese espionage agents in Queensland has never been satisfactorily established, but previously secret documents released in 1982 clearly indicate that the master Japanese spy was a man named Professor Ryonosuke Seita.

Seita was 58, and a highly placed and influential secret agent when he was appointed Professor of Japanese at Brisbane's University of Queensland in 1938. He had been nominated by the Japanese Foreign Office, which, as we have seen, was deeply involved in the organization of Japanese espionage activities abroad. Australian counter-intelligence agents had become suspicious of Seita soon after he arrived with his daughter in the country, because the professor easily and quickly became the nominal leader of the large Japanese community then living in the city. Australian counter-intelligence agents also discovered that Seita was a man of some considerable importance. During a visit to the Japanese Consul-General in Sydney, he reportedly had sufficient authority to give the Consul-General a dressing down over the lax way in which he was allegedly carrying out his duties.

Indeed Seita knew all about diplomatic duties. He had been appointed to Germany in a senior diplomatic post and he spoke fluent German. He was often seen in the company of a known Japanese espionage agent and he worked diligently in distributing pro-Axis propaganda leaflets. He was paid for his espionage work via a Japanese company then operating in Sydney. Amazingly, he was later given the position of translator in the high security Brisbane Censor's Office. At that post he was in a position to read every Japanese communication in and out of the State. Various attempts were made to have Seita removed from his position, but an obstinate and blinded bureaucracy was operating which refused to believe that Seita could have been a security threat.

After the attack on Pearl Harbor and Seita was arrested in the widespread alien swoop which quickly followed. Security agents now searched Seita's belongings. The search revealed a visiting card in the name of Mitsuru Toyama, the much feared head of the Black Dragon Society, a society which, as we have seen, did much to push for Japanese military expansion and the formation of Japanese espionage training establishments. Other documents were able to link Seita with another known Japanese agent, Marcelle Tao Kitazawa. Kitazawa had travelled with Seita to Australia aboard the Japanese ship *Canberra Maru*, and was later interned in New Caledonia under suspicion of being the leading Japanese espionage agent on the island. More than a year after Seita's arrest, a Brisbane security agency issued a secret report which stated: 'It has now been established beyond reasonable doubt that Seita was a Japanese agent, and it has become a matter of urgency to check up on all his contacts.'[37]

An indication of the importance of Seita to the Japanese came some time later when the Japanese Foreign Office, through a Swiss intermediary, requested that Seita be considered for exchange with several Australian internees then being held in Japan. Australian Intelligence recommended that Seita be retained – he had been in Australia for several years and obviously was aware of many details – social, economic and military – which could have proved very useful to the Japanese. Whether by design or mere folly, the intelligence warning was not heeded. Seita and his daughter were both repatriated to Japan in August 1942.

It is also worth noting that the Australian people at this time were generally aware of the activities of the Black Dragon Society and the role it played in the Japanese war effort. During the war years the Australian press published a number of reports concerning the society. In January 1942, for example, the North American News association released details to the Australian press of an investigation which claimed that a file of secret Japanese documents entitled, 'The Three Power Alliance and the American/Japanese War', revealed in detail the alleged Japanese war plan which was to have reached a climax with the simultaneous invasion of the Panama Canal zone, Alaska, California and Washington State. The documents were said to have been obtained clandestinely in 1940 by an anti-Japanese Korean patriot, named Kilsoo Haan, from the possession of a high-ranking officer of the Black Dragon Society. The transfer of documents was alleged to have taken place in a Los Angeles hotel.[38]

Anti spy mania was now reaching new heights in Australia. In February 1942 intensive enquiries ordered by the Federal government revealed that several secret fifth-column radio transmitters were being used, primarily in Queensland, to transmit information of military value to Japan. At this time there was a large population of Italian sugar-cane cutters and shearers working in Queensland, many of them – those with proven Axis sympathies – had been interned at the beginning of the war, yet thousands remained free, and the authorities believed that some of these Italians were responsible for aiding the Japanese espionage nets. The North Queensland Returned Soldiers' League called for the immediate internment of all Italians, and also for the imposition of a mandatory death penalty for anyone caught engaging in espionage activities. Many of their demands were swiftly met. Shortly afterwards, on 13 February, the State and Federal governments rounded up a large number of suspects.

These suspects were mainly living in the Ingham and Innisfail districts of northern Queensland. More than 2,000 aliens were questioned concerning their affiliations and sympathies with pro-Axis and pacifist organizations. The Minister for the Army, F.M. Forde stated at the time that, 'any enemy alien or any other person engaged in subversive activities,' would be interned. In announcing the campaign the Minister stated that all such persons would get, 'short shrift', adding:

> ... the Japanese are obtaining vital information on Australia's security. Hundreds of letters are being received from all parts of the Commonwealth from people who believe that they could assist in tracking down sources of leakages. All suggestions will be carefully examined by military intelligence officers.[39]

The campaign continued. In June 1942 the Toowoomba branch of the Returned Soldiers' State Congress called upon the government to impound all short-wave radio sets in the possession of aliens; to ban the publication of any newspapers or periodicals in the languages of enemy countries; the collection of all firearms in the possession of aliens and the cancellation of fishing boat licences then held by aliens.

Campaigns were formulated to watch for Japanese spies being dropped by parachute, and shore watches were made to check on possible spy landings by enemy submarines. In Brisbane, the state capital, there were several instances of sabotage. According to secret files recently released, the United States Army transport ship *Holbrook* was sabotaged in February 1942, the steering gear was tampered with which almost resulted in the vessel running aground. The scrub which effectively camouflaged the installations of the fort at Cowan Cowan on Moreton Island was deliberately set alight, and intelligence investigators stated that it had definitely been an act of sabotage so that the installation could be easily seen from the sea. Other acts of sabotage included the insertion of large pieces of iron into cane which was waiting to be crushed at the Babinda sugar mill near Cairns, sand in ball bearings at another sugar mill, the disappearance of large quantities of precision tools, fires in warehouses carrying stocks of food for the defence forces, and the attempted sinking of several ships in harbour.[40]

NOTES

1. SRS 1657, 4 May 1945.
2. SRS 1658, 5 May 1945.
3. SRS 1616, 10 May 1945.
4. SRS 1616, *ibid*.
5. SRS 1665, 12 May, 1945.
6. SRS 1665, *ibid*.
7. SRS 1683, 30 May 1945.
8. SRS 1683, *ibid*.
9. SRS 1743, 29 July 1945.
10. SRS 1743, *ibid*.
11. SRS 1748, 3 August 1945.
12. SRS 1750, part two, 5 August 1945.
13. SRS 1755, 10 August 1945.
14. SRS 1757, 12 August 1945.
15. SRS 1761, 16 August 1945.
16. SRS 1761, *ibid*.
17. SRS 1762, part two, 17 August 1945.
18. SRS 1764, 19 August 1945.
19. SRS 1764, *ibid*.
20. SRS 1764, *ibid*.
21. SRS 1765, 20 August 1945.
22. SRS 1765, *ibid*.
23. SRS 1767, 22 August 1945.
24. SRS 1767, *ibid*.
25. SRS 1780, 4 September 1945.
26. SRS 1783, 7 September 1945.
27. SRS 1835, 1 November 1945.
28. SRS 1837, 3 November 1945.
29. Australian Archives, A981, item Consuls. 1911-1942.
30. Australian Archives, *ibid*.
31. *Truth*, 2 September 1945.
32. *Truth*, *ibid*.
33. *Truth*, *ibid*.
34. Australian Archives, Commonwealth Investigations Service. BP 242 1/2, correspondence files, single number with Q prefix, 1924-1954.
35. Australian Archives, *ibid*.
36. Australian Archives, *ibid*.
37. Australian Archives, *ibid*.
38. *Maryborough Chronicle*, 14 January 1942.
39. *Maryborough Chronicle*, 14 February 1942.
40. Australian Archives, *ibid*.

Conclusion

Throughout the war Japanese espionage activities directed against the West were only moderately successful, but perhaps it should be stated that whereas the German spies operating in neutral and Allied countries were often caught and punished, the Japanese generally seemed to have led charmed existences. Suma, Morishima, Kase, and many others could certainly have been arrested by their host countries on charges of espionage, and as those countries moved inexorably towards a stricter form of neutrality, the chances of arrest were considerably heightened. However, few arrests were ever made.

During the final weeks of the war, as the Swiss started to freeze funds and Japanese diplomats began salting fortunes away where they would not be discovered by American investigators, large amounts of official monies went mysteriously missing. Much of it has never been accounted for.

Evidence of widespread diplomatic looting and the illicit accumulation of wealth came in March 1946 when members of the American Eighth Army confiscated thousands of dollars of American currency, diamonds, jewellery and other valuables from the first group of Japanese diplomats returning home since the surrender. Japanese port authorities estimated that more than US$5 million worth of currencies and valuables was found aboard the repatriation ship *Tsukishi Maru*. (Also known as the *Tsukushi Maru*.)

The operation was carried out under the supervision of Major J.W. Duff of the 12th Cavalry Regiment. Under the US military ruling that their diplomatic immunity ended as soon as the ship entered territorial waters, passengers were met at the docks at Uraga, near Tokyo, and marched to a customs shed to be searched. 336 Japanese men and women were involved in the search, and while most of these were diplomats, the number also included several businessmen and journalists and their wives. Soldiers aided by interpreters and doctors examined each man, and US Army nurses searched the women passengers. All passengers were stripped of their clothing and placed in front of a fluoroscope in order that any items of value they might have swallowed could be detected. Major Duff subsequently reported that among the first group of twenty diplomats searched there were found three large diamonds concealed in a woman's kit and many bills of currency sewn into items of clothing. In the knee patches of one suit, the military authorities discovered a large amount of high denomination US currency. The clothing of one child was bulging with valuable wrist-watches, and toothpaste tubes were stuffed with jewels. Three thousand pieces of luggage were searched and large quantities of precious items were confiscated. Major Duff also stated that the US Army would be making investigations into obtaining evidence of bank accounts held by the diplomats in foreign countries.

Historians dream of being able to interview the subjects of their investigations, unfortunately it has been impossible to interview the leading protagonists of this story as they are now all dead. At the end of the war, the Japanese Ambassador to Hitler's government, Hiroshio Oshima was captured by the Americans in Berlin and sent to the eastern US state of Pennsylvania. At this time around 193 former Japanese diplomats and their dependants were interned in the city of Bedford under the conditions stipulated by the Geneva Convention for prisoners of war. He later returned to Japan and lived in Chigasaki City, Kanagawa Prefecture. He died on 6 June 1975.

Yakichiro Suma and Morito Morishima also survived the war. Suma lived at Minami-Ogikubo, Suginami-ku in Tokyo, he died on 30 April 1970. His eldest son, Michiaki Suma, also became a leading and successful Japanese diplomat. He retired from the diplomatic service in 1981 when he was the Ambassador to Canada. He now works as a counsellor for the Nippon Shinpan Company in Tokyo.[1]

Morishima lived at Yoyogi, Shibuya-ku in Tokyo, He died on 17 February 1975.[2]

The chief of the *TO* agency was never officially identified by the Allies during the war. The American authorities certainly believed that they knew his identity, yet all reference to him in the *Magic* messages has since been carefully deleted by US censors. This man, highly elusive and a talented spy, was often anonymously referred to by Suma, Suner and Jordana in their dispatches and correspondences. Suma once referred to him as a former press attaché to the Spanish Embassy in London, and, '... a cavalier – one who will do anything on earth for his friends and those he likes; of strong character but rather quixotic and hot-headed.' This agent played a vital role in the gathering of Axis intelligence, passing his information on to the Spanish government, the Spanish Foreign Office, the Germans and the Japanese. *TO* intelligence almost surely began in Great Britain under German direction and funding, but it was not until 1978 that Spanish diplomat Senor Angel Alcazar publicly admitted that he had led the organization in England. 'Franco knew every detail of my activities,' he stated.[3]

NOTES

1. Letter from Michiaki Suma to author, 5 March 1993.
2. Letter from the Consulate-General of Japan to the author, quoting information supplied by the Japanese Foreign Ministry, 19 February, 1993.
3. *The Times*, 21 October, 1978.

Bibliography

PRIMARY SOURCES

Most of the information contained in this book was derived from approximately 30,000 previously top-secret documents which comprise the *Magic* Summaries, National Archives of the United States, 1941-45. The following documents and publications were also of great assistance.

Previously secret and confidential reports
A981 item CONSULS 252 'Consuls. Spain at Melbourne' (1911-42). Australian National Archives.
A981 item CONSULS 254 'Consuls. Spain at Sydney' (1924-45). Australian National Archives.
A989 item 43/195/1/15/1 'Consuls. Consul Spain at Sydney' (1943). Australian National Archives.
A989 item 43/195/1/15/2 'Consuls. Consul Spain at Melbourne.' (1943-1948). Australian National Archives.
A1838/T13 item 1515/1/2/5 'Con. Reps. Spain. Alleged appointment of Mr P. Michelides as Hon Vice-Consul at Perth' (1925-52). Australian National Archives.
Commonwealth Investigations Service. BP 242 1/2, correspondence files, single number with Q prefix, 1924-54. Australian National Archives.

Secondary Sources
Attiwill, Kenneth, *The Singapore Story* (Muller, 1959)
Attiwill, Kenneth, *Banking Structure and Sources of Finance in the Far East* (Banker Research Unit, 1975)
Beevor, Antony, *The Spanish Civil War* (Orbis Publishing, 1982)
Bresnan, John, *Crisis in The Philippines* (Princeton University Press, Princeton N.J., 1986)
Brown, Brendon, *Crimes Against International Law* (Washington Public Affairs Press, 1950)
Callahan, R., *The Worst Disaster* (University of Delaware Press, 1977)

Charlton, Peter, *War Against Japan* (Time–Life Books in association with John Ferguson, Sydney 1988)

Clutterbuck, Richard, *Riot and Revolution in Singapore and Malaya 1945-63* (Faber & Faber, 1973)

Collier, Basil, *The War in the Far East 1941–45* (William Morrow & Co., New York, 1969)

Deaken, F.W. and Storry, G.R., *The Case of Richard Sorge* (Chatto and Windus, 1966)

Deakon, Richard, *A History of the Japanese Secret Service* (Frederick Muller, 1982)

Deakon, Richard, *Kempei Tai* (Beaufort Books, New York, 1983)

Farwell, George, *Mask of Asia* (F.W. Cheshire Pty, Melbourne, 1966)

Field, S.E., *Singapore Tragedy* (Angus & Robertson, Sydney, 1943)

Fitzgerald, Ross, *From 1915 to the Early 1980s, A History of Queensland* (University of Queensland Press, 1984)

Friend, Theodore, *Between Two Empires* (Yale University Press, 1965)

Hall, Timothy, *The Fall of Singapore* (Methuen, Australia, 1983)

Hart, Sir Basil Liddell, *History of The Second World War* (Phoebus Publishing, 1980)

Johnson, Brian, *The Secret War* (British Broadcasting Corporation, 1978)

Kanroji, Osanaga, *Hirohito – An Intimate Portrait of the Japanese Emperor* (Gateway Publishers, Los Angeles, 1973)

Kaplan, David E. and Dubro, Alec, *Yakuza* (Addison-Wesley, Sydney, 1986)

Keenan, Joseph, and Kennedy, Joseph, *British Civilians and the Japanese War in Malaya and Singapore* (MacMillan, 1987)

Kennedy, J., *When Singapore Fell* (MacMillan 1989)

Kirby, Woodburn, *The War Against Japan, The Loss of Singapore* (Her Majesty's Stationery Office, 1957)

Kwity, Jonathan, *The Crimes of Patriots* (W.W. Norton and Co., New York 1987)

Leasor, James, *Singapore, the Battle that Changed the World* (Hodder and Stoughton, 1968)

Lewin, Ronald, *The Other Ultra* (Hutchinson, London, 1982)

Liddell Hart, Sir Basil, *History of the Second World War* (Phoebus, London, 1979)

Manchester, William, *American Caesar* (Hutchinson Group, Australia, 1978)

Mayer, S.L., *The Rise and Fall of Imperial Japan* (Bison Books, 1984)

Montgomery, Brian, *Shenton of Singapore* (Leo Cooper, London 1984)

Newman, Bernard, *The World of Espionage* (Souvenir Press, London 1962)

Newell, William H., *Japan in Asia 1942–45* (Singapore University Press, 1981)

Philippines Reparations Commission Report 1956–58 (Manila, 1959)

Percival, Sir Arthur, *The War in Malaya* (Eyre & Spottiswood, London, 1949)

Perrault, Giles, *The Secrets of D Day* (Arthur Barker, London, 1964)

Piccigallo, Philip R., *The Japanese on Trial* (University of Texas Press, Austin and London, 1979)

Playfair, Giles, *Singapore Goes off the Air* (Jarrolds, London 1944)

Quirino, Carlos, *Quezon: Paladin of Philippine Freedom* (Filipiniana Book Guild, Manila, 1971)

Russell-Roberts, Dennis, *Spotlight on Singapore* (Times Press, Isle of Man, 1965)

Russell, Lord of Liverpool, *The Knights of Bushido* (Cassell & Co., 1985)

Simson, Ivan, *Singapore: Too Little Too Late* (Hutchinson, 1968)

Steinberg, David Joel, *Philippines Collaboration In World War Two* (Solidaridad Publishing House, Manila, 1967)

Swinson, Arthur, *Four Samurai* (Hutchinson, 1968)

Syjuco, Ma Felisa A., *The Kempei Tai in the Philippines 1941–45* (New Day Publishers, Quezon City, 1988)

The Background of Our War (Lectures prepared by the Orientation Course, War Department, Bureau of Public Relations (Farrar and Rinehart, New York, 1942)

Toland, John, *The Rising Sun* (Cassell, 1971)

Truman, Harry S., *1945 Year of Decisions, Volume One* (The New American Library, 1955)

Tsuji, Colonel Masaobu, *Singapore: The Japanese Version* (Ure Smith, Sydney, 1960)

Welles, Sumner, *The Time for Decision* (Harper and Brothers, New York, 1944)

Newspapers, magazines and periodicals.
Asia Week
Bristol Evening Post.
Courier Mail – Brisbane
Daily Globe – Manila

Evening Star – Manila
Fortune Magazine
Guinea Gold
Life Magazine.
Malaya Independent
Maryborough Chronicle
Newsweek
New York Times
Sunday Mail – Brisbane
Time – Australia
Time – USA
The Times – London.
Truth – Brisbane
Washington Post.

Index